BRIEF HISTORY OF THE PIONEERS OF THE CROMWELL, MINNESOTA AREA

BENNETT A. BECK

First edition: self-published in 1962 by Bennett A. Beck
Second edition: revised and edited, 2001

Carlton County Historical Society
Cloquet, MN 55720

copyright © 2001 Carlton County Historical Society

All rights reserved. No part of this book may be reproduced in any form, except short excerpts for review or educational purposes, without written permission of the publisher.

Printed and bound in the United States of America by Bang Printing, Brainerd, Minnesota.
Book layout and design by Marlene Wisuri

ISBN 0-9618959-5-0

Cover Photo: Cromwell Depot, 1910.

Published by the Carlton County Historical Society
406 Cloquet Avenue, Cloquet, MN 55720

ACKNOWLEDGEMENTS

The production of a book of local history requires the assistance of many people. The Carlton County Historical Society wishes to thank those who aided in the production of this book:

John Mark Skalko spent many hours during the summer of 2001 entering the text of the book into the computer for typesetting. This project would not have been completed without this valuable contribution of time and effort.

The Gerin-Fahlstrom Educational Fund of the Carlton County Historical Society Foundation funded a student internship grant which allowed us to provide a stipend to John Skalko for his services.

Daniel Naslund provided invaluable editing and proofreading of the manuscript. We are indebted to him for sharing his expertise and advice and his patient undertaking of this task.

Christine Skalko oversaw the production of the first computer copy and Roberta Malwitz provided final proofreading assistance.

The Cromwell Young Old Timers Club provided financial and moral support to the project.

Eino Heikkila loaned us photographs that contributed to the project.

Finally, George Balsness, step-grandson of B. A. Beck, provided the generous financial support which enabled the printing of the book. He prepared the index of names for the book and offered advice, encouragement, and information. Some of the photographs used in the book are also from his collection.

PUBLISHER'S PREFACE

A book of local history book can serve as the collective memory of a community and become an invaluable tool in preserving its legacy. As part of its collections, the Carlton County Historical Society owns many volumes of local history which are used by family historians and researchers to access information that is otherwise difficult to find and reconstruct. The Society has undertaken the task of reprinting some of the Carlton County local histories that have long been out of print and not readily available to readers.

The first such book was *The History of the Thomson Farming Area* by John A. Mattinen which was first published in Finnish in the 1930s. The book was translated into English by Dr. Richard Impola and republished by the Society in 2000.

This volume, *Brief History of the Pioneers of Cromwell, Minnesota Area*, was researched and written by Bennett A. Beck during the 1950s. It was self-published in 1962 with initial encouragement from the Carlton County Historical Society and the Minnesota Historical Society.

B. A. Beck writes of the time before white settlement when the Cromwell area was inhabited by native people. He describes the natural features of the land and recreates the lumbering era when the area was first settled—mainly by French-Canadian immigrants and descendants. He writes of the arrival of the first Bohemian, Finnish, and other Scandinavian immigrants and of the transition of the forest based economy to one based on agriculture, particularly dairy farming.

Beck outlines the organization and growth of local government, schools, churches, and businesses. The founding and growth of the co-operative movement of the Cromwell area mirrors that of Carlton County as a whole.

He covers the co-op creamery and consumer co-op development. He also provides some colorful stories about local residents that would have been known only to a community insider.

This material would be almost impossible to reproduce today had it not been gathered and organized by B. A. Beck. He undertook his task essentially alone, although he did have some assistance from neighbors and friends in gathering information about families. He also had help with the typing of the original book, which was mimeographed and nicely hard bound.

Often books of local history are written by amateur historians and writers who have a passion for their subject matter and a deep conviction that their task is essential to the preservation of particular facts and material. In many cases, these local historians do not have the luxury of proofing and editing services. Such was the case with *Brief History of the Pioneers of Cromwell, Minnesota Area*. We know some errors exist in Beck's material and that it would be impossible to research and correct them all at this time.

Before undertaking the book project, we had to make a decision about editing and corrections. While we have attempted to maintain B. A. Beck's voice and style, we have done editing for grammatical clarification, sentence structure, and punctuation. We have attempted to provide correct spellings of names by cross referencing with county directories and census records. Of course, these records are not always totally accurate with regard to spelling either. We apologize for any errors that may still be a part of the text and ask that readers put the book into the context of Mr. Beck's time and the circumstances of its creation.

The photographs used in the book are from the collections of the Carlton County Historical Society and several Cromwell area residents. They are in no way all of the images that exist of Cromwell families and scenes, but should give a representative flavor of the community. There were no photographs in the original edition.

The Carlton County Historical Society has a tradition of publication that includes volumes such as *Crossroads in Time: The History of Carlton County, Minnesota; Reflections of Our Past: A Pictorial History of Carlton County, Minnesota;* and *The Fury of the Flames* that we believe is of great importance to our mission of collecting, preserving, and disseminating Carlton County history. We certainly hope you will enjoy this look at the hardy pioneers of the Cromwell area.

      Marlene Wisuri
      Director
      Carlton County Historical Society
      October, 2001

Cromwell, Minnesota, 1933

ABOUT THE AUTHOR

Bennett A. Beck was born near Kolding, Denmark, on April 22, 1873. He attended the Kolding School and as a boy often swam in the Baltic Sea.

A half-sister of Ben's had come to the United States about 1880 to pioneer in the new land. Ben completed a two-year course in animal husbandry and some training in a brush-making factory. In 1889 he set out for "America." He landed in Detroit, Michigan, at the age of sixteen. After working in Detroit for about a year, he went on to the Twin Cities. He then contracted the dreaded typhoid fever and nearly died. Slowly recovering, he worked on a farm in Fridley (north Minneapolis). The next year he worked for the city, "and in the woods," in the winter. In the spring of 1893, Ben came north with Oscar Homstad who was proving up on his farm near Cromwell. Oscar and a Mr. Erickson had contracted to clear some land on the F. A. Watkins farm, three and one half miles south of Carlton. Ben did some fencing there and worked at times for James M. Paine and Stanley Walker, then living on Chub Lake.

Here are my first memories of "Ben Beck", whose kindly nature endeared him to all who knew him. I was five years old and nearly worshipped this strong, soft-spoken Dane who so recently had come "across the seas." I believe Ben was with us the next year (1894) when the Hinckley Fire roared up from the south that dry September. The lamps were lit at 3:00 p.m., for the smoke had darkened all the sky, filling the air with its coughing fumes. I remember how frightened my mother was. My father was away, but fortunately got home that evening. Blankets were ready to wet down at the

Lake (Venoah) where one hope of escape was possible. The horses and carriage were ready for immediate need, but where could one hope to drive? Yes, Ben Beck was a big comfort to many.

Ben Beck was married in 1905 to Mrs. Mary Balsness, a widow with three children. In 1910 they farmed at Cromwell, building up a noted herd of Guernseys. He shipped milk and cream to Bridgeman Russell in Duluth. (Ed. note: His first wife died in 1935.)

By 1912, the Co-op Creamery took plans and was started. It will complete fifty years of continous running this summer (1962). Ben was a great co-op booster as well as a leader in educational activities. In 1936, Ben married Mrs. Anna Nesso and carried on farm activities where he lives today.

This book modestly tells some of these stories, of early pioneer days when brave hearts dared build up homes in the wilderness and of the past eighty years. Ben carries on (now alone) with faith, in his Lord. Our prayers are with you, Ben Beck!

L. H. Watkins, Vice President

Carlton County Historical Assoc.
Carlton, Minnesota

Ed. note: Bennett A. Beck died in his home of natural causes in December 12, 1965, at the age of ninety-two. His obituary speaks with pride of his accomplishment in writing *Brief History of the Pioneers of Cromwell, Minnesota Area*. He left several step-children and step-grandchildren to mourn his passing.

MEMOIR

A Brief Biography of the Pioneers and Their Families

I want to express my appreciation and thanks to Mr. Andrew Parviainen for supplying me with the family history of all the early pioneers of the township of Eagle. Mr. Parviainen is a member of the Finnish Historical Society and fluent in the Finnish language.

I have also written a complete history of the spiritual life of the village of Cromwell and since the Finnish brought their Christian denomination with them, I have written a complete history of their spiritual life. The spiritual life of a nation determines the character of its people.

I am dedicating the history of the village of Cromwell and the township of Red Clover, the Congressional township 49-Range 20, and the township of Eagle, 48-Range 20, a political subdivision of Carlton County, to the memory of my old friends and fellow pioneers who first came here about 1885 and established their homes on homesteads and to the later pioneers who came here and bought wild, cut-over land and established their homes and cleared small farms up to about 1904. Nearly all of them have gone to their eternal rest and I am a little lonesome. Yes, I miss them. However, I appreciate the friendship of the first and second generation of the first settlers—most of them were immigrants and more than eighty per cent of the immigrants came from Finland. Some people have said that the old people live in the past and the young people live in the future,

so there is a reason for discord and the inharmonious "Philosophy of Life."

Bennett A. Beck. Cromwell, Minnesota

CARLTON COUNTY HISTORICAL ASSOCIATION
CARLTON, MINNESOTA

OFFICERS:

President, J. C. Long,	Cloquet, Minn.
Vice Pres., L. Harlow Watkin,	Carlton, Minn.
Secretary, Mrs. Ruth McCausland,	Carlton, Minn.
Treasurer, Mr. C. C. Hanson,	Barnum, Minn.

DIRECTORS:

Kenneth Braatlof,	Cloquet, Minn.
Robert Goodell,	Barnum, Minn.
Evelyn LaVoie,	Carlton, Minn.

Our Aim:

To preserve our early maps and records; the skills and equipment; and the pioneer aims and stories that gave birth to our County's first life; and challenged the early immigrants who prized their liberties, to build for better days for their families and loved ones who would follow.

This is a continuing factual history, a story of patience and advancing skills, of hope, of faith in God and in our fellow man.

This is a tying-together of earliest dreams, and the day of small beginnings, with growing accomplishments, into a fulfilling chapter of abundance for all, and the growing day of Peace, to all who labor on....in faith, believing.

(1962)   L. H. W.

TABLE OF CONTENTS
KNOW THE GENESIS OF YOUR TOWN AND COMMUNITY

Publisher's Preface	iv-vi
About the Author	vii-viii
Memoir	ix
Carlton County Historical Association	x
Table of Contents	xi-xii

Part I

Pages:

Chapter 1: History of Eagle and Red Clover Townships   13-24

Chapter 2: Flora and Fauna   25-28

Chapter 3: Harvesting Timber; Crops Upon Which Man Bestowed No Labor   29-35

Chapter 4: Organization of Local Government by Pioneer and Permanent Settlers   36-43

Chapter 5: Organization of Local Government II   44-48

Chapter 6: Brief Biography and Accomplishments of Early Settlers. Some Finnish Pioneers in the Original Township of Red Clover   49-136

Part II

Chapter 7: Preamble to the History of the Finnish People of the Town of Eagle   137-147

Chapter 8:   Brief History of the Genealogy &
             Biography of the Finnish People of Eagle
             Township and Their Accomplishments as
             Original Pioneers   148-161

Chapter 9:   Story of Romance   162-167

Chapter 10: Second and Third Advent of Finnish
             People   168-199

Chapter 11: Origin and History of Christian Church of
             Eagle   200-207

Chapter 12: Commercial Life of Cromwell   208-263
             Co-operative Movement   233
             Fraternal Activities   247
             Earliest Citizens   249

Chapter 13: Spiritual Life in Cromwell and Area
                                              264-278

Maps: 279-281

Index: 282-286

Suggested Reading: 287

A FACTUAL HISTORY OF THE ACCOMPLISHMENTS
OF
THE EARLY PIONEERS WHO WERE KNOWN TO
ME, PERSONALLY:

Bennett A. Beck,

Cromwell, Minnesota

CHAPTER ONE

History of Eagle and Red Clover Townships

The geological origin of the surface strata of the townships of Red Clover and Eagle in Carlton County, Minnesota, will be of special interest to the present and future inhabitants of these political divisions, which are geographically located on the northeastern edge of the red drift. It appears from observation that the glacial moraine deposits, clay, sand, and silt were very unevenly distributed, leaving large areas that were probably under water for a long time. Except for the present lakes most of the land of lower elevation has been filled with decomposed moss and other vegetation in the continuous process of growth and decay, which constitutes our present deposits of peat.

Island Lake at Cromwell, Minnesota

Some of the higher and comparatively level lowlands were filled with alluvial deposits of sand and silt, interspersed with gravel deposits derived from the hills beyond. According to a geological survey the approximate south half of Red Clover and all of Eagle Township is underlaid with a bed of gravel and sand, with the coarser gravel on top and the greater the depth occurs, the finer the sand becomes. Approximately the south half of Red Clover and most of Eagle Township is covered with a crust of red moraine clay, from the depth of a few feet down to the water table. About a foot below the surface, this clay becomes so firmly packed that it is termed hard pan. Underneath this clay crust, but on top of the underlying gravel is a layer of mixed strata composed of stones, sand, and gravel fused with metallic minerals that have been exposed to terrific pressure and heat, an indication that the movement of the glaciers must have been rapid to generate sufficient heat to cause this fusion. Approximately the northern half of Red Clover Township is covered with a sandy gravel on the surface and is quite level in elevation, due to the action of water and possibly the influence of geysers. These strata are practically free from stones.

An interesting feature of Red Clover Township is Skunk Island, three miles north of the village of Cromwell. This high elevation rises abruptly above the surrounding swamp and a small lake on the north. This island might have been created by a geyser and is formed from sand and gravel. A plausible reason for the higher crust on the northeast corner of the island is that a prevailing southwest wind sprayed the water in that direction. Originally, a crater existed on the top of this island, suggesting the former presence of a geyser. Evidence of the crater remains. Other high elevations in this area indicate geyser action. Adjacent to this area, only one mile north of Red Clover is a range of hills which are the dividing line between the red and gray drift. This range is the dividing watershed between the Mississippi and Saint Lawrence River systems. Prairie Lake is located in the southern part of this range area and is seventy feet higher than Island Lake at Cromwell. Prairie Lake drains into the Mississippi River system.

This entire geological area described above is located within the Mississippi River watershed and barely enclosed in the confines of the northeastern border of the historical Louisiana Purchase of 1803 when this territory was secured by the United States from France. Previous to this time it had been undisputed Spanish territory. However, this territory was not open to settlement or development until acquired by further treaties with the Chippewa Indians. In 1854 a treaty was made covering the township of Eagle and other lands south and east. Supporting this conclusion is the fact that a contract was let by the U.S. Department of Interior to Milton Nye to make a sectional survey of the township of Eagle on July 21, 1857, but the survey was not made for reasons such as the intervention of the Civil War. On August 11, 1870, the survey contract was re-let to Jewett and Howe and the survey was completed April 6, 1871.

The history of Red Clover is of similar interest. This township was acquired from the Chippewa Indians by treaty in 1898. A contract was made by the U.S. Department of Interior with Jewett and Howe to make the sectional survey on August 11, 1870, and the survey was completed April 18, 1871. The surveys for both Eagle and Red Clover townships were made by the same two surveyors, Jewett and Howe. Following the completion of those surveys the Chippewa Indians were transferred to the Fond du Lac Reservation, but were permitted the enjoyment of hunting and fishing, as well as other legal privileges of American citizens. They were governed by their chiefs according to their tribal customs.

Two Indian families and their offspring remained in this vicinity to the beginning of the 1890s; namely, the Grasshopper and the Beargrease families. White men (woodsmen and lumberjacks) were becoming squawmen as they married Indian girls. Now, I plainly want it understood that squawmen as recorded here is no reflection on their character, as many Indian girls became good wives and homemakers. Many families followed the lumber camps. The last being those who lived at Prairie Lake and around Barney Clowgh's lumber camp on the north side of Prairie Lake in log houses comparable to those of white settlers. They worked in the woods in the winter and on the river in the spring, driving logs down from Prairie Lake to Big Sandy. The last log drive went down in the spring of 1907 and this camp closed down, moving on to Poupore and toward Brookston. But one Indian, John Foot, remained and resided on the west end of Prairie Lake as long as he lived.

Mrs. Grasshopper outside of her wigwam.

It was customary for them to make pilgrimages

every fall to pick cranberries. There was always a good crop in the swamps until the swamps were drained by extensive ditching. The only thing the extensive ditching accomplished was to kill the cranberry crop. The remains of an Indian burial ground could be seen on the large island in Prairie Lake as late as 1915-1916. The Indians traveled long distances through the woods on tote roads and logging roads. The Indians would travel single file, the bucks, sometimes two or three or more of them in the lead, with their Springfield muskets. They were always on the lookout for game birds and other game. Following them would be the old squaws, packing a big bundle of bedding consisting of buckskins and camp blankets, which were used for their bunks or their beds, and for their temporary tents or wigwams, also called tepees. After them would follow the younger Indian mothers with their papooses on their backs, and following them the younger and free Indians, carrying packs loaded according to their strength and age. There would be from ten to twenty or thirty Indians in the pilgrimages. They would have old camping grounds or sites to go to and all that remained there was a big pile of rocks or stones which were used for their fireplace in the summer and fall. They would build a small tepee around the fire by setting up a few tripods and covering them with blankets or buckskins.

    The number of tepees would depend on the number of the Indians there, and in the winters they would build wigwams. They were larger—up to sixteen or eighteen feet each way. They would use quarterposts in such a manner that would leave an opening of three or four feet on top for the smoke from the fireplace to escape, and the pile of rocks and stones would be in the center. There would be bunks for sleeping all around and just a small opening for a doorway covered with a blanket. The rest of the outside would be covered with buckskin or with balsam boughs hung and lapped over each other on the sides of the wigwam up to a foot in thickness. There would be small poles crosswise on the corner posts about one foot apart, fastened with a buckskin cord, and that was the base for the balsam bough. And so after they had settled down, you would not be surprised if you would meet a buck or a squaw a long distance in the woods, even on the darkest night.

I will record an incident recalled by a woodsman. He was driving a tote-team from camp late one night with a big lumber wagon. It was very dark and he could not see the road, but the horses knew the way and could not have gone off the road if they had wanted to. The road was very rough and he was having a time by himself to stay on the wagon when he was aroused by a bloodcurdling yell and scream. The teamster stopped his team and expected to find he had driven over some drunken lumberjack who had fallen by the wayside (which was not an uncommon occurrence then.) To his surprise, something crawled into the back end of the wagon; it looked as if it might be a big black bear. But not so. It was a big squaw; he asked where she was going and if she would sit on the seat. She said they had a campfire some distance in the woods. Her name was Mary and she wanted a ride. She lay down in the back of the wagon, but it was not long before she had all the ride she wanted. She got out of the wagon and returned to her wigwam.

I have introduced you to the real American pioneers, who have not exploited the natural resources of timber, and minerals, and all kinds of game. These people were satisfied with their way of life.

But with the advent of the white man with his system of exploitation of all the natural resources to its furthest extent, the Indian could no longer live on the natural increase in the animal kingdom and vegetation on the limited area of their reservations.

A geographical survey by the government was made in the 1860s in a general way and it was expected that a complete survey would be made soon. Squatters might have staked out permissible claims before this time. There were four ways of acquiring land from the government by an Act of Congress in May, 1862:

    (1) Citizens and prospective citizens could stake out and file on a 160 acre homestead.
    (2) Preemption claim for 160 acres.
    (3) Timber claim for 160 acres, under the Stone and Timber Act.
    (4) Soldier script to honorably discharged Union soldiers.

Congress enacted a law granting to honorably discharged Union soldiers, a "negotiable script," which entitled the owner or holder of the script to 160 acres of land anywhere within the government domain. Such script no doubt is still existing. Some Confederate soldiers in this way became owners, acquiring some by bartering or trading as the script had no great value. The land was plentiful and cheap, so some of the old soldiers would find old friends who had used their homestead rights and would transfer their rights for a glass of beer. No residence was required. Neither was any residence required on a stone and timber claim, but they were required to prove that such a piece of land was more valuable for stone and timber, than it was for agriculture. This was very easy to prove in those days, as agriculture was then considered impractical in this district. However, they were required to pay $1.25 per acre then, but it is believed some of this land was acquired earlier for much less. It is believed the early lumber companies acquired much of this land, indirectly by the Stone and Timber Act, the soldier's script, or by homestead. They would have a lumberjack file on a homestead in his own right and build a small log cabin and put in a small cook stove, some tin pots and pans, and a bunk with blankets so he would be able to sleep there. A single man was required to sleep there for three or four nights, twice a year, and had to have a curbed well to establish residence. The well was easy to dig, as it was necessary to dig only six or eight feet to water. Water was always easy to find next to a swamp. Next he looked up a small open spot that would make it easy to clear five or six acres of land on his 160 acre tract. He would clear that, he leave the stumps, sow some grass seed, and then he would have completed all the requirements to qualify. He could qualify in three years by paying $1.25 per acre or wait five years and not have to pay any money, except the land office fee and the cost of publishing the notice of final proof three times. In due time he would get his U.S. patent (or deed). It would take from six to eight months or even ten months for this to come through. However, final proof had to be made within seven years, or the rights to the land were forfeited, and refiling would be necessary to reestablish a claim to the land.

 I have known some instances where a lumber company had cut the timber on government land and hired a lumberjack to file on the homestead, or induced him to do so by promising him they would pay for the stumpage when he qualified on the homestead. In another case, a logging contractor cut timber on a homestead and was caught at it. He avoided the penalty by filing on the claim and putting up a cash bond to insure he would qualify. When he did, his cash bond was refunded. If he failed to pay, the penalty would be three times the market value of the stumpage cut.

I will record another instance to illustrate how qualifying could be done. This concerned a married man, his wife, and two children who filed on a homestead. They built a fairly large camp and outbuildings, there being room to care for six horses. He moved his family to the camp, lived there in the winter, and cut timber in the fall and winter. He sometimes had two or three men working for him cutting timber, not always on the homestead, but cutting on stumpage he had bought close by. He would use his homestead as his camp and in the winter would have two or three teams of horses hauling his timber out to the railroad. When spring would arrive, he would write to the land offices stating there was no road for him and his family to get out. He would then make an application for permit to leave his homestead for the summer months. The permission was always granted. When fall came again, he would move out to the homestead and cut timber for the coming fall and winter. So he continued year after year. He cleared five acres in the swamp and sowed some grass seed; he had a well for the camp and after five years qualified for his claim. After qualifying, he moved away and let the land go for taxes. In the early days, there were many such cases.

Finally by an act of Congress in May, 1862, all the swamp land was ceded to the state on certain conditions which I will not record here. This act did not grant title in full until they had held it for twenty-one years. This could be contested by any citizen or prospective citizen by proving such parcel of land not exceeding 160 acres was more than fifty percent high land. This meant that one half of each forty acres was to be high land, and it is not known that the state objected unless there was a known mineral deposit existing on such land.

Following this (in the late 1860s), the federal government by an act of Congress gave a land grant to the Mississippi & Lake Superior Railway Company which later became the St. Paul and Duluth Railway Company. The railroad was given a choice of every odd numbered section in this locality of Red Clover and Eagle Townships. Later the state of Minnesota, also by legislative act, gave land grants to the railway company. The state also set aside two sections in each township for school purposes, to wit: section 16 and 36 (called school sections) from which our state school trust fund originated.

There remained approximately only twenty homesteads of 160 acres in each township, and were generally scattered all over. All the state lands were and are yet exempt from taxation. The railroad lands were exempt from all taxes until such a time as the state by legislative act would require them to pay such tax. This was started in Minnesota about 1896 and was contested in district court. Four years after an appeal to the Minnesota Supreme Court, the act became effective in 1901. It was not possible for the railway company to levy on their business enough for real estate taxes. It would have to be charged against their operating expense and paid out of the freight and passenger income. Also, it would need the approval of the Railroad and Warehouse Commission, and this, the Commission could not grant.

The railway company then organized the Northwest Improvement and Immigration Company. This was located on township 49, Range 20 (Red Clover). They in turn transferred their holdings to Boston and Duluth Land Company, a newly organized real estate sales company headed by former Mayor of Duluth Mr. Snively. The Winona and St. Peter Land Company acquired title to all the land owned by the lumber company, principally the St. Anthony Lumber Company. This company owned practically all the valuable pine timber land in the township of Eagle. They later bought all the railroad land and started an organization project by surveying their land, building several miles of roads, and then selling it on long terms to actual settlers.

The Northern Pacific Railroad was built in the late 1860s and was completed in the early 1870s. (sic) The first train to go over the line was in 1872; a section house was then built. It was a large house for two families, served as a hotel, was called "The Eating House," and in the beginning employed a regular cook. The trains stopped here to fuel as they were woodburners in those days and the passengers and crew also had to be fed. The station, according to Northern Pacific Company records was established in 1870, and was named Island Lake Station. This name was changed in 1883 to Cromwell so as to agree with the post office and in honor of James L. Cromwell of Duluth, Minnesota.

Mr. Cromwell was identified with the West Duluth Land Company and the Reuben Carlton Lumber Company. The first agent they have a record of is E. A. Woodward, 1881-82 (might have been in 1883). Island Lake was the first station which later became Cromwell. The post office was in the depot and the agent was the postmaster. Thomas Tripanier of Wright was the postmaster and the section foreman brought the mail to Wright on a hand car every day. Cromwell was the only station between Northern Pacific Junction or Komoko which was the first town site plated about one mile west of Northern Pacific Junction and Kimberly. A stationary steam engine was kept here by the railway company who kept the water tank filled. A similar tank was kept full in Kimberly in the winter. The section crews were kept here to maintain the track east to Corona and west to Wright station, as it was called in honor of George Wright, Sr. and his son, John H. Wright. It is believed that Enoch Arden and Peter Parson were the first section foremen. The railroad track bed was new so the railroad crew was required to maintain and improve its track and railroad bed. This crew was required to keep a work train and an extra gang employed every summer for more than thirty years to bring the tracks to present standards. It required an additional large amount of money and forced the Northern Pacific Railway Company into bankruptcy in 1894. They were in the hands of a receiver for a period of more than ten years and most of the original investors and shareholders lost most of their investments.

CHAPTER TWO

Flora and Fauna

The wild plant life and animal life in Eagle and Red Clover was similar, as the original timber on the high land was dominated by pine, white pine, and in the northwestern part of Red Clover, Norway pine. As Indian lore has it, a big forest fire had burnt over most of Red Clover, the northwest part of Eagle, and possibly all of it. This killed the original pine, leaving only scattered clumps of trees here and there. Most of them were large trees, more than four to five feet on the stump, and would be 500-700 hundred years old. The fire must have been in the late 19th century (1870), about the time the first railroad train went over the line. There is evidence that such had occurred. The largest of these trees in 1894 would indicate their growth to be nearly a century old. None of this second growth timber was considered suitable for lumbering in those days. Logs were not accepted unless they were twelve feet in length and had an eighteen-inch top. General length was twelve, fourteen, or sixteen feet, with a special length of eighteen to twenty-four feet. Most were of special length and were Norway pine. No other timber was logged and sent down the rivers. The market price was a top of nine dollars per thousand logs, scaled and delivered on Big Sandy Lake to be floated down the Mississippi River. All logs landing on the upper Kettle River were then floated down the St. Croix River.

All the second growth timber that was left after the pine was cut included such species as balsam (or white fir); white and blue spruce; white and yellow cedar; white and blue larch commonly called tamarack

(tamarack is American black larch); white and yellow birch; some rock maple and black bark hard maple and several species of soft maple; red and black oak; a few white oaks and several species of blue oak; several species of elm and black ash; some basswood; some second growth white pine, Norway and jack pine; aspen, commonly called "poplar" predominate and many other weed trees that are common in the northern latitudes. The most prominent grasses were the blue joint which grew very rank to a height of more than three feet and was to be found along all river bottoms and all open lowlands. This came in or seeded itself on the logging roads. When cut early, it made good hay. There was a flat grass which had no feeding value. Later the blue joint gave way to wild red top which made fairly good hay. Wild blueberries, raspberries, juneberries, wild strawberries, logan berries, and highbush cranberries were plentiful.

    Various kinds of timber became valuable after the removal of the best white and Norway pine. A market for tamarack railroad ties at a price of twelve to fourteen cents per tie on railroad track. There was a demand for cedar paving blocks eight feet long, and sold by the cord at five to six dollars per double cord. Cedar posts sold at a price of one and one half cents above a three-inch diameter, so that a post seven feet long with a three-inch top would bring four and one half cents. A four-inch top would bring five cents, and so on. Posts were mostly shipped to North Dakota and Nebraska. Telephone poles were twenty feet long, with a four-inch top and sold at four cents per foot. A thirty-foot pole with a six-inch top sold for five cents per foot.

    About 1898, paper mills started at Cloquet and

other locations. With them came a demand for spruce pulpwood at three dollars per cord. Four or five years later they bought balsam for about the same price. In the early days of this century, there were operators of tie and cedar camps. Old lumber camps were used where there was a good stand of cedar, tamarack, and spruce. Later, all operations were by settlers and although there were some tie camps, they were not a very profitable industry.

Game was plentiful, especially deer and rabbits, with some moose. The snowshoe and cottontail were the most common rabbits. Upland game birds included ruffed grouse, woodcock and other birds while the wetlands were summer homes for a variety of ducks including mallards and bluebills. The lakes were full of fish such as pickerel, pike, bass, and suckers. Small birds such as woodpeckers and bluejays were always around the camps, as well as other common birds. There were timber (but no brush) wolves and also a few bears, wildcats, bobcats and red fox. Of the fur-bearing animals there were the skunk, mink, some otter and raccoon, weasel, and the most valuable of all, the muskrat. Hunters and trappers camped in the woods most of their lives making their living. In the summer they would kill deer just for their hides and let their carcass go to waste. The hide would bring a dollar. Game laws were not very

Cora Morse hunting near Cromwell.

strict and were not enforced then, unless someone made complaints.

There was an incident of two hunters coming here from Little Falls on the morning train. They took their ammunition and hunting packs and went into the woods about three miles from Cromwell. Here, they built a hunting camp, stayed eight days, and came back with sixteen deer to ship home to Rices, Minnesota. Their kill was hauled by Charles Morse with his old gray mare, Kate, and a jumper (a small wooden sled).

Fishermen with their catch—l to r: Fred Stone, Lief Ilstrup, Iver Lynne

CHAPTER THREE

Harvesting Timber Crops

    Logging operations in Red Clover and Eagle were first located in Section 22-48-20, on Kettle Lake. The earliest camp might have been owned by the St. Anthony Lumber Company and operated by a fellow named Bean. It was later operated for many years by Sauntry Cain. The earliest logging here was done in the early 1880s. For many years Martin Cain had charge of the camps. He cut nearly all the pine south and east of Eagle Lake. He cut the pine on the eastern part of 49-19, and as far north as two miles into Township 50-19. It was a nine-mile haul. He used trailer sleds with four horses, and made 1 1/2 trips in a twelve-hour day. A trailer sled was two sleds, one behind the other. They would be nine feet wide, have eighteen-foot bunks, and were used on iced roads. He would haul from ten to twelve thousand feet on a load. The loads were landed on or below Kettle Lake and went on to Stillwater. The last log drive down to Stillwater was about 1897.

    Murphy and Bonus had a big logging camp on Section 7-48-20. They cut all the pine in the town of Eagle, north of Eagle Lake and west of Cromwell Lake. They landed their logs in Tamarack River and through Flower Lake. In the town of Red Clover, the main lumber camps were on Section 10, one on Section 24, and one on Section 33 on the north end of Cromwell Lake. They were operated in the early 1880s by the Grant brothers for several years. They also had a small sawmill and logged a good part of Red Clover. Later the camps were used by other contractors and jobbers. The last logger to use any of the camps was the one on the north end of

Cromwell Lake used by Arthur Dotton. He used it in the winters of 1891-92 and 1892-93. He cut his logs mostly in Red Clover, some in Eagle, and then would land on Flower Lake.

Logging camp near Cromwell, ca. early 1900s

The last drive to go down the Tamarack River was in the spring of 1893. Barney Clough had a camp on the north side of Prairie Lake. From here he logged some Norway pine on Section 9-40-20 as late as the winter of 1896-97. He landed his logs on Hasty Brook, as far up as Section 10-49-20. The last drive down Hasty Brook was in the spring of 1897. They were driven down Hasty Brook to Prairie Lake, then down Prairie River to Big Sandy Lake. The last drive to go down Prairie River was in 1907 by a jobber by the name of Sands. These logs were bought by Minneapolis mills on Sandy Lake. They were taken over by the Boom Company of Minneapolis, as well as all the logs along the Tamarack River.

In the eastern part of Red Clover, the earlier pine timber was logged from as far south and west as Section 25-49-20, plus a good deal of the pine in the western part of Progress 49-19 by the Cloquet and Nelson Lumber Companies. The timber was hauled by rail to Stony Brook, then floated down Stony Brook to the St. Louis and on to Cloquet. The railroad came up southwest to Section 20-49-19, the town of Progress, as late as 1896 or 1897. The J. M. Paine Lumber Company of Carlton also logged some pine in Red Clover and Eagle. It was hauled to the railroad tracks and loaded on their own logging cars. The Weyerhaeuser Lumber Company also had some timber in Red Clover and elsewhere. After the Cloquet Company had sawed all their pine timber, they sold their sawmills to the Weyerhaeuser interest and operated two mills for some years after that. They also had some pine timber in northern Red Clover which they cut and floated down Prairie River to Little Falls before they had the mills in Cloquet.

The logging people working for the lumber companies were mostly from New Brunswick, the state of Maine, and later from Michigan. They worked under logging contracts, establishing camps, and hiring men to work in the logging business. These men were mostly of English, Irish, and French descent. They were all good woodsmen as there was no place for a tenderfoot. A man slept on his own innerspring mattress made of small poles lengthwise in his bunk and covered with balsam boughs with a little hay over the boughs. If you had one blanket on top, you had a good bed.

Now there were some lumberjacks with storybook characters, but the great majority of them were of good average character, the same as you will find today in a crew of working men. They stayed with the camps from early fall until the camps broke up in the spring. This meant work from early dawn until late at night at a minimum wage of twenty-six dollars a month up to forty-five dollars for good, four-horse teamsters. This was in the good old times—I should say good old Democratic times under Grover Cleveland when wages went down to less than eight dollars a month. If you quit before camp broke up in the spring, you would receive only a piece of paper certifying the time you worked and the amount due. This time check was negotiable; you could sell or assign it to anyone who would buy it. There were buyers in saloons who would buy them for a few glasses of beer and fifteen percent discount. Banks would take them for a fifteen percent discount, but you had to have someone to identify you if you were not known. One could not

An unidentified lumberjack.

enforce the collection of payment until camp work had broken up in the spring and the logs were sold and delivered, usually about the first of May.

Now we come to the time of the beginning of the actual settling of the first pioneers, in about 1870. One of the first was one Thomas Finn or Finch, an Irish Canadian, who came here in 1869 and homesteaded on what later was known as the George Wright place. It is thought Finch had something to do with the construction of the railroad, as the place he homesteaded—the piece of land described as Section 4-48-20—was built about that time. It appears that he was closely associated with William Dunlap and acquired considerable land where Carlton is now located and in Cloquet, which was called Knife Falls in those days.

Besides the crews that worked on the railroad, there were people who followed the workers for gambling and drinking. No license was required in the early days, so people lived pretty much as they pleased. The record makes it appear that in 1874, Thomas Finch sold his land to George Wright, Sr., who owned the same until he died about 1898 or 1899. He hired Indians to cut the timber on his land and let the timber lay to be burned every spring by fire. George, Sr. had two sons, John H. and Thomas, and a daughter, Maggie. After George Wright, Sr.'s wife died in early 1880, Thomas was brought up by an aunt in Duluth and Maggie kept the house for her father until she married and moved to Montana to live.

George Wright, Sr. built the first frame house in Cromwell after the depot and section house were built. It remained until 1894 when it was burned by the

Hinckley Fire. John H. and Thomas were telegraph operators and worked for the Northern Pacific Railway Company. John H. was working at the depot in 1892 when he was dismissed from his job on the railway. The reason for his dismissal was that he had some cattle and one of the cows was killed by a passing train. He wanted the railroad to pay for the cow. But instead of paying him, they dismissed him, as operators were not supposed to have outside jobs. The cattle he kept were the only ones this side of Carlton. After his dismissal from the Northern Pacific Company he became a conductor on the Duluth-Winnipeg Railroad. This was a new railroad being built between the two cities. It was built as far as Deer River, where the original builders ran out of capital. About 1899 or 1900, the Great Northern Railroad leased that road and extended it from Deer River to Fosston, Minnesota, and from Cloquet through Carlton to Wrenshall and on to Superior. They abandoned that part of the road from Cloquet through Harney to West Duluth.

About 1896 George Wright had a paralytic stroke which made him helpless for more than two years before he died. Because his father had been employed by the Northern Pacific Company from its beginning, John H. was hired again as a telegraph operator. He moved his family back to the old Wright home so he could take care of his father. Later the same year he was promoted to agent and remained so until he retired from the railroad in 1914. His brother, Thomas, was also an operator and worked in the dispatcher's office in Duluth where he was considered to one of the best.

In 1894 the American Railroad Union went on strike. The union had been organized in 1893 by Eugene

V. Debs in a loose sort of way. The elections were made by mass meetings and Thomas was elected the secretary of the union in Duluth. When the strike was over, the officers in the union were blacklisted by the railroad company. Thomas was demoted to operator and came back to Cromwell with his family. He had just moved back when the Hinckley Fire came along and burned all his possessions. The Northern Pacific rehired him at the dispatcher's office after the fire. He worked there for about ten years. He then moved out west where he would later die.

A train of the type that would have gone through Cromwell in the early years.

CHAPTER FOUR

Organization of Local Government by Pioneer and Permanent Settlers

Until 1893 this territory was part of the township of Moose Lake. In about 1893 the township of Red Clover was organized, which included all the townships of Beesman, Lakeview, Eagle and better than half of the western part of Progress or over to the western line of the Fond du Lac Indian Reservation. The organizer was John Savage, who was also elected the chairman at the first election of officers for the township of Red Clover. Horace B. Paine was the first town clerk; Woodbury Whitten, treasurer; Mike Erkas of Wright Station and Arthur R. Newton were the first supervisors. There were thirteen votes cast and three more settlers who could have voted; Thomas and David Trepanier and Solomon Morancii. Those who voted were John Savage, Woodbury Whitten, A. R. Newton, John Bellivue, Ben Pepin, Alex Bellanger, Jerry Royer, Louis Roderick, Frank Lamier, E. P. Duffy, George Wright, George Merwin, and George Flaugher. They were the settlers in this area at the time. The Arthur Newton family was the first white family that settled in the town of Eagle as it is now organized.

A few years later Eagle Township was organized taking all of 48-20 and becoming an independent township. Then followed Lake View and Beesman, leaving Red Clover with 49-20 and the west half of 49-19. Red Clover also withdrew and organized their own township, but not until the Reservation was opened to settlement in about 1907.

School District 13 was organized in 1891 when John E. Green was County Superintendent of Schools. George Wright, Sr., gave one half acre of land out on the southeast point of his property. When the schoolhouse was built south of the section house, there were no roads except tote roads. There was a tote road running south from the depot past the schoolhouse. (The school was located about where John H. Wright built his new house). The tote road ran south near the lake then branched off. One branch went in a southerly and westerly direction to Eagle Lake and the other east across the narrows on the north end of Island Lake. It followed a rocky reef on the east shore of Island Lake about 1 1/2 miles, then south and east out to the lumber camp by Bean Dam on Kettle River. There was a footbridge made of poles which made it possible to walk dry-footed across the narrows.

The first teacher was Barbara Eher from Moose Lake. The enrollment the first year was six: Lydia and Daisy Paine, Jerry and Minnie Bellanger, and Erwin Newton and his sister. The first officers were A. R. Newton, director; John H. Wright, clerk; and Woodbury Whitten, treasurer. This schoolhouse (the little green schoolhouse) was the only building that remained after the Hinckley Fire which went through on the first day of September, 1894. The schoolhouse was used as an emergency dwelling by the people. This school building burned in June, 1900.

The Board of Education consisted of Charles Morse, John H. Wright, and B. A. Beck. As there were many new settlers coming in and some roads had been built, the Board of Education felt that we were able to maintain a semi-graded school. We could get a little more state aid, but we were required to have at least two classrooms with one principal and another teacher having a much higher education and training than formerly needed in the one-room school. We had only two semesters of three months each in the beginning. In two or three years-even up to five years, there would not be any more children to go to school. We had a special election to authorize the school board to go ahead by approving a bond issue from the state trust fund. Now we had more trouble, as our taxable valuation was low and all we could get from the state was fifteen percent of our taxable valuation. So we were forced to sell private bonds. State loans were a little less than two thousand dollars and the estimated cost of the school was better than three thousand.

Cromwell School in 1905.

Mr. H. Oldenburg of Carlton helped us draw up the papers and sell the bonds. The new schoolhouse was built west on higher ground where the Legion Hall is now. The first principal was Miss Van Every, the second teacher was Miss Clausen, and the second principal was August Rolf. We opened with an enrollment of about forty pupils. By this time there was another school district organized (number 30). They took nearly one half of our taxable area. Later another new district was organized (number 31) taking another big slice of territory to the south and east and part of District 21. District number 13 was left with nearly all of the children, and less than 30 sections of land. Some of that was state land and was not subject to taxes.

There was another movement started to the northeast to organize a new district, but we appeared in opposition to their petition before the County Board of Commissioners who rejected the petition. We had to agree to build them a schoolhouse in the southwest corner of section 26-49-20 and it was maintained about five years. The school laws were such that, where there were six children between the ages of five and sixteen years they could demand a school for their children if they were more than two miles from the central school. The School Board was authorized to board the children near the school, but only with the consent of the parents.

In the fall of 1910 we were still having a semi-graded school district. The School Board was composed of three members: Edward Benson, Ida Morse, and B. A. Beck. They realized that something should be done to save our taxable valuation or we would be left with all the children and with only about seven or eight sections of land on which to levy taxes.

There was an invitation extended to us by the

commercial club of Duluth to a meeting—a kind of open forum—a free discussion on how we could improve the laws governing our schools. The Governor and representatives from the state Department of Education were there for the two-day meeting. B. A. Beck represented the local board at the meeting. They were all aware that the present laws governing our present system of organizing our school districts were not in the interest of improving and bringing a higher school education to the rural school children. After much discussion, it was agreed that we needed a new law that would permit the consolidation of several school districts. The consolidated district would become an independent district. A bill was prepared and presented to the legislature to that effect and was passed. The office of rural school director, who in cooperation with the county superintendent of schools could promote consolidation of rural schools, was also created. B. A. Beck, with the cooperation of the members of the board, started a movement for consolidation by circulating a petition, getting the required number of signatures, and presenting it to the county superintendent of schools. A special election to vote on the consolidation was called and it was carried by a big majority.

This meant reorganization, and so another special election to elect six members to the School Board and approve bonds was held. Three old and three new members were elected. The six members being elected were Edward Benson, Ida Morse, B. A. Beck, John Lindquist, John Hackamaki, and E. T. Walker. Next we had to have at least two acres for the school ground, which we bought from Joseph Kubat, and is the present school site. We hired a young architect, Clyde Kelly of Duluth, to draw plans for the new school building. A contract for the construction of the building was let to Jacobson Brothers, building contractors of Duluth and Chicago and the building was completed in April of 1913.

The faculty consisted of four members: Superintendent, John Wall; Principal, Lettisha King; and teachers, Sadie King and Nora Gilstad. The King sisters had been with us five or six years. We had the misfortune of having our old school building burn down before the new one was completed. The fire occurred during the end of Christmas vacation, about January 1, 1913. This school was located where the present American Legion hall now stands. A temporary school was set up in the old Morse store and warehouse buildings by the lakeshore. No school time was lost and the year was finished in the new building.

The next year we had a new superintendent, B. C. Winkleman. We also acquired two new teachers; Miss McIntyre was a domestic science teacher and the other was Miss Gates. Miss Gilstad stayed over, but the King sisters left because of Sadie's health. We also started a manual training course. Great stress was put on these two courses—domestic science and manual training—but they soon changed to home economics and agriculture and lead up to a fully accredited high school that would be a credit to a much larger community. The school that we had built was acquired through much sacrifice and cost by the people. They had to pay through higher taxes, go through the trouble connected with such an enterprise, and experience the travail, strife, and contention entailed. Some were motivated by jealousy and personal dislike, while others by honest fear of excessive taxes and the centralized control of school management, as this new system gave the power of levying the tax needed to operate the school.

Students at the Cromwell grade school—1st row: Marion Carlson, Helmi Hogbakka, Lila Larson, Helen Reimer, Bernice Hanson, Melvin Maki; 2nd row: Lydia Kamunen, Mamie Crocarrelli , Frances Svohada, Arnold Dahl, Helen Koskinen, Leon Line; 3rd row: June Gustafson, Marcella Hill, Hazel Glavanich, David Markusen, Tena Svohada, Toivo Makelson; 4th row: Audrey Ilstrup, Bertran Wilson, Donald LaMay, Arne Maki, Frances Gravelle, Nannie Carlson; Teacher: Martha Nordquist. Students absent: Emily Peterson, Florence Lundstrom, Ethel Smith, Arthur Martwig, Henry Smith, Guy Wilson.

    Here are some of the problems our new school system brought us. We had to transport the children within five miles of the central school and those beyond with the consent of their parents. If the parents did not consent, we had to provide school facilities for those children with the approval of the county superintendent of schools and the state Department of Education. This forced us to maintain a school up north in the southeast corner of Section 5-49-20, and also a school in the northwest corner of Section 12.

These were old simple frame buildings built before consolidation and they would not meet approval. There were no roads and nowhere for the teachers to board. There was quite a settlement moving south of Corona and they were looking for a school for their children. Now we did have a problem, with no road, up to sixteen pupils, and a prospect of thirty or more in a year or two. We rented a small building with the approval of the county superintendent of schools—mainly for two seasons. We had to have at least two acres of ground. The state Department of Education had now set up a building department and supplied us with plans and specifications for various sizes of buildings, depending on the number of pupils. The schoolhouse and grounds were finally approved. We then had to submit to the voters for their approval with a special election. People from Corona voted while the Cromwell district failed to vote. It carried unanimously or nearly so. There might have been one vote against it but that was all. Two or three years later, there came a protest. All of the protesters had had an opportunity to vote and give their expression of opposition in an orderly and respectable manner. The blame was put on the board of education when the responsibility really rested with them. If a mistake was made, it was made under the compulsion of a legal requirement.

CHAPTER FIVE

Organization of Local Government II

Now we refer to the time in the late 1880s, when permanent settlers began to settle the area. Some were a happy-go-lucky kind while others were of a serious disposition. All of them were visionaries and good neighbors. All the social events were held in the homes with singing and dancing. The music was furnished by someone who could play a violin or mouth organ. They would play such old timers as "Turkey in the Straw" and "The Irish Washer Woman." Some others included "Two Little Girls in Blue," "Annie Laurie," "Tommy Asleep at the Stitch," to name just a few. At times there would be a small keg of beer at the small cost of one dollar. All would have a good time and go home happy and rejoicing in the good old home and community spirit.

Most of the people were French and nearly all came from the same community near Quebec, Canada. They liked to talk about a legendary giant or a big wrestler, what we now call a heavyweight champion wrestler, who would come from afar. It so happened that there was another big wrestler down in the eastern part of Canada, probably from New Brunswick, for there were many men there who gloried in their strength and might. He had heard the big giant was coming to challenge him to battle and he was afraid of him and did not want to wrestle. He made it a point to be out plowing with an ox when the giant would arrive. The challenger arrived and came out to the field to inquire where Joe Mafraw lived. Joe Mafraw Junior took his plow in one hand and lifted it up in gun fashion and pointed it toward a shanty some distance away and said, "My father is over there." In so pointing the plow, he lifted the ox up so that his front feet just touched the ground. When the challenger saw how strong the son was, he made up his mind to return east.

No wonder they feared Paul Bunyan. There is also a story about the first Frenchman coming out to look over this country. He met a very big man with a blue ox. When the little Frenchman saw Paul Bunyan with his Canadian boots (Highlows, twelve-inch tops halfway between ankle and knee) it nearly scared him to death. Paul Bunyan asked him where he came from. The Frenchman said he came from Canada, about 280 acres from Latuque (280 acres is about ten miles). Paul noticed the Frenchman had a cross-cut saw, an axe, a two-inch auger, an old Springfield rifle, and a one-gallon jug. When Paul asked him what he wanted the saw and axe for, he said he wanted to build himself a shanty in the bush. Then Paul asked him what he wanted the rifle for and he answered, "to make the keyhole in the door." Next Paul wanted to know what the auger was for; the Frenchman said to bore holes in the doughnuts. "What about the big jug?" asked Paul. This, he explained was for his pea soup. So Paul Bunyan called the little Frenchman "Pea Soup" and many called the Canadian-French pea soup for many years afterwards.

The Canadian French were not an agricultural people, but excellent woodsmen and most of them very amiable. The Canadian French would clear five or six acres of land and plant between the stumps. Their first crop would be Canadian field peas, some potatoes, and other garden crops. They would get a hold of one or two pigs and a cow so they would have milk and pork for their own use. There were no general stores so it was necessary for them to lay up a six-month supply of groceries such as flour, sugar, and other household supplies. There were no roads usable in the summer. The only means of transportation was the pack sack and no one enjoyed that. Most of the supplies came from Aitkin.

The men would work in the woods making railroad cross ties, cutting fence posts, telephone and telegraph poles, and cedar for street paving. This was mostly piecework. In later years they cut cordwood. They were men who worked hard and were intelligent although they had very little schooling. Some of them became successful loggers and operated logging camps of their own, employing as many as forty to fifty men in the winter.

This reminds me of a story about one logger, Pete LaGou, who was a logger in Wisconsin. He had a large camp and hauled his supplies with a tote team which was an all-day trip. Food supplies were shipped and stored in the warehouse. The teamsters would get orders from the cook for the food and from Mr. LaGou for such things as axes, canthooks, chains, or other repair parts. On one occasion Mr. LaGou had a grindstone on his order which was illustrated by a circle with a hole. For an axe or chain he drew illustrations of the article desired. The teamster returned to camp that night. The next morning Mr. LaGou looked for his grindstone, but instead he found a big cheese. Then he wanted to see the order he had given the teamster. He looked it over carefully and at last he exclaimed, "By golly, I forgot to put the hole in it." So that was that.

There were some who came from New Brunswick and some from Ontario. Many became jobbers (small loggers). There were also some Swedes and Germans. I have recorded some stories about the French so I must not forget the Swedes and Germans. There were many dramatic stories about the Swedish and German people as well as other nationalities.

It has been said that the first Swede was Ole Olson. He got a job in the lumber woods and newcomers were nearly always given the job of swamping, and so was Ole. Not being able to speak English, they had much fun with him. On one occasion he was sent to a camp some three miles away to bring out a canthook. Well, Ole got home to camp and looked all over for something that "could not hook." The last place he looked was in the hovel (stable) where he saw a mule ox. He took him out in the woods. The crew all burst out laughing and Ole saw there was a mistake somewhere. He said this is the only thing he could find that could not hook. He stayed there all winter and in the spring he returned to Minneapolis which was called "Swede Town" in those days. When he was reunited with his old friends they asked about his experience in the woods. He told them and this was his answer. "When I come they started to call me son of a mule, and I tell them that was wrong—that son was the last part of my name and not the first part. Then they started to call me dumb head all winter. Ha! Ha! Ha! And my name was Ole Olson all the time."

There were only a few Germans here then. Here is a little story about a German homesteader. There were just two of them, a man and his wife. They had a neighbor who was a bachelor and came over sometimes to visit. One day Fritz came home and found his neighbor standing in the middle of the room hugging his wife.

Fritz said, "Hanna, you tell him to stop that." She said, "Ha! Ha! Ha! You tell him yourself—you speak better English than I do." So, they lived happily ever after.

By this time the original timber was gone and the Soo Line Railroad Company built a branch through Moose Lake, McGregor, Swatorye, up to Federal Dam and opened a new timber frontier. The French people were woodsmen, so they moved to Swatorye, the Thunder Bay district, and some up to Timeskoming, Canada.

Cromwell, Minnesota in the early 1900s. Visible in the photograph are the Co-op store, bank, and Morse store.

CHAPTER SIX

Brief Biography and Accomplishments of Early Settlers

George Flaugher is believed to be the first white man to settle in Red Clover. He was born in Indiana in the 1830s. He had been in the Confederate army as a regular or as a bushwhacker (guerrilla) and he bore the mark of a wound in his forehead that resembled a bayonet wound or stab.

He would never talk of his past. He may have come here to work on the railroad when they were building the Northern Pacific Railroad in the late 60s. (ed. note: Groundbreaking for the NP was February 15, 1870.) He was a big strong man. He filed on a homestead in about 1875 on the S1/2 NW1/4 Sec. 32-49-20 and made his home there until 1894 when the Hinckley fire destroyed his house. He had qualified up on this claim in due time some years before this and had also sold this land for forty dollars to one named Mitchel who was then the depot agent at Carlton. He had obtained soldier's script that he used to get title to the N1/2 SE1/4 Sec. 32-49-20 where he built a log cabin and made that his home for the next twenty years or more. When he became nearly blind he was made a charge of the town of Red Clover and they sent him to Scanlon to a boarding home where he died. Mr. Flaugher was not very industrious. He never worked for anybody, but made his living by hunting and raising a garden. He would purchase about one acre of land, plant his garden, cut some wild hay on the creek bottoms and sell it to the lumber camps. Outside of this, he had lived with the Indians in the early days and might have had an Indian wife.

Woodbury Whitten homesteaded in the early 1880s in Sec. 6-48-20 and made it his home all his life. He was supposed to be a single man of good character and a good neighbor. He sold the pine off his land—cutting it himself so it gave him a little money. He farmed some, mostly raising hay put up by hand which he sold to the lumber camps. In this way he made his living. He was born in Ohio and had served in the Union army. He died from the effects of an operation in a Duluth hospital in the fall of 1894. He had sold five acres in the northwest corner of land that was the north part of the Northern Pacific right-of-way to George Westbrook, who lived there two or three years and then left. It is not known what became of Westbrook. After Mr. Whitten died, his brother, Daniel, came out from Ohio, took charge of his estate, and settled north of Wright. Two women came out from Ohio who claimed they were the wife and daughter of Mr. Woodbury Whitten. They contested the right of Daniel Whitten and the lawyers got the estate.

Arthur R. Newton, a brother-in-law of Woodbury Whitten—non-French, but a Yankee, came from near Boston and filed on a homestead E1/2 NW1/4 Sec. 10-48-20 in 1888. He lived there about five years and qualified, but his claim was not accepted as he had not moved on the land and made it his home within one year as provided by law. Also, he had sent his family of one boy and two girls back east before he qualified and had gone back himself as soon as he qualified. So a year later when he received the notice that his claim was rejected, he sent his son, Erven, to file on this claim again. Erven held it about two years and then sold his right to Louis Lungreen who later qualified and sold out to Emil Rypka.

Horace B. Paine came to Cromwell in 1879. He cooked on the railroad boarding cars and later in the section house or "Eating House" as it was called. A year or two later he settled down here to live and made his home on a homestead, the SW1/4 Sec. 4-48-20. He made his living by cooking in the lumber camps. He did not do much farming, but raised a good garden every summer and did some hunting. He was raised as an orphan by his aunt in Wisconsin and had at least a high school education. He had a large family, six girls (one died in infancy) and five boys. In about 1898 he sold the west eighty to Jacob Pohto and in about 1906 he sold the balance to Joe Waverin and the Kubats and moved out to Washington. He lived there about one year. He came back to Cromwell and bought a small farm about four miles west of Cromwell and lived there until they burned out. Then they bought a small house east of the lake on Highway 210. Mr. Paine served as town clerk of Red Clover and as Justice of the Peace. When the village of Cromwell was incorporated, he served as village recorder and Justice of the Peace. At last, he retired from all active work and lived to be more than eighty years of age. His wife and three daughters and two sons preceded him in death.

Mr. and Mrs. Jacob Pohto were born in Finland. They came to this country as young people and were married in upper Michigan. Mr. Pohto worked in the copper mines for some years. Later he worked in Superior, Wisconsin. Three daughters were born to them. In 1898 he bought eighty acres of land from H. B. Paine. They came to Cromwell in 1903 and built a house and dairy and livestock farm. Mr. Pohto was very active in public affairs and served on the village council for many years. He also served on the creamery Board of

Directors and for part of that time served as secretary and treasurer.

In the early 1930s his wife suffered a paralytic stroke and was partially paralyzed for about five years before she died. The farm was then rented to a family who lived there for some time and Mr. Pohto moved to California and made his home with his daughter in Oakland. He died there at the age of eighty years, leaving three daughters to mourn his departure. The Pohtos were a very highly esteemed family.

Mr. George H. Merwin was born in New York. He had been a schoolteacher and served as an officer in the Union Army. He came up the Kettle River from Stillwater sometime in the early 1880s to watch camp for the St. Anthony Lumber Company on Kettle Lake in the summer. In the winter he would hunt (maybe for the lumber company) and trap. Later, the lumber company gave him forty acres of land. He lived there for many years. He married in 1897. They had no children and he sold his land to Olaf Johnson and moved to town to live about 1920. He lived there until he died about 1925. He lived mostly on his pension and took little interest in public affairs. He did serve several terms on the town board when Eagle and Red Clover were united and he served on the school board of District 31 at the time of consolidation, but in the later days of his life his memory failed. He wandered out in the woods and was found dead the next morning. His wife lived for several years after at Fort Snelling where she died.

Alex Bellanger left Canada as a young man just married and settled in northern lower Michigan where he worked in the woods and sawmills. He came first to

Wright and then to Cromwell, filing on a homestead W1/2 SW1/4, W1/2 NW1/4 Sec. 34-49-20 about the year 1885 or earlier. He had a family of two girls and three boys. He had quite a bit of good pine timber which he logged and sold in the winter of 1892 and 1893. He might have received about a thousand dollars for the stumpage which made him independent for a few years. Later he sold sixty acres to Edward Simmons, a Norwegian.

Mr. Bellanger had some livestock and carried on some farming, but a few years after Mrs. Bellanger died he sold out and went to California where he had the misfortune of being struck by a car or truck and was killed. Mr. and Mrs. Bellanger were good neighbors and kept an open house for everybody and many social gatherings were held in their home.

Minnie Bellanger

The Hinckley fire missed Bellanger's house and barn, but it burned over all of his land and killed all of his cattle and one ox team. Mr. Bellanger built the first large log house and the first big barn in Red Clover and Eagle.

Jerry Royer was a French Canadian and worked in upper and lower Michigan before he came to Minnesota. He came to Wright first and filed on a homestead E1/2 SW and E1/2 NW1/4 Section 34-49-20 in the late 1880s. He was a single man and cleared about five acres. He did not farm but sold his pine timber in 1892 to a lumber company who cut the pine in the winter of 1892-93. He had close to 300 to 1,00 feet at three dollars per thousand and he worked as a jobber. He had a contract to cut the logs and swamp all roads at one dollar per one thousand feet, and he made good. He qualified and shortly after he sold out to Charles Swanson, who lived there about three years. Jerry Royer bought forty acres from Fred Johnson, the NW1/4 of SW1/4 Section 10-48-20, and held that two or three years. He then left this community; it is not known where he went. He sold this forty acres to Ole Haugland who lived there about five years.

Dan Frazer, a French Canadian, was a locomotive engineer for the Northern Pacific and was a good handy man. He came to Cromwell in 1891 and filed on a homestead, the N1/2 NE1/4 Section 2-48-20. He married in 1892. He cleared some land and built a good sized log house and a large barn for that time. He qualified his homestead in due time and then had some matrimonial trouble. He and his wife parted and Frazer went to the Iron Range. There were no children and the homestead was left to Mrs. Frazer.

John Billeveau, a French Canadian, came to Cromwell from Michigan about 1885 and filed a homestead, the SE1/4 Section 34-49-20, and lived there as a single man for many years. He sold his pine timber about 1891 and worked for a while in the woods and sawmills. Later he did some farming and had eight or ten milk cows. He sold all his land except for forty acres and married shortly after, about 1920. He then moved to

Pine City where he died some years later. The Hinckley fire did not burn over his land.

Frank LeMier, a French Canadian, came from Michigan about the early part of 1887. He filed on a homestead, the NE1/4 Section 34-49-20, about 1888. He sold his pine timber in 1892, did no farming, and sold the forty with the buildings to Philip Dezonia in about 1894. Mr. Dezonia lived there until his death. Mr. LeMier sold one forty to Charles Morse, one to Ole Benson, and one to Dan Coty. Frank LeMier bought a strip of land from Ole Benson where he lived until he sold out to Joe Holecek. He had married some years earlier when he went back to Canada to visit his old home. He came back to Cromwell with his wife and they lived there until he sold out. They moved to Eagle River, Wisconsin, and lived there the rest of their lives having no children.

George Ambeau, a French Canadian, came from Michigan in 1888 where he had worked in the woods for several years. He filed on a homestead, the N1/2 NW1/4 and S1/2 SW1/4 Section 2-48-20. He cleared a small farm of about twenty acres or more and made it his home. He married about 1907 and shortly after sold out to Edward Yerean. He then moved to British Columbia where he remained and raised a family of six or seven boys. He died there a number of years later leaving his wife and boys to mourn his passing.

Arthur Dotten came from New Brunswick, Canada, about 1890. He was a lumber man and had a logging camp on the north end of Cromwell Lake. He logged all the pine around Cromwell in 1890 to 1893. His logs were landed on Flaugher Lake and driven down to Minneapolis sawmills. About this time (1893) he filed on a homestead, the W1/2 NW1/4 Section 10-48-20. After this he also carried on some logging and, beginning around 1897, he operated a sawmill on the east side of the lake at Cromwell for five or six years. He had, as he said, taken "all the cream of the community" before moving to Louisiana. He lived there until he died leaving his wife and a step-daughter to mourn his passing. It has been reported that Mr. Dotten quit the hard work of logging to start the "softer" job of raising cotton. We know that some fruit becomes hard and bitter with age while other fruit becomes sweet and mellow as they mature. I am sure this can also be applied to mankind.

Amasa Dotten came here from New Brunswick, Canada, in 1891 and worked in the lumber camp for his brother, Arthur Dotten. The next summer he worked in a sawmill in Minneapolis. In the fall of 1892 he sent for his family, consisting of his wife, two boys, and two girls.

The Amasa Dotten Family—Amasa, Oscar, Earl, Maude, Laura, Mary.

They moved here and worked in the lumber camps that winter. He filed on a homestead, the E1/2 NW1/4 the W1/2 NW1/4 Section 26-49-20 and made his living by cutting timber every winter until the early 1890s when his wife died. He then moved to town where he had built a house a few years earlier. It had been rented by Louis Larson who used the front for a general store and the back for bachelor quarters. Mr. Dotten built a second house a few years later. They were the first homes of construction built by private citizens that could be rented. Except for a short time in Iowa, after he married the second time, he lived there until he died in 1920. He did not do any farming and his hauling was done by ox team. He had raised a large family—four girls and three boys. He helped organize and build the Methodist Church in the late 1890s.

Ben (Billium) Pepin was a French Canadian who came here as a woodsman (a cant hook man) from Michigan in 1891 and filed on a homestead, the S1/2 NW1/4 Section 4-48-20. He remained a single man and made that his home for many years doing some farming until he retired and died. He had a brother in Minneapolis who was a fireman with a family of two sons and one daughter.

Ben Pepin

Peter Morrison, a French Canadian, filed on a homestead about 1892, the N1/2 of SE1/4 Section 8-48-20. He improved the land by clearing some of it but never lived on it as he made his home halfway between Wright and Cromwell. Around 1894, he sold his right to John Derosier, a French Canadian blacksmith, who came here from a French settlement at Hardwood Creek, Minnesota. He had separated from his wife and family to work as a blacksmith and handyman in the lumber camps. He built some good buildings and cleared a nice little farm and lived there until he sold out to Otto Lust in about 1904.

Mr. Lust made a good farm out of the eighty acres as a general farmer and was a successful dairy farmer until his and his wife's health failed due to arthritis and they were forced to retire. They sold their farm and moved to town to live until about 1940.

John Savage, an Irish Canadian, came from the northern part of Ontario. He had traveled over a good part of the country as a lumberjack and timber estimator. He came to Cromwell in about 1900. He filed on a homestead in 1892, the W1/2 SW1/4 and S1/2 NW1/4 Section 26-49-20. He helped locate many on their homesteads and worked hard to get settlers in here. He was a single man in his fifties working in the lumber camps. He helped organize the town of Red Clover which then included townships 48-20, 48-21, 49-20, 49-21 and the west half of 49-19 or that part of 49-19 west of the Indian reservation. This was all part of Moose Lake Township at the time.

Mr. Savage worked hard and laid out most of the roads where they are now established and have become our main highways. He was a man of sterling character. He married in 1904, but they parted some three years later and divided the land. She kept the land with the buildings and he kept the three forties. He sold all of his land to Patrick Mahar. In 1902-03 he was the first chairman of the Board of Directors of the town of Red Clover. He also established Forest Hill Cemetery as a public burial ground. Prior to this, the dead were buried where they died. Mrs. Savage lived there for some years after and married Claude Wilson. They remained on the place a few years when they sold out to John Erkkila. They moved to Long Prairie where they lived until Mr. Wilson became ill with diabetes and then they returned to Cromwell. He died about two years later and Mrs. Wilson married Frank Wagner, a shoemaker, and they lived happily ever after.

Mr. and Mrs. John Erkkila were born in Finland and came here as young people. They were married in Superior, Wisconsin, and came to Cromwell in 1903. About two years later they bought the old Savage homestead and made this home for some years until they sold out to Henry Smith. From here they moved to a homestead in Sec. 10-49-20 and established their home there until Mrs. Erkkila died. John then turned the home over to his daughter and son-in-law and left to work as a woodsman. The Erkkilas had two daughters.

Henry Smith and family moved to Cromwell in about 1905 from the southern part of Minnesota. They lived with Mr. Smith's uncle, Lee White, for a year or two until they bought the farm from John Erkkila in 1907. Mr. Smith lived on this farm for about ten years, but not doing much farming. Soon thereafter he started to work on the section. He worked there until his health failed him and he had to retire. They sold the farm to Edward Dahlman of Duluth who moved onto the farm in the spring of 1918. In that fateful fall of 1918, a big forest fire burned over the northern part of Red Clover and came close to Mr. Dahlman's buildings. By hard work he saved them, but the effects of the smoke and over-exertion brought him down with pneumonia. He died in a short time, leaving Mrs. Dahlman and two sons and one daughter to mourn his departure. Mrs. Dahlman continued to live on the little farm and kept her family together. She raised her children to be honorable and industrious citizens, who later married. The two sons took over the farm and bought more land making it a large stock and dairy farm. Mrs. Dahlman retired to her own little home on the farm. So, time moves on and one by one we are left behind. Sooner or later, the memory of us will be forgotten, whether it is good or otherwise.

John H. Wright, the son of George Wright Sr., came to Cromwell with his parents in the early 1870s. He became a telegraph operator and later depot agent. He left Cromwell in 1892 and became a conductor on the new Duluth and Winnipeg, working there until the fall of 1896 when his father suffered a stroke. He then came back to Cromwell as telegraph operator. He became depot agent on January 1, 1897, and was the agent for many years. Mr. Wright and others incorporated the village of Cromwell and he entered the saloon and hotel business. He continued this for many years until the buildings burned down. Mr. Wright also organized School District No. 13 in 1891. He was elected a county commissioner and served as chairman of the County Board of Commissioners for part of the eight years he served on the board.

Mr. Wright also operated the old Wright farm and bought all the lakeshore land on the west shore of South Lake from Edward P. Duffy. Later he sold ten acres of his lakeshore land to Charles Kanerva who started a chicken ranch. The balance of the lakeshore property was also sold, part of it to George Wright. Mr. Wright did not farm much but kept some cows and livestock for some years until his health failed him. He was in poor health with a heart ailment for many years. He had built himself a good modern home after the hotel had burned down and lived there until he died, leaving his wife, two sons, and two daughters (one daughter preceded him in death) to mourn his passing. Mrs. Wright lived several years and survived nearly all her children. She sold all her property in Cromwell and moved to Louisiana to live with her youngest daughter, Mrs. Rolph, where she later died. Her daughter died shortly after as well.

Charles Morse and his brother, James Morse (of English descent), came from the state of Maine as young men to Frazee, Minnesota, and filed on a homestead. Charles married Elizabeth Pierz, also English, in 1886. He farmed some in the summer raising grain. In the winter, he and his brother-in-law logged in the woods around Frazee until about 1890. He logged in the upper

The Morse family at home. l to r: Ida, Charles, Horace, Elizabeth, Cora, and "Scotty."

Prairie River near Prairie Lake. The first winter he logged and the second winter he had a contract to cut logs and skid them. Skidding means to pile logs on the skidways along the logging roads ready to be hauled to the landing. It was mostly Norway pine on what is known as the Schin and Gradberg farms. Most of the logs were landed on Hasty Brook.

The next winter Charles Morse was in partnership with Arthur Dotten and had a contract with Brown and Wood of Detroit (now Detroit Lakes), Minnesota , to get out several railroad cross ties with the right to cut on all railroad lands. It had been a good winter with an early start about the middle of November. He did well so that spring Mr. Morse bought government lots 6-7-2 which are now the Morse farm and the north part of the village of Cromwell. This was the spring of 1894 and in June of that year he entered a partnership with E. P. Duffy and started the first general store in Cromwell. I will give a history in another chapter. However, for now I will say that it was small building—about ten by twelve feet.

Charles Morse

About noon on the first day of September, 1894, the Hinckley fire hit Cromwell, and in less than ten minutes all that was left of the town was the little green schoolhouse south of the section house. A few of the people left on the freight train that was there at the time, but most of the people went out in the lake and no lives were lost. Shortly after the fire, Mr. Morse built the west part of the present Morse home and the next summer he finished building it. He used it as a hotel, this becoming the first private hotel and public stopping place in Cromwell.

Morse Hotel in Cromwell. Pictured on the porch, l to r: front, Ida Morse, Mary Brett, Pat Corbett; back, Claude Wilson, Charles Morse, Elizabeth Morse, Anton Bergman; on lawn, Lottie Wright, Ethel Wright, Cora Morse.

About three years later Mr. Morse sold his farm at Frazee and then he built and started a general store north of the railroad tracks on the lakeshore. He conducted business there selling merchandise and dealing in forest products such as ties, fencing, telephone and telegraph poles, pulpwood, and cordwood. In about 1907 he built a brick, two-story building on the main street. The main floor became his store and the upper floor was used for public purposes. In 1905, he built a sawmill north of Tamarack River on the west shore of Cromwell Lake. He carried on some logging and was in the lumber business for many years. He also operated the Morse Mercantile Co. until his death in the 1920s. His wife, two daughters, and one son survived him. He was considered "well-to-do," but as his property consisted mostly of real estate, one thousand acres of wild land, it yielded no income. The estate kept paying the taxes on it for some years. Mrs. Morse conducted the business until she became ill with pernicious anemia and was bedridden for about a year before she died. Her oldest daughter was with her and took charge of the business, selling the merchandise and renting the store building and home to Mr. Evenson who conducted the business for two or three years. Mr. Evenson sold the merchandise to Mr. Goldstein, including a lease to the store building, and he continued for about three years until the building burned down. The ruins have been an eyesore ever since. The farm was leased to Charles Martwig for a number of years. He was the first one around here to use a tractor for farm work.

Edward P. Duffy was born in Ohio and came to Cromwell in 1892 as depot agent. Charles Morse and Edward Duffy started a little store north from the depot in the spring of 1894. The previous winter, they had been getting out railroad ties and operated under contract to D. L. Young of Aitkin, Minnesota, who had a contract with the railroad company for all their ties. The railroad canceled their contract in early February so that left Young with all these ties on hand. They were more than Young could pay for so they offered to take them in payment for the ties on his promissory note for one year. Mr. Morse and Mr. Duffy took many notes with the understanding that the settlers would trade them out in goods. They in turn sold the notes to Stone, Ordean and Co. in Duluth for merchandise to stock the small store, which was the first store in Cromwell, but the Hinckley fire burned it and Duffy and Morse lost everything they had. The total capital of the store was about one hundred dollars. After the Hinckley fire, Mr. Duffy bought some land on the west side of the lake, the W1/2 SW1/4 and SE1/4 SW1/4 Sec. 4-48-20. He sold the latter to Samuel Elliot in 1895 who cleared about twenty acres of the land.

Samuel Elliot was born in Ontario, Canada. When he had cleared his land, he returned east and married. He then worked in the woods in Michigan for eight or ten years. He came back and built a house on the land and made it his permanent home until he died from heart failure some ten years later. He also bought a strip of land, Government Lot No. 1 Sec. 33-49-20 from Judge Bradley, the probate judge of Carlton County, who had owned this land for many years. He sold it to Mr. Elliot about 1906 or 1907.

Mr. Elliot held the land about five years and sold it to Edward Simmons, who built some buildings on it and cleared all the land along with sixty acres he bought from Alex Bellanger. He farmed it for many years with hired help. Mr. Simmons was born in Norway. He lived in Superior, Wisconsin, until the time of prohibition where he operated a restaurant and saloon. He then moved to Cromwell making this his home. His wife died in Superior about 1910. They had two daughters.

Edward T. Walker came from the state of Maine about 1891. He was a single man and worked in the woods down near Barker where he met John Savage who located him on a homestead, the N1/2 SE1/4 and the E1/2 NE1/4 Sec. 26-49-20. Mr. Walker made that his home until about 1925. In 1899 he married a school mistress. They had two boys and one girl. He did some farming but engaged mostly in the timber business consisting of cordwood, cedar posts, and poles. He built the brick garage in Cromwell, but after his wife died, he was not so successful and he lost all he had in the late 1920s. He remarried and moved to Minneapolis where he lived until his death in February, 1953. His second wife preceded him in death.

Michael O'Brien was from St. Johns, New Brunswick, Canada, and came to Wisconsin, Michigan, and Minnesota to work in the woods. John Savage located him on a homestead in 1892, Sec. 20, the NW1/4 Sec. 20-49-20, on which he built a shanty and lived with his two brothers during the winter of 1893. They had no stove and did all their cooking and baking out on an open fire. They baked their bread in a cast iron kettle. We had lots of snow that winter so they had plenty of fun. In the spring of 1895, however, O'Brien committed suicide after the Hinckley fire burned his timber. He was buried on his homestead about two hundred feet from his shanty.

Mr. Joseph Rogers was born in Michigan and came here in 1894 and was located on a homestead by John Savage in Sec. 20-49-19 in the NW1/4. He lived there long enough to prove up his claim. He sold his pine timber in 1896 and then sold his land to a real estate company in 1900. Mr. Rogers did not farm but might have done some hunting and trapping. He was not very industrious. He married at the time he filed on the homestead, getting his wife through a matrimonial advertisement. He got a good wife, but she did not have the benefit of a beauty shop. This reminds me of when eight or ten young men were gathered at the NP depot, which was the only social center then. John Clar, who made his home with Harry Paine when not working in the woods, was there. They were talking on the subject of beauty in the presence of Mr. Rogers, who made the remark that beauty was only skin deep. Said Mr. Clark to Mr. Rogers, "If that is so I would go home and skin my wife if I were you." He had said that she was a perfect wife but lacked one thing; she did not know how to tan buckskin. Maybe he was not very successful for he did not stay around Cromwell very long after that.

Gust Webber was born in Sweden and settled in South Dakota about 1896. He lost his wife there and then moved to Superior, Wisconsin, and came to Cromwell about 1897. He bought the SE1/4 SW1/4 and SW1/4 SE1/4 Sec. 8-48-20. He had a family of two boys and one girl. He cleared some land and built a small house and barn. After the barn was built, he got sick. When he had nearly recovered, however, he committed suicide by shooting himself. He had assured himself that his children would be taken care of. He was buried two or three hundred feet northwest from his house, south of a maple tree.

Oscar Homstad, a Norwegian, was born in Coon Prairie, Wisconsin, in the first Norwegian settlement in the state. He had been working in different parts of the state of Minnesota as a woodsman and railroad builder. He was located on a homestead by John Savage in the year 1893, the N1/4 Sec. 24-49-20, and he made it his home until about 1914. He cleared a small farm and spent part of his time farming and the rest of his time in the woods getting out ties, posts, and cordwood. About 1906, he married and had two sons. About 1913 he disposed of the farm and moved to the NW1/4 of NE1/4 Sec. 34-49-20 which was part of the old Frank Lamier homestead. He had worked on and helped build the first court house in Carlton in 1891-92 when the county seat was moved from Thomson to Carlton. (ed. note: The county seat was moved in 1890.) He also worked in Carlton in the sawmill. Mr. Homstad, in partnership with a Mr. Erickson, cleared twenty-two acres of land on the F.A. Watkins farm in the summer of 1893, 3 1/2 miles south of Carlton, Minnesota.

Mr. Thomas Anderson was born in Scotland and had worked in the sawmills at Carlton for the J. M. Paine Lumber Co. for many years and later in Cloquet for the C. N. Nelson Lumber Co. He located on a homestead with the help of John Savage in 1894—the SE1/4 of SW1/4 Sec. 2-48-20. He never lived there, however, so he lost his right to Harvey Walters who filed for it in 1901 and lived there for some years before moving up to Hibbing, Minnesota. He later sold the homestead. He did no farming but sold all the pine timber.

Niels Maston, a single man from Michigan, bought eighty acres in the late 1890s, SE1/4 SW1/4 and SW1/4 of SE1/4 Sec. 26-49-10. He built a little house and lived there a few years and sold this land to John Erkkila. Mr. Erkkila, lived there for about ten years and then moved up north on Sec. 10-49-20 where he took up a homestead.

David Emerson, a Norwegian (his original name was Bracken), was an ox teamster for the Sauntry Cain Lumber Co. He worked there for many years. In 1891 he filed on a homestead in Sec. 14-48-20 and proved it up in due time and then sold the land to Charles Morse. He did no farming but worked in the woods until he died.

John Pohl was born in Germany and came to this country with his parents about 1877 and settled in or near Port Huron, Michigan, and grew up there. He started early in life as a lumberjack and worked in the woods in Michigan and Wisconsin. He came to Cromwell in the fall of 1893 and worked in the woods here. For some time he clerked in the store for Edward P. Duffy and did some farming. He married *Lydia Pohl, wife of John Pohl.* in 1898 and then he worked for the NP railroad as a bridge carpenter for some years and then bought some land, the S1/2 NE1/4 Sec. 8-48-20. He cleared the land but never built any buildings on it. He operated a threshing machine and a portable sawmill for some years. He retired to his home in Cromwell and worked as a carpenter. Mr. and Mrs. Pohl had two daughters and one son who made their homes in Detroit, Michigan.

Willis Cool was born in Wisconsin and came to Ricos, Minnesota, about 1890 and worked there as a carpenter. He was also a great hunter. He and his brother-in-law came to Cromwell to hunt deer in the fall of 1893. They located their hunting camp in the center of Sec. 27-49-10 and in one week pulled out with sixteen deer. The next spring Mr. Cool came back with the intention of starting a general store. He bought one acre of land from George Wright and built a small house that fall. In the spring he sold the house to John Pohl. Mr. Cool and his family moved back to Wausau, Wisconsin, where he worked in the paper mill.

Louis Pohl was born in Germany and around 1876 came to Michigan as a young boy with his parents and grew up there. He worked there until about 1895. Then he came to Cromwell and worked around there and the Iron Range for some years. He bought eighty acres, the S1/2 NE1/4 Sec. 8-48-20. His father and mother came to Cromwell and built a house after having sold their property in Michigan. They lived their declining days there. After they died Louis got married and started farming which he continued to do for some years. He then sold out and started working out again. His wife died and he continued to work here and there for other people and at last went to Detroit, Michigan, where he worked for some time. He had the misfortune to lose both of his hands. He continued to live in Detroit and died there two or three years later. Mr. and Mrs. Louis Pohl had no children of their own but they adopted a baby and raised Louis Pohl, Jr. to manhood. Mr. Pohl left part of his farm to his brother, Ed Pohl, and the balance of his land to his foster son.

Jack Gill was born in Kentucky. He was a cook in the lumber camps and he filed on a homestead in 1891 on the NW1/4 Sec. 22-48-20. He made this his home, proved up, and built a log shanty on it. That is about all the improvements he made. He was a single man, but he took a common law wife a year or two before he proved up. She was called "Momma" and he met her in Barnum. When he had proven up, he sold his land to Hogan Hanson. Hanson moved onto the land right after he was married in Barnum. He lived there two or three years.

Mr. Hogan Hanson was born in Norway and came to Stillwater with his parents as a small boy of six.

He started to work in the woods at an early age as an ox teamster and later as a camp foreman. He was the foreman for the Sauntry Cain Lumber Co. up on the North Shore for many years. He moved back here and made his home on this land. He and his sons kept a large herd of Guernsey cattle. He made this his home until he died, leaving his wife, four sons, and one daughter. Mrs. Hanson and her two youngest sons are maintaining and operating the farm. The oldest son, Norman, married and is one of the leading citizens. He is very active in soil conservation and other cooperative activities.

Hogan Hanson

    Mr. James McDermot was born in Canada and was Canadian Irish. Mrs. McDermot was Canadian French. They moved to Cromwell from Barnum about 1898 and bought forty acres of land from J. M. Paine, the SW1/4 of NE1/4 Sec. 3-48-20. He built a house and other small buildings and cleared a little land for a garden. Mr. McDermot was a cook in the lumber camps and worked at that for some time. He was the first rural mail carrier in the town of Eagle and worked on this job until his health failed. He retired and died shortly afterwards from dropsy. Mrs. McDermot and his step-son survived him and she died two or three years later.

    Mr. Edward Ekstrom was born in Finland and was believed to be the first Finlander to settle here. He worked around Thomson as a timberman building log houses and barns. He never married. He filed on a homestead in 1891, the E1/2 NW1/4 and E1/2 SW1/4, Sec. 32-49-20. He lived there off and on until he proved up but worked at Thomson most of the time for a few years until he took up blacksmithing at Cromwell. He lived here until he died. He sold that part of his homestead south of Tamarack River, about ten acres, to Oscar Isaacson. About 1905, his brother, Erick Ekstrom, came over from Finland. He lived on the Edward Ekstrom homestead and farmed it for more than twenty years. He died of a heart attack around the same time as his brother, Ed.

Mr. Oscar Isaacson was born in Finland and was a motorman on the streetcars in Superior, Wisconsin. He came to Cromwell about 1898. He bought ten acres and a building from Edward Ekstrom, the NW1/4 of SW1/4 Sec. 32-49-20. He lived there two or three years and operated a general store for a few years. He then sold his business to a Mr. Korhonen. Mr. Isaacson moved to Sawyer about 1906 where he lived until he died. He had sold his land to a Mr. Peterson, a brother-in-law of Alex Wherela. Peterson lived on the land for two or three years and then moved back to Superior, Wisconsin. He was born in Finland, had two children, and died a violent death.

Mr. Bennett A. Beck was born in Denmark and went to the public schools, taking up a two-year course of training in animal husbandry. At the age of sixteen he came to Detroit, Michigan, and worked there for about one year. He then came west to the Twin Cities in 1890 and worked there until the fall of 1892 when he came to Cromwell to work in a lumber camp on the north end of

Cromwell Lake. He also worked in Carlton, Wrenshall, and Cloquet, Minnesota. He filed on a homestead, the W1/2 SW1/4 Sec. 28-49-20, in 1894 and made that his home. It was a general farm but mostly a dairy and livestock farm. Mr. Beck was considered a successful dairy farmer for more than forty years.

He was very active in organizations. He helped to organize the Carlton County Farmers Mutual Fire Insurance Co. in 1903. About 1910 he helped to organize the Producers Co-operative Market Association of Duluth, Minnesota, and was a member of the Board of Directors. About this time he also worked on the organization of the Consolidated School District No. 13 which was organized in 1912. He also helped to organize the Co-operative Creamery and many other organizations which made Cromwell noted for its co-operative enterprise. In the 1890s he was active in the building of roads, and in 1896 he helped build the first turnpike road in the northwest part of Carlton County. This later became the main street of Cromwell and is now U.S. Highway No. 210. He helped to organize the English Bethany Lutheran Church in Cromwell and was ready to support every good cause that would improve the community. He assisted in organizing the local telephone company and was its first secretary. He also helped organize the Carlton County Potato Growers Association of which he was Secretary and Treasurer.

Mr. Edward Larson was born in Norway. He was a married man and farmed some in the northwestern part of Minnesota (the 13th township it was then called). He had lived in Superior, Wisconsin, some years before coming to Cromwell as a carpenter in 1898. He bought forty acres, the NW1/4 of NE1/4 Sec. 33-49-20, and improved it by building a good house and barn and clearing all the forty. He had a large family of six boys and three girls. He made this his home as long as he lived. His wife preceded him in death by about two years.

      Mr. Ole B. Benson was born in Norway and came to this country as a young man, first settling in Iowa and South Dakota and then in Brainerd, Minnesota, about 1892. He was married in 1893 and came to Cromwell in 1894 to work on the NP section. In the summer or fall of 1894, he bought the SE1/4 and SW1/4 of Sec. 33-29-20 and made his living by farming. He lived there the rest of his life, raising a highly respected family of one girl and three boys who became leading citizens. The boys became creamery managers at Cromwell and Wright, Minnesota. Mr. Benson made a trip back to Norway about 1920 to visit his old home and his brother, Ben, who had also been at Cromwell for a number of years. Ben had worked on the railroad in the 1890s before returning to Norway to marry his old love. He remained there to establish a home and farm, raising a family of several children.

      Mr. John Hendrickson was born in Finland and came to this country as a young man. He worked in Michigan, Wisconsin, and Duluth, Minnesota, before coming to Cromwell in about 1896. He bought forty acres, the NW1/4 of the SW1/4, Sec. 31. He built a nice home on it and was doing well until he burned out in 1915. He was a married man and had three boys and two girls. Along with others, in 1900, he helped in the organization of School District No. 30 which had all been part of School Dist. No. 13. Later, in 1912, it became part of Consolidated Dist. No. 13. Mr. Hendrickson was so strongly opposed to this that he and two others appealed the election and took it to District Court. They lost the appeal. He then sold his farm to Tony Gregory and went to the Dakotas and was there two or three years before coming back to Cromwell where he remained for three years. He later moved to Duluth, Minnesota, where he died.

Jacob Nyrhinen was born in Ylistaro, Finland, in 1869 and his wife, Mary, was born in Nurmoo, Waasan Laani in 1864. They came to this country in 1898, first to Massachusetts, then to Pennsylvania, then Detroit. They came to Cromwell in 1901, filed on a homestead, the SW1/4 SE1/4 Section 8-49-20, and made that their permanent home. He had to pack all his provisions on his back and his wife had to pack their oldest girl on her back all the way to and from Cromwell, a distance of nearly five miles. There were no roads then and Mr. Nyrhinen worked on the town roads and took contracts ditching on the road sides. While he was working on a road ditch he had the misfortune to have a hemorrhage of the brain and he died two or three years later. He left a wife and three girls. Mrs. Nyrhinen remained on the homestead and raised her three girls to noble womanhood.

Matt Mannikka was born in Finland and came to this country in the 1890s. He filed on a homestead about 1900, the NE1/4 NW1/4 Sec. 30-49-20. He was a single man all of his life. He cleared a good deal of land and made his living mostly by selling hay and other farm products, but had no cattle.

John Hakamaki was born in Finland and came to New York Mills with his parents sometime in the 1880s. He came to Cromwell in 1896 to work on the section and filed on a homestead that summer, the SE1/4 NW1/4 Sec. 6-48-20, and made that his home. He was single. His brother, Felix, came and stayed with him and later his father came and made his home with him also. He bought more land and cleared a nice farm. He had another brother, Frank, who filed on a homestead, the E1/2 SW1/4 and the W1/4 SE1/4 Sec. 80-49-20, but he did not stay very long and he relinquished his right to his brother, Felix, who moved on the homestead with his father. They made it their permanent home. John married a widow with two boys and they had one son, Felix. John cleared a good farm. He later went with his son, Felix, and operated a threshing machine and performed other custom work until he retired and turned his farm over to his son. John was known as John Maki and later as John Hakamaki. He had walked all the way from New York Mills and asked for a job on the track from every section foreman along the way. When he came to the section foreman in Cromwell, he was hired and so he stayed in Cromwell. After he had lived on his homestead for three years, he walked back to New York Mills and got a cow from his father or some other relatives. He walked all the way back to Cromwell with the cow—a distance of over a hundred miles.

Mr. John Eastman was born in Sweden. He was a married man with two boys and one girl. He came here as a section foreman and bought forty acres, the NW1/4 SW1/4 Sec. 33-49-20, and built a house and a small barn and cleared some land and did some small-scale farming. He had lived there three or four years when he sold out to Edward Benson and moved to Superior, Wisconsin.

Axel Swanson, a single man, was born in Sweden.

He came to this country in the late 1880s and worked on the railroads mostly as a section hand. He came to Cromwell about 1895 and worked on the section that summer. The next winter he worked in the woods for Sauntry Cain. In the spring he filed on a homestead on which Mr. Cain had cut the pine. This was to clear them of trespassing. This was the NW1/4 of NE1/4 Sec. 14-48-20 which Swanson held for two or three years until he relinquished his right to Bertram Cates of Stillwater who built a log house on it but no other improvements. Cates held the homestead for about two years and relinquished his rights to Samuel Brigan, a married man from Stillwater with a large family, four boys and three or four girls. Brigan moved on the homestead and made it his home for many years. Shortly after his wife died, he sold out to Ole Holmes.

After Axel Swanson had given up his homestead he bought the SW1/4 of the SW1/2 Sec. 33 and made his home there for many years. He farmed, keeping some cows but raising mostly chickens. About 1900 he sent home to Sweden for his boyhood sweetheart. She came and they were married in Cromwell and one daughter was born to them in the 1920s. He sold his land to David Carlson and moved to Nevada where he filed on a homestead. He died there some years later.

Shortly after he was married, Axel's brother, Swan Swanson, came over and bought forty acres, NE1/4 of NE1/4 Sec. 4-28-20. He built a small house and cleared some land. Swan went to North Dakota and worked there. He sold his land to A. Blaha. Blaha lived there only a few years, returning to Chicago and selling his land to Ivar Dahlquist and John Swanson, step-son of Axel Swanson. He bought eight acres of land, the W1/2

NE1/4 Sec. 5-48-20, and cleared fifteen or twenty acres and then sold it to Peter Dahl who has made good of it.

Alfred (Fred) Johnson, born in Sweden and newly married, came to Cromwell where he filed on a homestead in 1894, the SW1/4 Sec. 10-48-20. He established a home on the claim by hiring one Louis Lundgren who lived on the claim for some time and built a small shanty and also a log house. Mr. and Mrs. Johnson made their home there for many years. A son was born to them. They made their living by cutting and hauling cordwood. They cleared a nice little farm for general farming, dairying, and some poultry. Mr. Johnson was an electrician and had worked at this trade for many years in Duluth. Mr. Johnson, with others, helped organize School District No. 31 which was later consolidated with District No. 13 in 1912. Mr. Johnson was the mail carrier in the horse and buggy days in the town of Eagle for twenty years. They made the homestead their permanent dwelling place and home for all their living days. They sold one forty in the early days to Jerry Royer who in turn, after fixing the house, sold it

Alfred (Fred), George, and Annie Johnson

to Ole Hougland, a married man from North Dakota with a family of a wife, one boy, and one girl. They had two or three cows but did no farming as Mr. Hougland worked as a carpenter in North Dakota every summer. They lived there about five years and then sold the farm to Mr. Schroeder who lived there many years doing general farming and dairying.

Mr. George Schroeder, a German, had moved up from Minneapolis and had a family consisting of a wife and two girls. They lived here several years and were active in public affairs. He served on the Board of Education one term. They sold the farm and moved to Chicago.

Mr. Dan Cody, a Canadian French, was born in the state of Maine. He came to Cromwell about 1898. He was married and had three daughters. He was a woodsman and worked for Charles Morse most of the time. The first years he was in Cromwell he built a house in the village and had lived there about three years when the house burned down. Then he bought forty acres from Frank Lamier, the NW1/4 and NE1/4 Sec. 34-49-20, building a house and barn on this land. A son was born to them. Dan was very industrious and soon had a large clearing. He worked out most of the time and did some farming for years. His wife then built a small shanty and lived there about four years. He finally traded his farm with Max Hackensmith for sixty acres in Sec. 15-48-20. He later married a widow with three daughters. One child was born to them, but the marriage did not last. They were separated and so Dan Cody lived alone for many years; clearing the sixty acres and cutting all the timber into cordwood. After loosing two homes by fire, he lost his life when his last home burned of unknown causes.

Mr. Frank Nord was born in Sweden and came to this country as a young man marrying in Superior, Wisconsin. He had one daughter and worked in Superior and Duluth for many years. He bought some land, the N1/2 SW1/4 Sec. 9-48-20, about 1896 from the St. Anthony Lumber Co. and moved out on the land in 1900. He made this his home, building a house and barn, and clearing a nice farm. He farmed some twelve years or more. His wife died and he remarried soon thereafter, sold his farm, and moved out south of Grayling where he farmed until he retired when he was in his late eighties.

Mr. John Schei, a married man, was born in Norway. He had five boys. Mr. Schei had worked in Superior, Wisconsin, for many years. He bought some land about 1896 from the St. Anthony Lumber Co., the N1/2 and SW1/4 of SW1/4 Sec. 4-48-20, and by hard work built a large home. He farmed—raising potatoes, dairying, and raising livestock. They lived there all the days of their lives. Mr. Schei was a hard worker with a reserved disposition. Mrs. Schei was very active in organizing the Bethany Lutheran Church and Ladies Aid and was an officer of same until she died very suddenly. Mr. Schei had the misfortune of falling from a load of hay and broke his neck. He lived some five years and used a brace on his forehead and neck. He could work around the farm until the very last. He died from pneumonia, leaving five sons to mourn his departure.

Mr. August Newquist, a married man, was born in Sweden. He and his wife came to this country in the early 1890s and worked in Duluth. They bought some land, the SE1/2 and the SE1/4 and the SE1/4 SW1/4 Sec. 3-48-20, in 1898 or 1899 and moved onto the land in 1902. He built a house and other buildings, cleared a nice farm and lived there until he retired—turning over the farm to his son, Martin Stoner. They had three sons and one daughter in the family.

Mr. Christ Skramstead came to this country when he was a young man and married soon after. He first settled at Eau Claire, Wisconsin, and then moved to Superior, Wisconsin, in the early 1890s. Mr. Skramstead worked in the Great Northern car shops for many years until his health forced him to retire. About 1900 he bought eighty acres of land from J. M. Paine Lumber Company and came to Cromwell in 1902. He built a house and other out buildings and cleared a small farm. Mr. Skramstead continued to work in the car shops in Superior until he retired two or three years before he died. The farm was turned over to his son, Gunnard. They had two boys and three girls, but one of them died in infancy. Mrs. Skramstead and the other children survived him and she died several years later.

Mr. Peter Osberg was born in Sweden. Mrs. Osberg was born in Norway and they came to this country as young people and were married at Eau Claire, Wisconsin. They went to Superior, Wisconsin, in the early 1890s and Mr. Osberg worked there for many years. He bought forty acres of land from J. M. Paine Lumber Company about 1899, the SW1/2 of SE1/4 Sec. 3-48-20. They moved to Cromwell in 1902 and built a house and other buildings on the land and cleared a small farm where they both lived all the days of their lives. Mr. and Mrs. Osberg were good neighbors of a reserved disposition. They had three daughters, but one died some years ago. His wife and two daughters survived Mr. Osberg. The youngest daughter, Ruth, married Hans Hanson and they live on the farm now.

Mr. Andrew Balsness was born in Norway and married there. He came to Marshfield, Wisconsin, about 1890 where he worked for about two years. Then he sent for his wife and one son, Thomas, who came to join him in Marshfield and shortly thereafter they moved to Superior, Wisconsin. Mr. Balsness worked there for some years and in 1902 they came to Cromwell and bought a farm from Charles Swanson, the E1/2 SW1/4 and the E1/2 NW1/4 Sec. 34-49-20. He later sold one forty, the NE1/4 NW1/4, to John P. Dalen. Mr. Balsness cleared a good deal of land. He contracted tuberculosis and was sick about two years and died in 1904. Later the farm was turned over to his son, Thomas, who held it for some years. Not being a farmer, but a photographer by trade, he sold the farm to Edward T. Walker.

Mr. Caspar Slezak, a widower, was born in Bohemia (now Czechoslovakia) and came to this country in the early 1880s and settled in or near Owatonna, Minnesota. He farmed there for many years. He had been married, but his wife died some years before he came to Cromwell in 1900. He filed on a homestead, the NW1/4 Sec. 8-48-20. He proved up but did no farming and he died shortly after this time in Owatonna. He had three daughters who survived him.

Mr. Frank Rypka came from his native land of Bohemia in the early 1880s. He married, worked, and did some farming in or near Owatonna. He lived in the Red River Valley for some time also, but returned to Owatonna and stayed there until 1900. Then he and his family came to Cromwell and bought some land from the Boston and Duluth Land Company, the SW1/2 and other land in the SE1/4 Sec. 29-49-20. He made this his home, building a house and other out buildings. He cleared some land and started farming. He lived there about four years and then sold this land to a man named Bjorae from Clarkfield, Minnesota. He moved over on the NE1/4 of the NE1/4 Sec. 32-49-20 where his son William had built a house and cleared some land two or three years before. They lived there five or six years and cleared some more land. In 1910 the house burned down and they moved over to live with their son, Emil, who had bought eighty acres of land, the E1/2 NW1/4 Sec. 10-48-20. In about two years they rebuilt the house that had burned down on the same foundation and moved into the new house about 1912 and lived there about two years. They sold the little farm to Mr. Brakos, an elderly Bohemian, who came from Owatonna with his wife and one son, John, then about six years old.

The Frank Rypka family again moved over on the Emil Rypka family farm and they later moved up to their son-in-law's, Edward J. Colovin, who married their oldest daughter in Mahnomen County, Minnesota. They lived there for some years and then returned to Cromwell and bought a little strip of land in Sec. 32-49-20. They built a little house and moved there to spend their declining years. Mr. Rypka died at an age of eighty-six years. Mrs. Rypka lived a few years longer and died at the age of ninety-four years, leaving three daughters and two sons to mourn their loss.

Mr. Emil Rypka bought eighty acres of land, the E1/2 of NW1/4 Sec. 10-48-20, and built a good house and out buildings in 1903. About this time he married a woman from Owatonna. They had one child, but it died in infancy. Mrs. Rypka was a victim of consumption and died shortly after the baby was born. The baby was buried here in Cromwell, but the remains of Mrs. Rypka were taken to Owatonna. Sometime later Emil remarried to Lydie Violett. They moved to Owatonna to live, making it their permanent home. His brother William, took over his farm until he sold it to Mr. Laubach who lived there for a number of years.

Mr. Prakos had bought the Frank Rypka's farm and lived there about two years. The second winter he was there Prakos died, leaving his wife and son, John, to mourn his death. A year or so later she married Joseph Patrick, an elderly Bohemian, who worked around here for four or five years. They lived on the little farm a few years and he worked out for the farmers and had a few cows. About 1916 or 1917 they sold their farm to Olaf Jenson from Duluth.

Mr. Olaf Jenson from Duluth was a Norwegian who came over from Norway as a young man. He married his sweetheart from the old country and lived in Duluth for a number of years. They had five children, one boy and four girls, when they moved out here on the farm. Mr. Jenson drove the school bus in the days when horses were used. When he was a janitor in the schoolhouse, Mrs. Jenson died of pneumonia very suddenly. The next year Mr. Jenson sold the farm and moved to Minneapolis and remained there.

Mr. and Mrs. Joseph Kubat were born in Bohemia. They came to this country in the early 1880s and settled in or near Owatonna, Minnesota, where they were married. They had five sons and one daughter and came to Cromwell in 1900. He filed on a homestead of one hundred sixty acres, part of the W1/2 Sec. 18-49-20, and established their home there, proving up the claim and living there about five years. He came back into the town of Cromwell and purchased the Harry Paine homestead in partnership with his son-in-law Joseph Waverin. They lived on their half of the eighty acres until Mr. Kubat

Joseph Kubat in town with his horse and ox.

became ill and was taken to Owatonna where he died. Mrs. Kubat returned to Cromwell and lived there for many years, later going back to Owatonna for medical aid before she died.

Mr. Milo Kubat, oldest son of Joseph Kubat, filed on a homestead, the E1/2 of NW1/4 and the W1/2 of the NE1/4 Sec. 4-49-20, which he later sold to John Kubista. He then moved to Minneapolis, Minnesota, taking up his trade of watchmaker. He remained there until he died.

Their youngest son, Joseph E. Kubat, also took a homestead in Sec. 14-49-21 and then sold it and relinquished his right to Joseph Kubista and left this community for some years. He married and lived in Wisconsin for several years when he came back to Cromwell about 1914. They made their home in the house that his father built. He farmed and worked in the creamery.

Mr. Joseph Waverin, brother-in-law to Joseph Kubat, lived in the Paine house for a few years and then moved to Carlton where he became janitor in the courthouse. He remained there until he died.

Mr. Joseph Holecek came to Owatonna, Minnesota, with his parents (or he might have been born there). His parents came from Bohemia (now called Czechoslovakia). They came to Cromwell in 1901 and filed on a homestead in Sec. 10-49-20 and he made the required improvements to prove up in due time. Being a single man he was not required to make it his permanent residence and when he had proven up his claim he married his boyhood sweetheart. They settled down in Cromwell and bought their present home from Frank Lamier who moved to Eagle River, Wisconsin.

Mr. Charles Lipa was born in Bohemia and came to Cromwell from southern Minnesota. He bought one half section of land in Sec. 13-49-21. He was a married man and had two stepsons and one stepdaughter who lived here with them for some time. They moved on their land, built a house and other out buildings, and cleared some land. There were no roads so it was very hard on all of them. Mrs. Lipa suffered from tuberculosis and lived only about two or three years after. Mr. Lipa moved away from here but his son, Rudolph, came back here and farmed several years.

Mr. and Mrs. Edward Benson, Norwegians, were born in or near Rushford, Minnesota. They were married about 1886 and moved to Clarkfield and settled on a farm. After farming there about six years they sold out and came to Cromwell in 1902. They bought the NE1/4 SW1/4 Sec. 33-49-20 and built a new house and other out buildings. This is now the present Ernest Kempi home. Mr. Benson was a good farmer and he worked hard and cleared a good farm. He had a general farm, but did mostly livestock raising. Mr. Benson was very active in all public affairs. He took an active part in organizing the Consolidated School District No. 13 and was the president of the school board for many years. He also helped to organize the Co-operative Telephone Association and Co-operative Creamery. He served on the creamery board of directors for some years and was active in many other undertakings. Mrs. Benson died in 1940. They had one son and a daughter, both of whom grew up, married and left this community to establish their own homes.

     Mr. and Mrs. Frank Krakora were born in Bohemia and came to this country as young people and married. They came to Minnesota sometime in the 1880s and settled on a farm near Staples, Minnesota. They farmed there until about 1901 when they sold out and came to Cromwell. They bought the homestead rights from Emil Rypka to the NW1/4 Sec. 20-49-20 and built a house and other out buildings and cleared a good deal of land, making this their permanent home. They made their living by general farming and raising livestock, living there as long as Mr. Krakora lived. They had three sons and two daughters; however, one of them died before coming to Cromwell. Shortly after Mr. Krakora died the farm was turned over to their youngest son, Joseph John, and land was purchased for the other sons—for Frank, three forties in Sec. 8-49-20, and for John Joseph, three forties in Sec. 20-48-20 where he now lives and farms.

     Mr. and Mrs. Miko Krakora (a brother of Frank)

were born in Bohemia and came to this country as young people, and were married and settled in a central Minnesota town and lived there until about 1903 when they came to Cromwell, buying the S1/2 NW1/4 Sec. 20-49-20. They built a house and other out buildings and cleared a good deal of land making a good start on a farm. About 1917 they sold out to a Mr. Whiton and retired and bought themselves five acres south of Cromwell in the SE1/4 of SW1/4 Sec. 4-48-20, building themselves a house where they lived until Mr. Krakora died. They had two daughters and one son. When their oldest son, George, came home from World War I he bought the balance of forty acres and started a chicken farm, operating it a few years and then sold out to Gus Carlson. He then started a chicken farm west of Cromwell in Sec. 32-49-20. A few years later he became a manager for Groth Lumber Company in Wright, Minnesota. His mother remarried and moved down to her old home in central Minnesota.

Mr. and Mrs. Joseph Gravelle, French Canadians, were born in or near Quebec, Canada, and came to Mountain Lake, Minnesota, with his parents in the early 1890s. They were married there and then moved to Poupour, Minnesota, and worked in the woods for a year or more when they moved to Cromwell and settled there to stay. They had a large family of four boys and six girls; however, three of the girls died of tuberculosis early in life. About 1900 they built a house on the NW1/4 of SW1/4 Sec. 2-48-20—forty acres he bought from George Ambau. They lived there for many years. Their children married and moved to various parts of the country. Mrs. Gravelle died in the early 1940s, leaving her husband, four boys, and three girls.

Mr. and Mrs. Henry Gravelle (Henry, father of Joe) were born in Quebec, Canada, and came to Mountain Lake, Minnesota, in the early 1890s They worked on farms until about 1898 when they came to Cromwell. He worked in the woods and bought eighty acres N1/2 of NW1/4 Sec. 3-48-30 from J. M. Paine Lumber Company. He built a house and other buildings and cleared some land and did some farming until about 1906 when he moved back to Canada. He stayed there about two years and then came back to Cromwell where he developed cancer and died shortly after, leaving his wife and four sons. Mr. Gravelle lived for some years after with her son, Joseph.

Mr. and Mrs. Joseph Richard were born in Quebec, Canada, and were married there about 1890 or 1891. They came to this country and settled at Mountain Lake, Minnesota, in 1893 and lived there until 1894 when they moved to Birch, Minnesota. He worked in the woods there until 1895 when they moved to Cromwell. He worked in the woods for Charles Morse and bought forty acres in the NW1/4 of SW1/4 Sec. 33-49-20 and built a house and other buildings, doing some farming and working out part time until he sold out in the 1930s and moved to Iron Mountain, Michigan. Mr. and Mrs. Richard had a large family of five boys and five girls. Two of the girls married and remained in Carlton County.

Mr. and Mrs. John P. Dalen were born in Norway and came to this country in the late 1880s and were married at Eagle Bend. Two daughters were born to them there. About 1903 they came to Cromwell and bought forty acres of land from Andrew Balsness. They built a house and other buildings on the NE1/4NW1/4 Sec. 34-

49-20, clearing some land and making this their permanent home. Mr. Dalen farmed some and worked a good deal cutting wood for E. T. Walker until he retired because of ill health in the 1920s. Mrs. Dalen continued to make this her home after he died until she had the misfortune to be badly burned and died in 1949.

Mr. Jack Mastomaki was born in Finland and came to this country about 1903, coming to Cromwell about 1904. He married and filed on a homestead in 1904, the NW1/4 of the NW1/4 Sec. 4-49-20. They established their home there, building a house and other buildings. They worked hard, clearing a good farm, and making this their permanent home until he retired. Mr. Mastomaki was a successful farmer. They had no children.

Mr. and Mrs. Rich M. Krogh were born in Norway and came to Montevideo, Minnesota, in the early 1890s, marrying there. They came to Cromwell shortly after in 1905. Mr. Krogh had bought eighty acres a year or two before but they did not move onto it until 1905. They established their home by building a house and other buildings and clearing a good deal of land, becoming successful farmers. They had a family of two boys and two daughters; however, their first daughter died in infancy. Their oldest son became a successful businessman and the youngest son an expert electrician and successful farmer.

Mr. and Mrs. Oscar Finnila, Sr. were born in Finland and came to this country in the early 1890s working in Ashtabula, Ohio, until around 1904 when they came to Cromwell and filed on a homestead, the S1/2 NE1/4 Sec. 2-49-20. Mr. Finnila worked in the woods most of the time after having built a log house and some other small buildings. He cleared some land, but did not do much farming as he was an elderly man. However, he proved up on this claim, but died shortly thereafter leaving his wife, three daughters, and one son. The homestead was turned over to his son, Oscar, who married and established his home there. He became a successful farmer and dairyman.

Mr. and Mrs. Joseph Anderson were born in Finland and came to Ashtabula, Ohio, in the 1890s from Finland. He worked there for some years and came to Cromwell in 1904 and filed on a homestead—the S1/2 of SW1/4 Sec. 2-49-20. They established their home by building a house and other buildings and lived there long enough to prove up and then sold out. Mr. Anderson was a Baptist lay preacher and moved to Duluth. They had one son and one daughter.

Mr. and Mrs. John Heikkila were born in Finland and it is believed they came directly to Cromwell from Finland in 1903 and filed on a homestead—the NE1/4 of NW1/4 Sec. 2-49-20. Mr. Heikkila worked some in the woods after having built a house and other buildings. He cleared some land and proved up on his claim in due time, but he died shortly after. They had three sons and one daughter. The children all married and settled here in their own homes.

The homestead was sold to Victor Hakkala, who in turn sold it to Mike Heikkila, the eldest son of John Heikkila, who erected good buildings, acquired more land, and made it into a good farm. He raised a large family of five boys and four girls. All of the children married and settled down around Cromwell on farms with the exception of a younger daughter. They were all very industrious and the boys were good machinists. They also were all good students in high school and graduated with high honors.

Mr. Mike Heikkila filed on a homestead on N1/4 of SW1/4SW1/4 Sec. 30-49-20 when he came here with his father in 1903. He built a house and other buildings and made it his home until he proved up on this claim. He got married and a daughter was born to them. His first wife died and he remarried shortly after to a girl who came over from Finland. They had ten children and Mike died in 1949 leaving his wife and all the children (except the first daughter by his first wife) to mourn his passing.

Mr. and Mrs. Abram Klavu were born in Finland and came to this country in the late 1880s or early 1890s. They came first to upper Michigan where he worked for some time and then came to Cromwell about 1896 or 1897 and bought eighty acres in Sec. 17-48-20 on the east shore of Eagle Lake. He built a house and other buildings, cleared some land, and started farming there. This became their permanent home for the rest of their days. They had three boys and three or four girls who all married and settled on farms in the community. One son died in young manhood.

Mr. Louis Larson, Mr. Klavu's brother, came here from Brainerd, Minnesota, in 1898 and lived with Abram, his brother, and started a small general store on his brother's land on the lakeshore. He operated this for two or three years when he moved to Cromwell and rented a house from Amasa Dotten. He operated a general store here for three or four years until he bought eighty acres from the J. M. Paine Company and built a big bricksided, two-story building and moved his store in the downstairs, living on the second floor. He operated this store for some time and married late in life. They had one son and six daughters who later settled in other parts of the country.

Mr. and Mrs. Henry Knuutila, Sr. were born in Finland (he was a teacher there) and came to this country in the early 1890s. It is believed he settled in Wisconsin first and then came to Cromwell and bought some land on the southeast corner of Eagle Lake, Sec. 17-48-20, and built a house there about 1896. He moved his family there the same year. They had four boys and one girl. Mr. Knuutila, one son, and one daughter died a few years later from tuberculosis. Mr. Knuutila died about the time of World War I. His oldest son, Henry, Jr., started a general store in Moose Lake and operated that business until the fire of 1918 when he along with others lost everything in the fire. His son, William, went into the banking business in Cloquet, Minnesota, and later in Cleveland, Ohio, where he died. His son, John, is still in business in Cloquet. Mr. Knuutila was a leader, a guide, a teacher, and highly respected by his countrymen. He also acted as land agent and located many of the first Finnish settlers, advising them in legal matters and being helpful in other ways.

Mr. and Mrs. John Oberg were born in Finland and came to this country in the late 1880s or early 1890s and might have settled in Michigan first. Mr. Oberg was a minister of the gospel and came to Cromwell about 1897 or 1898 and bought eighty acres of land on the east shore of Eagle Lake in Sec. 17-48-20. He built a house and other buildings there and cleared some land, making this his permanent home. They had two boys and four girls. One son and one daughter died early in adult life. Mr. Oberg went out on preaching missions in various Finnish settlements. He also worked as a stone mason, bricklayer, and carpenter. He was a good speaker and the latter part of his life he spent on a permanent call as pastor in North Dakota and upper Michigan where he passed away. His daughters continued to operate the old farm and his oldest son, John, started to operate a general store in Cromwell. Ill health forced John out of business and he died shortly thereafter.

  Mr. and Mrs. Daniel Sangola were born in Finland and came to Brainerd, Minnesota. It is believed they were married in Finland and came to this country in the 1880s or late 1890s. He worked in the NP shops in Brainerd until they moved to Cromwell in the spring of 1894. They settled in Kettle River, Sec. 26-40-20. They built a house and other buildings and raised much hay on the river bottom. He had a livestock farm. They made this their home until they passed away. The farm was turned over to their only son, Charles, who made this his permanent home after he got married. Charles was active in public affairs and served eight years as County Commissioner for Carlton County. He also held other public offices.

  Mr. Ole Dakken was born in Norway and came to Superior, Wisconsin, as a single man in the early 1890s. He worked there until about 1902 when he came to Cromwell and bought eighty acres of land from J. M. Paine Lumber Company, the SE1/4 NW1/4 and the NW1/4 SE1/4, Sec. 3-48-20, and built a small house and other small out buildings. The land was easily cleared as nearly all the timber had been cut. He sold his land in

1905 to Herman Olson.

      Mr. and Mrs. Franz (Frank) Herman Olson were born in Sweden and came over to this country early in life and first settled in Odanah, Wisconsin. He worked there in the sawmills for a number of years and came to Cromwell in 1905 and bought the Ole Dakken farm and improved it by building a new house and soon a new barn and enlarged the farm in general. About 1919, they sold the farm to John Swobota who lived there until he retired. Mr. and Mrs. Olson had a big family of twelve children—six boys and six girls. Two boys and two girls died in their youth. When they sold their farm they moved back to Odanah, Wisconsin, and lived there about five years when Mr. Olson bought some land at Maple, Wisconsin, and made a farm. He lived there until he was forced to retire because of ill health and then moved to Superior, Wisconsin, where he died in 1948 leaving his wife, four daughters, and four sons to mourn his passing.

      There were many others who came to Cromwell for a short time but did not establish a permanent home or residence there. I think I have listed all that I can remember. I will not claim that I have listed all the achievements of the early settlers; neither have I tried to give their complete characteristics but merely a little introduction to them and will have to leave to others to give a more detailed account of them all. But this I will record—they all had to suffer hardships in establishing their new homes. There were no roads and all the pine timber had been cut by the lumbermen who left the pine stumps and the stones and the small timber that had no market value. But the pioneers were a hardy lot of people though none had a superabundance of this world's goods. They had an abundance of ambition and a will to work hard. Some may not have exercised the best of judgment in all of their undertakings but perseverance helped them build good homes, clear good size farms, and become independent. All helped build the roads and churches and they also built a fully accredited high school that is a credit to any community and may be favorably compared to a much larger community.

This gives a record of all the pioneers in Red Clover and the north half of the town of Eagle from the beginning of the settlement, up to and prior to 1905. The following includes all that came later and had the benefits of roads, schools, churches, and other institutions that had been organized on the foundation laid by the pioneers.

A young man came up from Minneapolis with a mule team, following the Old Military or Stage Road up through Anoka and Elk River. He drove his team on through to Mora on the Military Road to a point northwest of Kettle River and north on an old tote road to Cromwell. He filed on a homestead, SE1/4 of SE1/4, Sec. 26-49-20, and built himself a little log cabin. This was about 1899. He advertised for a housekeeper and in due time a nice young lady came on a late train—about 9:30 p.m. He met her at the train with his mule team and lumber wagon and took her to his new home. He had invited his neighbors to be on hand to give her a rousing welcome. They danced until the early morning. The neighbors went home and his lady took her baggage and walked back about three miles to the depot to the 6:30 morning train for Minneapolis. She did not have enough money for her ticket, so she left her watch to insure that she would send the money for her ticket. My information is that she did so, and so our Prince Charming up and left with his mule team for North Dakota and later relinquished his homestead rights to Carl M. Peterson of Minneapolis, who filed on it and moved his family up onto the homestead. He established his home there about 1903.

Mr. Carl M. Peterson was born in Sweden and came to this country as a young man in about 1886. He worked in various places in Minnesota and South Dakota. He married his sweetheart and came back to Minneapolis, where he worked and ran a restaurant. When he sold it, he moved up to Cromwell. He cut cordwood and in time cleared forty or more acres of land and built a house and barn. He established a dairy farm and was active in organizing the creamery at Cromwell. Mr. Peterson had a large family of five boys and five girls. He prospered so well that he retired at the age of eighty and turned over his farm to his youngest son, Alfred.

Mr. George Kiel bought eighty acres of land, S1/2 SW1/2 Sec. 30-49-20, and built a house which he used for a camp. One winter he cut nearly all the timber. He made it into cordwood and left in the spring. The next fall he had all the wood shipped to North Dakota. His nationality was unknown, but he came from near Minneapolis. Two or three years later, in 1905, he sold his land to Anton Rosicky who moved onto the land with his family of five girls, three boys, and his wife. By hard work he cleared a good farm and at the age of about seventy he retired from active farming. He turned over his farm to his son, William, and died at about eighty years of age.

Mr. and Mrs. Rosicky were born in Bohemia and came to this country at an early age. All of their daughters married and remained on farms in this community.

Mr. Anton Gregor married the oldest daughter of Anton Rosicky, and bought eighty acres of land, S1/4 NW1/4 Sec. 31-49-20, and made a good farm of it. He had lived there about twenty years when he sold out to Swan Maki. Mr. Gregor went back to Chicago where he had worked for several years before coming to Cromwell. Two or three years later he came back to Cromwell and bought a small farm from John Hendrickson, SE1/4 of SE1/4 Sec. 31-49-20. Mr. Gregor was born in Bohemia and came to this country as a young man. Mr. and Mrs. Gregor have one son.

Mr. Mike Koncal came to this country as a young man early in 1890. He was born in Bohemia. Mr. Koncal worked in Chicago until 1904 when he came to Cromwell. He bought eighty acres of land, S1/2 of NW1/4, Sec. 32-49-20. He married one of the Rosicky girls and settled down on this land. He built a house, barn, and other buildings. He cleared a good farm and became a good dairy farmer and he is still active.

Another daughter of Anton Rosicky married Emil Graves, a telegraph operator, who went into business for himself for a short time. Later Mr. Graves bought forty acres of land, cleared it all, and built his home. They have a son and a daughter.

Arne Finberg married Rose Rosicky and they lived in New York Mills for a few years. They came to Cromwell and settled on a farm east of Cromwell in Sec. 2-48-20. They had two daughters and two sons. One son died early in life; the other, Maurice, died in World War II. Mr. Finberg is of Finnish descent.

The youngest of the Rosicky daughters married Jack Line. They live on a farm in Sec. 10-48-20 and have a large family and the end is not in sight yet. Mr. Line is of Pennsylvania Dutch descent, or may tell so. I have recorded all the Rosickys because they settled here and remained to develop the agriculture of this area.

Mr. and Mrs. William Raynols came here from Martin County and bought two hundred forty or more acres in the SW1/2 of Sec. 31-49-20. He cleared some land and did some building. Mr. Raynols sold the land to a Duluth lawyer about six years later. The lawyer, Mr. Davis, owned it for some years and made some improvements during weekend visits. Mr. Davis had Mr. and Mrs. George Krakora manage the farm for him until he sold it to Adolph Wydra in about 1894. Mr. Wydra has made it one of the best-improved farms in the area. He has fine buildings and a large herd of Guernseys.

Mr. and Mrs. Wydra were born in Bohemia and came to Chicago when they were young. They married there and for a number of years Mr. Wydra had a store. They came to Cromwell to engage in his first love— farming. They have a son and a daughter. Mr. Wydra operates his farm in partnership with his son.

Mr. and Mrs. Paul Oestriech were born in Iowa. They lived on a farm in South Dakota for a time and in 1905 came to Cromwell. Mr. Oestriech bought eighty acres W1/2 of SW1/4 Sec. 4-40-20. He built a house and other small buildings, cleared land, and raised potatoes and some livestock. He had a large family and having bought his land on time payment, the high taxes and failure of the Cromwell State Bank sealed his doom. He gave up the farm and a few years later bought some land in the SW1/4 of Sec. 4 where he established a permanent home.

Mr. Lars Jacobson, a single man, was born in Norway and came to Eau Claire, Wisconsin. He worked there two or three years and then came to Superior, Wisconsin. After working there in the woods for a number of years he came to Cromwell in 1902 and found a homestead which had been filed on in the late 1870s or early 1880. The homestead had been vacated—that is whoever filed on it, failed to prove up. In the course of twenty years the land was placed on the register for filing. Having found this pearl, Mr. Jacobson filed on Sec. 28-49-20, built a log house, and made it his home for eight years. He did no farming to speak of and in about 1909 sold one forty to Alfred Stone.

Mr. Alfred Stone came from Sweden in 1903 and married Olina Oien who came from Norway about the same time. They were married in Superior and lived there for a few years. Mr. Stone established a farm north of Cromwell in 1912 and raised potatoes and a herd of dairy cows. They had four daughters and one son and when Mrs. Stone died of cancer in 1944, he gave up farming. His son, Fred, took over the farm in 1946, when he returned from the armed services. All the daughters married and established their homes elsewhere.

Mr. and Mrs. John Reimer were born in Sweden and came to Superior about 1890. They were married there and two sons were born in Superior. Mr. Reimer came to Cromwell about 1910 and bought eighty acres of swampland from Lars Jacobson. It was about the hardest piece of land to clear in all of Red Clover. He hired some land clearers and in 1912 he built a small building and moved his family to the farm. He visualized a good farm.

    He saved some money and built his present home and part of the barn. By judicious hard work he made this farm one of the most productive in this community. Mr. Reimer was a good farmer and dairyman and kept a fine herd of Guernsey milk cows. By working hard and using good judgment in his business of farming he was quite prosperous, as prosperity was considered in this community. Mr. Reimer accomplished all this without the help of a capable wife, as she was an invalid for thirty years. She suffered with arthritis and was forced to sit in a wheelchair day after day. In the last few years Mr. Reimer carried her to and from bed every day. Mrs. Reimer was always pleasant and a good companion. She died in 1938 and left to mourn her passing, her husband, John; sons, Clarence and Henry; and daughter, Helen. He raised two sons and one daughter who were born in Cromwell. They are married and have established their own homes. They are independent, honorable citizens and good neighbors—always ready with a helping hand. A few years later Mr. Reimer married Mrs. Yates from Duluth. She was a cheerful helpmate and they were very happy. Unfortunately, she became sick with cancer and died two years later. Mr. Reimer took a good deal of interest in public affairs and served on the town board and creamery board for many years.

    Mr. Ely Wolf was born on a farm in the state of Indiana. He operated a farm there, married and had one son and two daughters. His son became a Christian missionary to the Phillipines. He may still be there. The two daughters were schoolteachers and came to Minnesota to teach school. They married in this state and may be living in Iowa now (1950). Mrs. Wolf died in Indiana. Mr. Wolf gave up farming when his wife died and started a general store in a small town. When he sold the store, he had two, good-sized farms. The Nelson Immigration Co. sold him about one hundred ten acres of swampland and Mr. Wolf gave them one farm in exchange or might have paid them in cash. There is a good deal of swampland in southern Michigan and northern Indiana which has been drained and made into very good farmland. Since Mr. Wolf had been born in Indiana he was well acquainted with the land and he had also been up north of Aitkin, where his son-in-law had located close to Crosby in 1903. That swamp was nearly all open marsh and so when it was drained it made good meadow land.

Ditchbank near Cromwell. They were never practical for irrigation.

Mr. Wolf believed that all this swampland could be subdued the same as the lowland at Aitkin, but he failed to realize that there is a vast difference between muck, peat, and moss. Many people down south and out east were led to believe that this swamp and moss or peat moorland was all the same and they were told that all they would have to do was just drain off the surface water and it would equal the best black agricultural land. Mr. Wolf; his brother-in-law, Mr. McArthur; and his son-in-law, Dr. Fox (who later became the owner); were persuaded that the swampland here was similar to the swampland in Indiana and Michigan, so they held the land and paid taxes on the land as long as they lived.

Mr. Wolf was a man of sixty-five years or more when he acquired all this land and he came up here to see the land in the winter when it was all covered with snow. He closed the deal and when he came back in the spring he found he did not have a piece of land he could build a house on. So he had to buy three forties more to get thirty acres of highland to build on. When he had explored his dominion and established boundaries he got up a petition to the county board of commissioners for a drainage ditch (under the new drainage law). A ditch about six miles long became Carlton County Ditch No. 1. Now Mr. Wolf was nearly seventy years old and a widower at that, so he had undertaken a big job to subdue all this swampland.

In the first place, the ditch they dug was not deep enough; second, they did not follow the natural water course, so the net result was that it did not drain the lowlands that would have been good agricultural land. Sometimes it cut off the water supply from the natural water course that flowed down there in the spring to cleanse them, as the spring snow water would flow down the streams. With this source cut off there remained no more water to supply a current to keep them open and so they grew full of willows and moss so that you could not find where they had been.

Now that Mr. Wolf had his ditching completed and Carlton County had sold bonds to pay for the ditch (bearing 6% interest, I think). The landowners were not required to start payment on the lien on all the land that was benefited by the ditch, which amounted to an average of four dollars per acre. At the end of five years he had a lien on every acre and at four dollars, plus twenty cents and five years interest that made the lien five dollars and twenty cents. Divided into ten equal payments of five dollars and twenty cents would require a payment of eighty-three cents per acre annually for ten years. In addition to this, the taxes needed for the school, town tax to the roads, county tax, and state tax. I do not have the exact amount per acre a year, but it would mean a tax of forty to sixty dollars per forty acres and that on wild land that produces no income. No wonder we have so much delinquent tax land. I paid forty-one dollars and twenty-five cents on forty acres of wild land. Mr. Wolf had some money when he came here and he had his other farm to sell in Indiana and I do not know how much he got for that farm.

This I do know, and I will record this as a warning to many farmers here to see to it that they have a clear title to their land and when they sell the land on a contract for the deed, or give a warranty deed, to be sure to understand the deed. If there are any reservations whatever, be sure to make them on the transfer of the title. As I have stated, Mr. Wolf had sold his first farm in Indiana to a real estate and immigration company. In return, he had received all this swampland and might have paid some cash besides. Now, Mr. Wolf believed he had a clear title to the farm and gave a warranty deed to it. Two or three years later it developed that the mineral rights had been reserved many years before and maybe the minerals had been removed many years ago and all had been forgotten. Presumably coal was several hundred feet below the surface. Mr. Wolf might have had a warranty deed and the former owner or owners had failed to insert the reservation of mineral rights in his prior transfer of title. I do not know, but he was held responsible. He received the notice of a demand to make good the warranty deed he had given and they brought a lawsuit against Mr. Wolf. It cost him five thousand dollars to make the deed good. That relieved him of his liquid capital and now he was up against it. His brother-in-law, Mr. McArthur, came to his rescue by advancing money to pay his taxes and maybe for subsistence also and then he finally bought the land outright from Mr. Wolf. Mr. Wolf retired after a long, strenuous and active life and moved to Iowa to live with his daughters where he died two years later.

Mr. McArthur took over and built a house and cleared some sixty acres of easily cleared land along the ditch. He also was an old man but he lived long enough to pay up the ditch lien. We, here in Cromwell and all through Carlton County, should honor Mr. McArthur as he was the only large landowner that paid up the ditch lien in full. He lived here only one summer, after which he returned to Ohio where he died shortly afterwards. Upon his death, the land was transferred to his son-in-law, Dr. Fox, who held the land for some time and did intend to develop a stock farm, but he took sick and died while still a young man. Mrs. Fox decided that after father and husband had stuck all of their money in this land without getting any return, it would be foolish for her to speculate with her insurance money, so she let it go for taxes. So it also became delinquent tax land. One Henry Smith took up eighty acres of it, the NW1/4 NE1/4 Sec. 28 and SW1/4 of SE1/4 Sec. 21-49-20, and Henry Peterson bought two more forties of that tax delinquent land and that is all that has been reclaimed of the McArthur empire. And so let Mr. Wolf, Mr. McArthur, and Dr. Fox, the big capitalists, rest in peace forever.

George H. Bodell was born in Michigan and was a meat cutter by trade. He first went to Fargo, North Dakota, where he worked in a hotel and met and married a little French girl. This was about 1908 and two years later they moved to Superior where Mr. Bodell got a job as manager of a meat and grocery business. He bought the store in 1911 and in 1912 came to Cromwell and bought the Lars Jacobson farm in Sec. 28-49-20. He did not move onto the farm until 1918 when he sold his store in Superior. He built a house and barn which are still standing. Mr. Bodell raised a dairy herd and in 1932 Mrs. Bodell died of cancer. In 1945 he sold his farm to Arthur Peterson who is now operating the farm. Mr. Bodell moved to Michigan and died three years later at the home of a brother, Louis.

Hiram K. Schafer was born in Pennsylvania and as a young man went out to Kansas. He worked as a sheep herdsman in western Kansas and Colorado for more than twenty-five years. During the winter months he made his home in Salina, Kansas, where he worked as a section hand. It is believed that Mr. Shafer had been married down east before he went west, but he and his wife had separated. In the fall of 1901, he came to Duluth and bought forty acres from the Boston and Duluth Land Co. He had not seen the land and had no idea where it was located, but he had the legal description of the land and knew it was near Cromwell. It was good land but low and swampy, covered with tamarack and cedar windfalls, and had very few trees standing. He built a log cabin on the land and "batched" there for five years. He cut tamarack into cordwood and made fence posts of the cedar. These he hauled to Cromwell with a small pair of steers and sold it. While he lived here the estate of his father was divided equally between Mr. Shafer and his brothers except the mineral rights which had been reserved and were sold after they had agreed on the price. The deal was closed and the company was told they could remove the coal now that they owned the land. Their reply was, "Don't worry about that; it was mined several years ago." That cleared the case. Mr. Shafer decided to return to Kansas to spend the rest of his life, and upon his arrival in Salina, he traded his property in Cromwell for some property there.

 Anton Richarva was born in Bohemia and came to Owatonna as a young man. He worked around there for some years, saved his money, and planned to invest in real estate which would increase in value. Some friend of his of the same nationality, located him on three forties, one hundred twenty acres in the NW part of Sec. 20-49-20. It was nearly all swampland. He then returned to Owatonna where he worked for two or three years. Unable to find a buyer for his land, he returned here and made his home on the land, lived a meager existence until he was old enough to draw old-age assistance. He raised a garden. Mr. Richarva did some trapping, but lived only a short while after he got old-age relief. The only one that profited by his plan was the person who located the land for him. It was then the custom of the Boston and Duluth Land Co. to pay a commission of fifty cents per acre to anyone able to sell land to someone else after they had bought land from the company.

Andrew Anderson was born in Denmark and came to Martin, Minnesota, when he was a young man. His brother had a farm, and Andrew, a blacksmith by trade, farmed there a few years and then came back to Minnesota about 1902. He bought 160 acres of land, the SE1/4 of Sec. 9-49-20, and then stayed away from Cromwell for some years. He came back about 1914 and made some improvement on his land and sold the north half to his brother, James, who was a molder in a foundry in Madison, Wisconsin. James Anderson moved up here to establish his home on the land. Andrew, at the age of 55, enlisted in the army and went overseas to fight the Kaiser. He came back and built a home and lived here some years and at last he rented the farm out. He went back out west to Idaho, as he still had a timber claim out there.

James Anderson made some buildings on his land; he and his wife were good farmers and hard workers. They had three children—two daughters and one son. When one daughter and the son were still home, they purchased a new car but misfortune struck when their car was hit by a train at the crossing in Moose Lake. Their son, Victor, who was driving, was killed and the car was a complete loss. Mrs. Anderson was so upset, they sold out all of their stock and moved to Rockford, Illinois. Mr. Anderson went back to work as a molder in the foundry. His health gave out and again they moved to Cromwell where they farmed for two years until Mr. Anderson's death. About this time Andrew returned to his farm here and did blacksmith work. A good blacksmith was hard to find in these days. Andrew had never married, but about three years after his brother's death, he married his widow. He became subject to a heart ailment and did not live long. Now, Mrs. Anderson had two farms, one of which she rented out for about two years. She later sold it when she moved to Chicago to live with her oldest daughter. That is the sad ending of a bright beginning.

Theodore Swanson came to Cromwell about 1912 and bought the old Joe Holececk homestead in Sec. 10-49-20 with his brother, Charles Swanson. They established their home here in about 1913 and made some improvements, but being railroad men at heart they did not care for farming. Theodore was a section foreman on the NP in Wisconsin and Minnesota.

The Swanson brothers were raised on a farm in Sweden and came to this country about 1897. Theodore worked in the Duluth area a few years but feminine attraction called, so he returned to Sweden and married his sweetheart. They remained in Sweden for three years, when Theodore came back to America alone. He worked on the section for a year and then sent for his wife and son who came to Carlton about 1908. Mr. Swanson continued on the railroad until they moved to Cromwell in 1914. They lived on the Holececk homestead until about 1935 when they moved onto the old Rypka farm which had been vacated by J. P. Larson who had been the last owner of the farm, having bought it from Olaf Jenson in 1928 and sold it to Swanson. The Larsons moved to Barnum.

Mr. Swanson prospered here for some years until his herd of Guernseys contracted Bangs disease and he lost the entire herd. Mr. and Mrs. Swanson then retired from farming and moved to Grand Rapids, Minnesota, to live there near their daughter. They had one son and one daughter. As stated before, Charles Swanson came here with his brother, Theodore, but he left, raised some cattle, and worked in the woods. Mr. and Mrs. Swanson had three sons and two daughters. His son, Fredolph, was killed in World War II. Mrs. Swanson died in the early 1930s and ten years later, Mr. Swanson gave up the farm.

Charles Martwig came from south central, Minnesota with his brother, William, and bought the SW1/4 of Sec. 5-49-20. He was a single man and established his home there. He built some small buildings and cleared about sixty acres of the land. He married a girl from Finlayson, Minnesota. He cultivated this land for several years and in 1910 sold it to Charles Ashley who came here from North Dakota. Mr. Martwig moved to Cromwell, purchasing the property just west of the schoolhouse and engaged in the trucking business. Later he leased the Morse farm and operated it for five or more years, while living in his own home. He sold his property and rented a farm in Iowa. He died there as a young man. Charles Martwig was the first man to farm exclusively with tractor power in this vicinity. One son, Michael, and one daughter, Bertha, were born to this union.

William Martwig came here with his brother, Charles, and bought eighty or one hundred acres in the SW1/4 Sec. 9-49-20. He might have cleared some land but he did not build any buildings and later sold this land to his mother and stepfather, Mr. and Mrs. Cornelius Schin. In 1917, Bill married Miss Garesch and they established their home in Cromwell. This home later became the telephone exchange with Mrs. Martwig as the operator. Bill was a natural automobile mechanic and worked for many years repairing cars and trucks. He also did some trucking. To this union was born one son, George, and one daughter, Frances.

    Cornelius Schin was born in Luxembourg in 1870 and came to Minnesota in 1890. He worked on a farm at Rose Creek, Minnesota, for several years. He then became the renter of the farm. About 1902 he and Mrs. Rose Martwig were married at Dexter, Minnesota. In 1910, two years after his stepsons, Charles and William, settled here, Mr. and Mrs. Schin came and bought William's land and established their home there in Sec. 9. Mr. and Mrs. Schin were hard-working people and good farmers so that in a relatively short time they had cleared land and good buildings. They continued to prosper and were well situated when health failed them. Rose Schin passed away after several years of illness. Cornelius Schin passed away in 1951 after many years of suffering. Surviving this couple is one stepson, William Martwig, and two sons, Mathew and Peter Schin. Peter continues to operate the home farm. Mr. and Mrs. Schin were good neighbors and honest, hard working people, always ready to lend a helping hand. May their souls rest in peace.

    Andrew Gradberg was born in Sweden and came to the state of South Dakota where he worked at the trade of bricklayer and stone mason. He met and married a girl from his hometown in Sweden. Three children were born to them—one son and two daughters.

Andrew purchased land in the NW1/4 Sec. 9-49-20 in 1914. Several years later the family moved to this land and established a good home operating a general farm. Mrs. Gradberg died about 1930 and the children sought other occupations, so Andrew quit farming although he continued to live in the home and work at his trade.

John Kubista and his two brothers, Joseph and Frank, were Bohemians who came here from Owatonna, Minnesota, and each bought homestead rights from the Kubat brothers. They had inherited some money from their parents. John lived in the center of Sec. 4-49-20 for some years and he married the daughter of Charles Ashley, a widower. John lived in the Ashley home and farmed in partnership with Mr. Ashley until they sold the farm in 1920. They resided in Moose Lake for a year and then moved to North Dakota.

Joseph Kubista settled on the east part of Sec. 4-49-21, but then moved to the land owned by Frank, the NE part of Sec. 4-49-20. They built simple buildings and were very successful, as far as farming goes, for bachelors. Frank had an adventure in marriage but it was not successful and then Joseph married. So Frank moved back to his brother Joseph's farm and remained there operating a general farm and raising dairy cattle.

Carl and Oscar Swanson were born in Sweden and came to Superior, Wisconsin, where they worked for some years. They bought land in Sec. 4-48-20 which had been a part of the John Kubista farm so they had some cleared acreage. Neither of the men married but were successful farmers, specializing in potatoes and high grade Guernsey cows.

Clement Gravelle was born in Canada of French parents. He came to Cromwell with Mrs. Gravelle from Mountain Lake, Minnesota, in 1908. They bought eighty acres from George Ambeau in Sec. 10-48-20. They built buildings and did general farming. The Gravelles were well along in years when they came to Cromwell. Mr. Gravelle died and Mrs. Gravelle moved to Cloquet where she lived with her daughter. One son and three daughters were born to this union.

Matt Vasanoja came from Stockholm, Sweden, to the Iron Range in Minnesota in 1904. In 1905 he bought eighty acres of wild land in Sec. 20-48-20. He built a two-room log house and in the summer of the same year Mr. Vasanoja continued to build buildings and improve his farm in many ways until he had the most artistic home in this community and maybe in all Carlton County.

Ben Vasanoja in front of the fireplace at the Vasanoja farm.

Mr. Vasanoja was a carpenter from the old country and made many other improvements in his very beautiful farm home. Mrs. Hilda Sophia Vasanoja passed on in February, 1928, at the age of sixty and Mr.

Vasanoja passed on in February, 1929, at the age of seventy. They left five children—two sons and three daughters to mourn their passing.

The children inherited Mr. Vasanoja's artistic ability; the daughter, Siami, is a painter in oils and Benhard is a genius at woodcarving and painting. He never married but continued to operate the farm home on a very successful basis. His flower gardens are of statewide interest. Segrid, another daughter, expresses her artistic temperament in classic rugs and other hand work. Hertta is also very clever. A grandson, Henry Syverson, is a commercial artist and cartoonist, whose work has been accepted by some of our most popular magazines.

Edward Yerian was born in Indiana and came to Mountain Lake, Minnesota, in about 1898. He met the girl of his love that he wanted to marry, which might have been the string that was drawing him out to Minnesota in the year 1908. He purchased George Ambeau's farm. He was a charter member of the Cromwell Co-op Creamery and served on the Creamery

The Edward Yerian Family.

Board of Directors for a term of three years. Mr. Yerian was appointed deputy sheriff of Carlton County in 1920 and served for about eight years. He then ran as candidate for sheriff and was defeated. At the time he lived in Carlton. After being defeated in the election he and Mrs. Yerian moved back to Indiana. There, he worked as manager of a creamery. He had the misfortune of losing his wife about three years later and Mr. Yerian died shortly after.

Felix Hakamaki, a brother of John Hakamaki, filed on a homestead in Sec. 8 that had previously been homesteaded by his brother, Frank, who gave it up and moved away. Together Felix and his father developed a good sized farm. Five years later Felix's father passed away and Felix farmed alone for five years before he passed away. Adam Kempainen, an uncle to Felix, took over the farm and operated it for ten years. He passed away, leaving his wife and five sons to mourn his passing. Three of his sons are now operating the farm.

Erick Karppinen was born in Finland and immigrated to this country as a young man in the early 1890s. He worked around Duluth and Thomson until about 1903, when he married and came to Cromwell. He filed on a homestead in Sec. 10-49-20 and built a small log cabin and established his home. About a year later his wife died leaving a small baby. Mrs. Oscar Isaacson took the baby. Erick vacated the homestead and moved back to Thomson. Here, he met and married a widow with five children. He moved back to Cromwell and bought forty acres of land in Sec. 5-48-20. He built a small farm, and made this his permanent home. He lived there about twenty years before he died, leaving his wife and eight or ten children behind.

Emil Heikkila came to Cromwell from Finland, with his parents, the John Heikkilas, and his brother, Mike. He worked around Cromwell for a number of years until he married a girl from Superior. He then bought eighty acres of land in Cromwell in Sec. 5-48-20 and established his home there. A few years later he was stricken ill and ailed for about two years before his death. His wife continued to make her home on the farm. They had no children.

Mr. Wyeat was a single man who came to the Cromwell area from North Dakota in 1910 with one horse and a wagon. How, I do not know, as there were no roads, only the old road south of Cromwell which is now State Highway 73. He settled on the old Amasa Dotten homestead for some time and lived on several other places that were vacant. He may have cut a little cordwood, but otherwise I do not know how he subsisted. He was a very peculiar character. The poor old man was mentally unbalanced, and was so judged and committed to Fergus Falls home for the insane.

John Skonders was a single man of Bohemian descent who came to the southern part of Minnesota as a young man. He later came to Wright station and settled for some years. He came to Cromwell about 1925 and lived in the town of Red Clover and at last on the McArthur farm in Sec. 28-49-20. He started to build himself a little house in Sec. 21-49-20 on a little piece of land that McArthur gave him. He became insane and was committed to Fergus Falls where he died a few years later. He had a very peculiar disposition—an eccentric character, I would say.

Mr. Mendenhall came from Stearns County about

1914. We called him "Old Man Mendenhall." He rented the Eli Wolf residence, which included part of Skunk Island, from the owner who lived in Stearns county. The owner had the land mortgaged to a state bank and the bank foreclosed on the mortgage. Later the bank failed and it became state land as tax delinquent. Mendenhall lived there for some years, working out as a day laborer now and then. He tried to make his living by truck farming and raising vegetables, but there was no market for garden vegetables. He then raised sorghum and he made his own sorghum mill to grind up his sugar cane. He made his own vat to boil it down to syrup, and good syrup it was. He sold it locally in one gallon cans. Later he moved to Illinois around 1920. Illinois was his native state. He had no family and was about sixty years of age when he left.

Jacob Nasso and his wife, Anna, came from Norway in about 1900 to Superior, Wisconsin. He worked there in a car shop until 1911, when they moved to Cromwell and bought forty acres of wild land. They rented the Balsness farm for three years and lived there while Mr. Nasso cleared some land and built a house and barn and made other improvements. He had been a skipper on Norwegian tramp ships for many years and even had his own ship on the Great Lakes as early as the 1880s. He became a victim of the deadly killer, cancer, and died in 1931. He left behind his wife, Anne, two sons, and three daughters. Mr. Nasso was a good neighbor and always ready with a helping hand.

Kenneth Mann's parents bought the Emil Sparring farm in 1931 and moved in. Kenneth married and lived with his parents. His father died in 1933 and his mother in 1944. Kenneth continued to farm there until 1951 when he sold all his stock and moved to Duluth to live. Mr. and Mrs. Mann have three girls and two sons—Sally, Maurice, Shirley, Paul, and Willis.

August Nilson lived in Minneapolis for several years and worked as a carpenter. He came to Cromwell about 1906 and bought eighty acres of wild land in Sec. 13, S1/2 SW1/4 of Sec. 13-49-20. He built a house and other small buildings here. He bought a portable sawmill, the first sawmill to be operated with a gasoline engine. It had an upright boiler for a cooling system, and sawed lumber. I believe Mr. Nilson would have been a success if his health had not failed him. He became a victim of tuberculosis and died in 1909, leaving his wife and two children. There were no means of subsistence for the family so they moved to Wisconsin to live with some of Mrs. Nilson's relatives. Their neighbors reported that they were good neighbors. They had to relinquish their hope of an independent home here.

Andrew Peterson is a brother of John Peterson Dallen (Dallen is the name of their birthplace). About this I will have to make some explanation. In Norway, as well as in some other countries, it is customary to have the name of their birthplace as an appendage to their name instead of their surname and so we find such names as Ole Johnson's children named and recorded as John Ole's son and their daughters as Olina Ole's daughter (this led to much confusion). They are only in church records and if they were not baptized there is no record of their birth.

Well, the Andrew Petersons came here from Iowa with their two youngest daughters in 1907. They had ten children in all. They bought forty acres of wild land in the NW1/4 of NW1/4 Sec. 34-49-20 from Charles Morse and built a small house and some small out buildings and made that their permanent home. They were elderly people and not in the best of health. Then in 1910, Mrs. Peterson died from a heart ailment leaving her husband and two daughters here along with seven other children in Iowa to mourn her passing. Mr. Peterson did not farm much as he was in poor health and suffering from heart trouble also and he followed Mrs. Peterson in 1917 from the same ailment. Mr. Peterson was of a very kind disposition and was a good neighbor and he left many friends. His youngest daughter married Oscar Homstad and remained in this area.

Emil Sparring was a native of Sweden and a carpenter. He and Mrs. Sparring came from Superior, Wisconsin, and bought forty acres of land and cleared the forty. They built a good house, barn, and other buildings. They farmed there until about 1930 when they sold the farm to Kenneth Mann. Then the Sparrings moved to Floodwood and built a farm northwest of there. Mr. and Mrs. Sparring had four children and they were good and helpful neighbors. The Kenneth Mann family farmed there until 1951 and then moved to Duluth and the farm is vacant now. They had five children.

William Good was a single man, who in the early 1920s came from Indiana to the Corona district and farmed south of there on the drained swampland, raising flax and winter rye in partnership with Norman Haugh who owned a lot of land there. He farmed there about two years and had fairly good crops in the dry years. But, flax was only a two-year crop on the same land at the most. We then had some wet years and that was the end of the flax production there. Mr. Good came to Cromwell and made a deal with Dr. Fox of Ohio, who had taken over the land of McArthur, his father-in-law in the 1920s. Mr. McArthur had built a house on it so Mr. Good moved onto the land about 1924 and cleared forty acres or more and put in many rods of small lateral ditches and plowed up maybe sixty acres along the Big Ditch on the east side of State Highway 73. Mr. Good did not raise any crops here. Being a single man, he hired a family man who had one daughter; the man to clear the land and the wife to keep house. The daughter was about sixteen-years-old and Mr. Good was between fifty and sixty. He married the daughter.

    Then Mr. Good went into a partnership with Norman Haugh of the State Bank of Cromwell and bought one hundred sixty acres in the SW1/4 of Sec. 9-49-20 and he cleared forty acres and plowed the same. The following winter they went up north of Floodwood and bought some timber there and started a timber camp. Mr. Good moved up there to take charge of the timber camp. I do not know what kind of timber but maybe pulpwood and mining timber. They operated there all winter. Then the State Bank was closed and Mr. Good never returned to Cromwell. In the course of time the receiver of the State Bank of Cromwell sold the land to Mr. Zalk. He was a cattle buyer from Duluth and St. Paul who improved it by building some buildings and pasturing the land by enclosing it with a high, woven-wire fence. For some years he had cattle, sheep, and horses. When his wife died after a long illness, Mr. Zalk sold his home in St. Paul and came up to Cromwell and made it his permanent home ever since. He made a good-sized farm out of it.

Mr. S. Meagher was a railroad man who bought 410 acres of land in Sec. 16 and 17-49-20 about 1920 and cleared one hundred acres or more and built a large barn and other small buildings and made a real stock farm. He kept a hired man the year-round and it appeared that he intended to make it his permanent home, but he died very suddenly of a heart attack. So Mrs. Meagher sold all the livestock and three years later sold the farm to Victor Maki about 1929. He came from Cloquet and, as there was no dwelling, Mr. Maki had to build a house. His house was large and made of cement block. He made the farm one of the largest livestock farms in Red Clover township. Mr. and Mrs. Maki were born in Finland and came to this country as young people. They have one son and one daughter.

Carl and Gust Brandt were born in Sweden and came to Cromwell as young men. They worked some years in North Dakota and came back to Cromwell and bought eighty acres of land with some clearing on it from Smith Collenson in Sec. 9-48-20 and built some good buildings and cleared all the land. They farmed in partnership and specialized in potatoes and dairying and were very successful for some years. Then Gust had to enter the army in World War I and served in Germany several months. When he came back he severed his partnership with Carl and worked in Superior, Wisconsin. There, he met the pearl of his eye and heart, or what have you, and they were married in Superior. However, she was a widow with five children—three girls and two boys. They moved to Cromwell and bought the Lindquist farm in Sec. 14-48-20 and carried on general farming and dairying. Gust is a good farmer and a hard worker. Mr. and Mrs. Brandt had two daughters and lived a very happy and successful life.

John Lindquist was born in Sweden and might have been married there. He and his wife came to Odanah, Wisconsin, as young people. Mr. Lindquist worked there in the sawmills for a number of years and the Lindquists had fourteen children—six girls and eight boys (four of them died in infancy). No wonder Mr. Lindquist wanted more living room when he came to Cromwell looking for it. He bought 120 acres in Sec. 23-48-20 about 1900 or earlier. He did remain in Odanah and worked in the sawmills there until about 1905 when he moved his family and a good deal of the Odanah population with him. He not only established his own home, but "Swede Town" also, and then started a sawmill out there and operated it for several years doing custom sawing. He had such a large family of boys that he did not need to hire much outside help. In the winter, they would cut timber logs and cordwood. He hauled the logs to the mill and the cordwood to Cromwell to be shipped out. This hauling was done by one of the boys with a team of horses.

Now, Mr. Lindquist found that the land he had bought first was low and swampy so he bought 120 acres in Sec. 14-48-20. This acreage had a good stand of hardwood timber. This land was north of the lake so he established his home there, cleared a good farm, and constructed good buildings. He and Mrs. Lindquist were very active until Mrs. Lindquist died in 1919 and then his own health began to fail him. He then made some kind of bargain with Emil Stranberg, his son-in-law, to buy the farm. His son gave it up and moved out to Oregon and Mr. Lindquist sold the farm to Gust Brandt. Only one of Mr. Lindquist's sons, namely Paul, and one daughter, Norma, remained here at Cromwell. When Mr. Lindquist died in 1932, he left three daughters and seven boys to mourn his death. Only Paul remained here to develop a good farm of his own and became a successful farmer. Note: John Lindquist was the first to buy a car in Cromwell. He bought a Ford in 1917; it was the first new car out.

Mr. and Mrs. Herman Carlson were born in Sweden and came to Odanah, Wisconsin. They were married there and Mr. Carlson worked in the sawmill

Herman Carlson Family, ca. 1920s

there for a number of years. They came with Mr. Lindquist and bought eighty acres in Sec. 14-48-20 and established their home there. Mr. Carlson worked hard and had a large family of twelve children and while they were very successful in multiplication in the family, they were not so in farming. This was the beginning of the age of specialization. The Carlsons were very good neighbors and always ready to give a helping hand. At last, the Carlsons, thinking they could improve their economic condition by moving to Indiana, sold their farm to

Albert Johnson, a single man from Duluth. He moved onto the farm and constructed new, up-to-date buildings. He made a good farm of it and engaged in general farming, livestock, and dairying until he died about 1952.

Mr. and Mrs. Albert Olson were born in Sweden and came to this country at an early age and settled first near Eau Claire, Wisconsin. They came to Cromwell in 1908, bought eighty acres of land in Sec. 22-48-20 and made some improvements, but then went back to Wisconsin and farmed a few years. They came back to Cromwell in 1920 and established their home on their land and built some good buildings and engaged in general farming with livestock and dairying. They were successful until Mrs. Olson became the victim of cancer. She died in 1930. After that Mr. Olson did not prosper so well, so he began to lease the farm with all the livestock and equipment. After that he leased the farm only, until at last he sold the farm to Hans Korpala about 1945. He retained a small plot of land where he built himself a little house and retired there to spend his declining years. He died in 1952. Mr. and Mrs. Olson were of a very reserved disposition; however, they are entitled to the credit of contributing to the development of Swede Town. He made a good farm and other improvements. They had no children.

John Hedman and his wife came from Sweden to Odanah, Wisconsin. They were married in Odanah. Mr. Hedman worked for some years in the sawmills and came to Cromwell in 1906. They bought some land on the south side of the lakeshore on Lindquist Lake and established their home there about 1907. They had a nice little farm and lived there until 1916. Then they sold their farm to Charles Anderson and moved to New York state. Mr. Hedman did not farm much, but was engaged mostly in getting out forest products. They had several children.

Mr. and Mrs. Charles Anderson were born in Sweden and shortly after they were married came (I believe, to Duluth) to this country and lived in Duluth until they moved to Cromwell in 1906. They bought the John Hedman farm. They built some good buildings on the farm and engaged in general farming, mostly dairying. Mr. Anderson operated the farm for about twenty-four years. Then he died in 1940 leaving his wife and one son to mourn his loss. His son, Everet, took over the farm and it is now operated by his grandson, Dick Anderson, and his wife. Mrs. Anderson and her son, Everet, and daughter-in-law make it their home.

Mr. and Mrs. Olaf Johnson were born in Sweden and came to Duluth as young people and in 1925 came to Cromwell. They bought the land owned by Oscar Johnson (the old George Merwen's land) and made that their home by building new, up-to-date buildings. They developed a good general farm and operated it as a livestock and dairy farm. Mr. and Mrs. Johnson had one son and one daughter. They were very amiable and consequently very good neighbors. When their son married they turned the farm over to him. They retired and moved to Duluth to live, perhaps, with their daughter.

Mr. and Mrs. Martin Lindholm were born in Sweden and came over in 1890 to Odanah, where they were married. He worked in the sawmill there for a number of years. They came to Cromwell in 1912 and bought eighty acres of land in Sec. 14-48-20. They established their home there, cleared a small farm, and operated a livestock and dairy farm until his health failed him. He died in 1929 leaving his wife, two sons, and one daughter to mourn his loss. This land had been homesteaded by a man named McCabe in the early 1880s who proved up in 1888 and sold all the timber pine and tamarack ties and timber in 1896.

Mr. and Mrs. Charles Stenberg were born in Sweden and came here as young people and settled in Duluth. Mr. Stenberg was a painter by trade and worked at his trade. He came to Cromwell about 1910 and bought eighty acres from a Mr. Sund or Lund who had bought the land from J. M. Paine Lbr. Co. of Carlton about 1902. He cleared about four acres of land, the N1/2 SW1/4 Sec. 3-48-20. Mr. Stenberg moved on his land and built himself a good house and other buildings and cleared more land. They had two sons and two daughters. In about 1920 they sold their little farm to Tony Kaubfire, a lithographist, who had been working on many different newspapers here and abroad. He did not intend to farm much but to maintain a home here. He died very suddenly of a heart attack on the lakeshore in the late 1920s. After five years, Mrs. Kaubfire sold the farm to Mr. M. L. Ferguson from Chicago, who moved here with his wife and started a poultry farm and built a large poultry house. He built a number of cottages to rent to tourists and also had boats to rent. He lived here for about ten years and then moved back to Chicago where he died three years later. Mrs. Ferguson then sold the farm to the present owner.

Mr. and Mrs. S. Melvold were born in Norway and came to this country as young people. They came to Superior where they married. Mr. Melvold was a salesman for many years in Superior and came to Cromwell about 1905. He bought 100 acres of land on the east side of Island Lake in Sec. 3-48-20 and later the point in Sec. 4. He maintained a summer home here for his family— Mrs. Melvold and three daughters. Later, when he retired on pension he would stay out here in the summers. They both passed away within a few weeks of each other in 1945. Their daughters Nora, Margret, Julia, and Louise are maintaining the estate and make it their summer home. The Melvolds were the kindest people and were very highly respected and were missed by all their old neighbors and friends.

Edward Vigness and his wife, Clara, were born in Fillmore County, Minnesota. Their parents were pioneer Norwegian immigrants in the southeastern part of Minnesota. Mr. and Mrs. Vigness were born in or near Northfield, Minnesota, where they were graduates of St. Olaf College. They moved to Mora in Kanabec County and lived there only a few years. Two sons were born to them. About 1920, they sold their farm, bought eighty acres of wild land in Sec. 16-49-20, built a good house and other outbuildings, cleared some land, and established their home there. Mr. Vigness served as bookkeeper at the creamery for one year or so. In the spring of the year about 1933, he and his youngest son were burning grass on their land. They were soon surrounded by fire and were so badly burned that the son died shortly afterwards and Mr. Vigness less than two weeks later. He left his wife and an older son, Enoch, to mourn his loss. At the time of his death he was the clerk of the school board and Mrs. Vigness was appointed to succeed him. Mrs. Vigness and her son operated the farm a few years together. Mrs. Vigness moved to the Iron Range and her son married and took over the farm. And that ended their high hopes of independence and thus brought to an end a sad story.

Louis Knutson was of Norwegian descent and came to Cromwell as a section foreman for the NP in about 1905. About two years later he married Miss Clara Skramstad and they, with his mother, made their home in the section house. About 1908, he quit the section work and bought forty acres in the southwest corner of Sec. 2-48-20 and established his home there. He did not do any extensive farming so he and his family moved to Hibbing, Minnesota. He worked in the freight warehouse there for about two years. He then returned to Cromwell and lived here for some time, then to Duluth where he worked a few years. Again, they returned to their old home at Cromwell and remained here for two years and then moved to Duluth where they finally made their permanent home. Mr. and Mrs. Knutson had one son and one daughter. They were good neighbors and always ready with a helping hand. As Mr. Knutson was an old railroad man it was a case of off the track and on again several times.

Ole M. Holm was born in Norway and came to Superior as a young man. He worked there on a dairy farm or as a milkman and later worked in the car shops. Shortly after, he married a young maiden, the apple of his eye. About 1912, they came to Cromwell and bought the farm home of Sam Brigan, the NW1/4 NW1/2 Sec. 14-48-20, and eighty acres, the N1/2 NW1/4 Sec. 15-48-20, and made that his home for several years or until about 1930. Then he and his family moved to Enderlin, North Dakota, and he went to work in the Soo Line shops as a wrecking foreman on the railroad until he died in 1945. He left his wife and seven boys and girls to mourn his loss. He was very active in the fraternal order of the Odd Fellows.

Charles Swanson was a single man who came to Cromwell about 1920. He bought eighty acres in S1/2 NE1/4 Sec. 15-48-20 and built a house and other small buildings. He cleared a small farm and conducted general farming there for a few years and made his living there. He died in 1940. Mr. Swanson was a bachelor and was considered a little eccentric as he did not mix much with other people. However, he was harmless and worked hard.

Mr. and Mrs. Albin Ruse came from Duluth in 1916 and bought the NW1/4 SW1/4 Sec. 14-48-20 from Martin Lindholm. They built a small house and made some improvements. Later they gave it up and moved back to Duluth. They had four children.

Mr. and Mrs. Emil Olson came from Duluth in 1916 and bought the SE1/4 SW1/4 Sec. 14-48-30. They moved onto the land, building a house and making improvements, but they lived there only a short time. They had four small children. They moved back to Duluth to their old home. I did not know any of them.

Peter V. Anderson was a single man who, I believe, came from Wisconsin about 1914. He bought a little farm, eighty acres in NW1/4 NE1/4 Sec. 13-48-20, and made his living there, mostly by cutting and selling timber. He died about 1938 and had no known relatives to mourn his loss.

John Arthur Selander was born in Sweden and came to Odanah, Wisconsin, as a young man. He had been a sailor in his young days. He came to Cromwell in 1907 with John Lindquist and others and bought the S1/2 of NE1/4 Sec. 15-48-20 and built a house and other buildings. It was all heavy timber and he did not do any farming until he married Salma Stoner, a neighbor girl. Since then, he has operated a general farm and has done some livestock farming as a co-partner with John Lindquist, Herman Carlson, and John Hedman. They operated a sawmill from 1907 until 1920. Mr. Selander is the only one of the original settlers left in the settlement. Mr. and Mrs. Selander had two sons and one daughter. They are good neighbors and highly respected by all who know them.

Mr. Pheffer, a contractor from Duluth, bought the farm of Emil Ripka in the 1920s—the E1/2 NW1/4 and the W1/2 NE1/4 Sec. 10-48-20— and built a big dairy barn and made other extensive improvements. A Mr. Laubeck and his family managed the farm for him for a number of years until he sold the farm to Ernest Mower in 1930. Mr. Mower owns and operates the farm now. This farm includes the old homestead of Arthur R. Newton, owned later by Louis Lundgreen. Mr. and Mrs. Newton were the first white family to live in the town of Eagle (outside Cromwell). They came here about 1886 and moved east to Manchester, New Hampshire, in 1895. They were highly respected people and good neighbors. He was one of the first officials of school District 13. One of his boys and one of his girls were among the first six pupils of the school.

Albert Blaha and his wife came to Cromwell from Rice Lake, Wisconsin. They were Bohemian immigrants and bought the N1/2 SW1/4 Sec. 11-48-20, built a log house and other small buildings, and made other small improvements. Most of the time Mr. Blaha worked out in the woods and about 1918, their house burned down. This left them in hard circumstances but with the help of their neighbors they built a small house. Not long afterwards, Mrs. Blaha got sick with some lung ailment and died about 1919. They had a large family of boys and girls and her death broke up their home. The baby, Louis, was adopted by Louis Pohl, who raised him and gave him the name of Louis Pohl.

Otto Adelgruber was of German descent and of old pioneer stock. His great-grandfather and great grand-mother came to Milwaukee as immigrants in the 1840s when Milwaukee was in its infancy and before Wisconsin was admitted to the Union in 1848. The revolutionary conditions in Germany at the time caused many to migrate to this country—some voluntarily, and others by compulsion. Some came on twenty-four hours notice to leave. That is the beginning of the history of Otto Adelgruber's grandparents. They were born in or near Milwaukee, and later, they were married. His grandfather enlisted in the U.S. Army and marched out through Wisconsin and Minnesota to Fort Ripley about 1871 and was stationed there on the Indian frontier. A few years after the Indian uprising (in 1862) and when his granddad was about a year old, his grandmother packed his mother in papoose fashion and came all the way from Milwaukee to Fort Ripley. There were only stage roads used to haul U. S. mail and for military transportation and some tote roads used by lumber companies, so there was no such thing as hitchhiking a ride.

As time went on, the Adelgrubers settled down near St. Cloud, maybe somewhere in what became Morrison County. Here Otto had his beginning, he married Esther Ida Johnson of Fairhaven, Minnesota, in 1919. He lived there about fourteen years and came to Cromwell in 1934 and bought the Ashley farm. That farm had fallen into the hands of the Federal Land Bank by mortgage and was held by the bank for a number of years (or maybe it was the state of Minnesota). The farm contained 160 acres and there were fairly good buildings and a large clearing on the farm. Mr. Adelgruber made a good farm of it and operated a general stock farm. Mr. and Mrs. Adelgruber are very industrious and are active in public affairs. They are very good neighbors. They had fourteen children—eight girls and six boys, nine of whom are living.

James Krotovel was born in Bohemia and came to Cromwell from Chicago about 1910 and bought eighty acres from Emil Ripka that he had bought for speculation. That was the E1/2 NW1/4 of Sec. 11-48-20. Mr. Krotovel was a single man and did not do much farming, but built himself a small house and lived there for many years.

Alfred Lundstrom came here from Duluth about 1916 and bought forty acres from James Krotovel. That was the NE1/4 NW1/4 Sec. 11-48-20 and he lived there until he retired in 1937 when he and his family moved to Chicago. He died there later leaving his wife and seven sons and six daughters to mourn his loss. Mr. Lundstrom was very active in fraternal organizations and was a good neighbor.

Mr. and Mrs. Nick Jerecovsky were born in Bohemia and came to this country as young people. They came to Crosby, Minnesota, about 1900 and moved to Cromwell in 1917. They bought eighty acres of wild land in the SE corner Sec. 3-49-20 and built a large, cement-block house and other small buildings. Later they built a large barn and have made their home there ever since. They have cleared a good deal of land and are operating a dairy and livestock farm and doing general farming. For many years they were engaged in buying and selling cattle and hauling by truck to Duluth and St. Paul stock markets, during 1939 and 1940. He also drove the school bus a few years when he first came to Cromwell. Mr. and Mrs. Jerecovsky have three daughters who are all married. The last children were twin boys and one of them died young while the other survived. He also married and lives on a farm east of Cromwell.

William Debolt came here in 1906 from Long Prairie or Eagle Bend. He came here with his three brothers: Vern, Charlie, and Ervin, in the deer hunting season and all remained here. William or "Bill," as he was called, went to work for James Violett's daughter, Beana. Charlie married Eva Cota and Ervin married Polene Cota, Eva's sister. Ervin moved to the Iron Range and Charley moved to Detroit, Michigan. Bill remained here and later their brother, Vern Debolt, and their father came and made Cromwell their home also. They all died young, leaving their father and their families to mourn their loss. Their widows are still living in Duluth and up on the Iron Range.

Mr. Jaster Lines came to Minnesota in 1882 with his parents from the state of Indiana. He came to Browerville and grew to manhood there and in 1899 married Blanche Phillips. They were blessed with six sons and four daughters. One son died in infancy and their son, James, died after they came to Cromwell. James was married and left his wife and seven children and his parents and four brothers and four sisters to mourn his loss. Mr. and Mrs. Lines and their family came to Cromwell in 1917 and bought 160 acres of wild land in the NE1/4 Sec. 1-48-20 and moved onto the land and built some small buildings and have made it their home ever since.

In the first years Mr. Lines drove the school bus—six years with a team of horses and two with a truck. Mr. and Mrs. Lines and the family have worked hard and have cleared about one hundred acres of land and made it a good productive farm. They built a good house and large out-buildings so they are enjoying a good home in their declining years. In the sunset days of their lives, they are living in comfort and independence. All of their sons and daughters are living on farms near the parental home and they all have greatly helped to develop the agriculture in this community. They are all raising large families which also helps to increase our population. Mr. and Mrs. Lines are good and helpful neighbors.

Ray Engelin was a single man who came here in the early days from Minneapolis. He was related to Ben Pipen and stayed with him in the late 1890s. He went up to Alaska in the Gold Rush days in the beginning of 1900 and remained there 15 years and then he came back to Cromwell. He bought 80 acres of wild land, the W1/2 SW1/4 of Sec. 5-48-20, and in about 1908 cleared a good deal of land. He built a small house and a big barn. He farmed here a good many years, raising potatoes, until his health failed him and he became a victim of cancer and died soon thereafter.

Mr. and Mrs. Oscar D. Davis came here from Aitkin in 1912 with their four sons and one daughter.

They bought the old Amasa Dotton homestead and made that their home for nearly thirty years. They farmed, raising some livestock and potatoes until Mrs. Davis died in the 1940s. After that his eldest son, Howard, operated the farm for some years. Howard was the only one of them that married. Mr. Davis moved to Duluth and lived with his daughter until he passed away in 1954. Mr. and Mrs. Davis were born in Illinois and were married there and then came to Aitkin, Minnesota. Mr. Davis was a cigar maker by trade and had some talent as a musician. There were four sons and one daughter. One of the sons served many years in the U.S. Navy until he retired. Mr. and Mrs. Davis were very jovial and happy people and were good neighbors.

Mr. and Mrs. Rex Herrick and his father came to Cromwell from Dakota in the 1920s and bought or contracted to buy 160 acres in Sec. 14-49-20, the NW1/4. They built a small house and moved their family there and lived there for four years, cutting timber in the summer and hauling it to Cromwell in the winter. Mr. Harrick was a prairie farmer, so after he had cut the timber he gave up the job of making a farm out of it. He then rented a small farm east of Prairie Lake in St. Louis County and farmed there a few years. Later he went to work on the county roads for St. Louis County as a grader man until he died from ivy poisoning. He left his wife and four children to mourn his passing.

Ronald Herrick came here from South Dakota with his wife and three daughters. He rented a small farm next to his brother's and lived there four years. He then rented a farm from James Anderson in Section 9 of Red Clover Township in 1930 or 1932. He lived there about three years when he moved to Cromwell and rented the Morse farm and operated that farm until his health failed him. In 1952 he retired from active farming.

Ivar Lynne and his brother came here from near Atkinson where they had rented a farm. They came here about 1925 and rented the old Ashley farm and rented livestock and machinery from Charles Menki of Moose Lake. At last, Mr. Menki sold his livestock and machinery and then the Lynne brothers operated the farm with their own livestock and machinery for about three years or until 1932. Then Ivar married Mrs. Bertha Jorstad and dissolved his partnership with his brother. Soon thereafter he moved off the farm and rented Emil Sparring's farm for one year. When it was sold to Kenneth Mann, Mr. and Mrs. Lynne moved over onto Mrs. Lynne's little farm just one mile north of Cromwell on state highway 73 where they lived until Mrs. Lynne died in 1947 or 1948. Then Mr. Lynne sold the farm to Emil Peterson, Sr. of Wright, Minnesota, and moved north of Prairie Lake.

Mr. and Mrs. Joseph Novotny were a newly married couple who came here from Rice County, Minnesota about 1920. They bought forty acres, the SE1/4 NW1/4 Sec. 21-49-20, and built a small house and other small buildings. They cleared about ten acres of land and made their home there for a few years. They were blessed with two sons, John and Joseph, and one infant that died in the late 1920s. Then they sold their little farm to John Carlson and moved to Wisconsin (Eagle River, I believe) and lived there two or three years and came back to Cromwell to make their home here. They bought forty acres in Sec. 35-49-20. Mr. Novotny is a veteran of World War I.

PART TWO

CHAPTER SEVEN

Preamble to the History of the Finnish People of the Town of Eagle, Carlton County, Minnesota

The earliest history indicates that Gomer, the son of Japheth, settled north of the Sea of Azof. There is a town there now named Berdiansk not far east of the Dnieper River, the Bread Basket of Europe today. The son of Gomer and grandson of Japheth settled west and north of Greece in the southwest corner of present day Bulgaria. His name is Riphath.

In the Caucasian Mountains of Georgia there lived a people that were known as Ibereans and we also hear of them, or a branch of them, living in Portugal. They were not Christians. Also, they were at war with a people who had heard and received the Gospel and were Christians in about 200 A.D. They lived southeast of Portugal in what is known today as Armenia. These Christians were defeated and most of the men and the old women were killed in battle. The young girls were taken and sold into slavery, which was a common practice then.

Here my story begins and it is based on tradition, the same as a good deal of our early history. Much of it may be authentic.

There was a young girl, not very good to look at nor was she robust, but a very devout and earnest Christian, as all the early Christians were. As she was not strong nor attractive, she was sold for a small price.

A young soldier got her as his compensation for serving in the army. He took her to his parental home some distance north in the mountain vastness where they lived. Their only support was their young men serving in the armies of their neighboring tribes. They did not traffic in human slavery as their neighbors did and so they treated her as one of their own. While they were not Christians, they had a high moral standard. She lived a lonely life among a strange people and she could not worship with them. The Lord was her only companion and she was faithful in her labors. She earned the respect and confidence of the family and all with whom she came in contact. Yet in her loneliness, she shed many tears. However, she did not lose courage or faith, which was not to be found among these people.

After an old and ordinary custom of those people, when one of their family was sick, they would take the sick member out to their neighbors and inquire if they had a remedy for the ailment. They believed that by showing the sick one to their neighbors, the neighbors would help. One day they brought a little infant who was sick with some unusual ailment; no one knew of any cure for it and so they wondered if there could be any cure. There were some who wondered if the strange girl would have some remedy for the child. After they had given up all hope, they carried the little child to the house where Naomi (the girl's Christian name) lived. She was called out of the house and asked whether she had a remedy for the child and she said, "No, but I know who has a remedy, not only for this ailment, but from death." The sorrowful parents asked who that could be and where he lived. She told them in the high heavens and He will gladly come to all that call upon Him and that He is full of love and grace. She called the parents, then went in and prayed for the infant, and when she came out she felt in her heart that God had heard her prayer, and that He had said "Amen." Then she saw the infant opening her eyes and smiling at her and she became well.

On their way home the parents had to stop and tell the neighbors about the miracle that had happened to their infant and by what process it was brought about. Yes, by the simple prayers of a simple Christian girl to the Almighty God.

It became known far and wide, and soon thereafter, the wife of the king heard about it. She had also fallen seriously ill and was brought to Naomi. When Naomi saw her coming, she was deeply moved in her heart and prayed for her also. Soon the wife also recovered from her ailment and so this is the beginning. The simple beginning of the Christian church and Christian civilization in Georgia, south of the Caucasian Mountains. The people might have been direct descendants of Gomer, grandson of Noah. All scholars are in agreement that somewhere in the southeast of Mount Ararat is the cradle of the human family. We are not in agreement as to the time. We will all have to admit that sometime in the past, we were all spewed out of that cradle, and had the same color of skin.

So we find a people called the Sumerians in the early days living north of the Persian Gulf and south of the Caucasian Mountains in the Euphrates and the Tigris valley, which was later called Mesopotamia. It is believed that they came from the north of Mount Ararat and may be related to a branch of the foster parents of the aforementioned slave girl. These people were opposed to human slavery and were living a life of strict-monogamy. They lived among a people that practiced polygamy and human slavery.

They were a very militant people and gave expression to their militarism by serving in the army of any ruler that would employ them. They nearly always settled on low swampy land along river beds where it was subject to seasonal overflow. This would leave a deposit of silt that left ready seed beds and was very fertile and produced good crops. These were also the characteristics of the Finnish people. It appears that all these people are directly related to the Ural Altaic family and their civilization with a similarity in their physiognomy. As they were a militant people, we find them or at least part of them, employed along the borders of the great Chinese Empire to protect the Chinese from attack by roving raiders. They might have been Tatars, the wild inhabitants of Tatary, and maybe some of them were Cossacks, a mixture of Turks and Tatars. How long they were employed there I do not know.

History records that they were settled there sometime between 2000 and 1000 B.C. and they made their living by hunting (compensation for border guardsmen), and some fishing and selling furs to the Chinese. If this assumption is correct the early Finns were loose groups of families organized into tribes and yet consolidated into one national group. They made their living by hunting, fishing, and tilling their swamp or river bottom lands with their young men serving in the armies of their western neighbors. It is also known that there was a continual movement and pressure from the east and southeast by the Huns and Mongols. Tatars might have forced the Finns to migrate northwestward and so the wandering Finns came west, many of them as far as the Vistula River, and some north to Pomeria settling there while the rest moved along the east coast of the Baltic Sea under pressure of the Asiatic Nomads. They may be kin of Tatars, Turks, and Huns, one of the ancient Tatar race which in the ninth century A.D. overran and devastated Europe, and the Slavonic family that later settled eastern Europe. There were also the Letts who came west and settled on the eastern shore of the Baltic Sea and forced the Finns to move farther north and conquered them. This forced them to move farther north to where their habitation is today. The Lapps are of the Ugrian Samoyed family and distinct from the Ural Altaic family. The Finns lived there some time until they were conquered by Sweden, in about the 9th century, 843 A.D., and became a part of Sweden until Russia took the Baltic provinces from Sweden. This they did by crushing the Swedish army at Poltava in 1709 and all the way up north to the Gulf of Finland. Russia got all of Finland from Sweden in 1815 A.D. and at the same time Sweden lost Pomeria to Prussia.

Prussia had already colonized a large land area and now they established legal claim to Pomerania. But we find some self-ordained Prussians, Professors of Ethnography and Ethnology long before this who before the 8th century stigmatized the Finnish people with the name Mongolian very successfully. Young Finnish men had been employed as border guardsmen on the Chinese borders. The same sources also tried to stigmatize the Norwegians by claiming that they came into Norway from the North and may be related to the Ugrian Samoyed family, hence the name Norwegian (when their name is Norge). The English have accepted the German interpretation of ethnology and ethnography and so they have made many people believe that the Norwegians are of the yellow race, and many highly learned professors hold that view today, all for the political purpose of creating a Prussian empire that would extend from the Arctic Ocean south to the Persian Gulf, or the Gulf of Oman. That was Bismark's ambition also. That would refute the claims of Denmark, Sweden, Norway, and Finland at that time.

I will quote from memory and from sagas and heroic tales of the ancient Danes and the hero Vigo (a Finn), the junior of the king's guard of twelve men.

About sixteen hundred years ago there was a Harold Bluetooth, king of Denmark. He had a bodyguard of twelve men; they were big, brave, and strong men. It was said of them that they were the equivalent of a whole army. They were specially chosen and they all had to make a solemn vow that they would avenge the death of their master, the king, by the ceremonial rite of handling the spear handle (eight to ten feet long and two inches in diameter) to the candidate as he would make his vow. Vigo was the junior guard, the youngest of twelve men.

At this time the southern part of Sweden and Baltic Island and the islands in the Kattagat and Jutland were not yet fully subdued. When the Saxons, so-called because they were the first of all the North Men or Goths to use a short steel sword (called sax) in their warfare, made a vow which was a sacred promise by the worshipers of Woden and Thor (their Gods). they would never break their promise. Now the king had given a banquet in honor of his friends and he might have been a little tipsy, so he became boastful and made a vow that he could conquer England with three small boats and his force of about thirty-five men, including his bodyguard. It was binding for him to live up to his vow. His wife made him a heavy leather suit that was supposed to protect him against the dart of the spear.

In the course of time they landed in England. The English were prepared for them and the battle was on. It did not last long; the English slew all but the King and Vigo. They cornered them with their shields and so they were captured and the king would not identify himself. They put him down in a pit full of adders or vipers (somewhat like our rattlesnake but without rattlers), and Vigo, remembering his vow, agreed to enter the bodyguard of the English king and so he had to go through the same ceremonial performance as before. The King of England handed him the spear handle taken from his former king. He said, "My former Lord always took the spear end in his own hands and gave me the handle and so I made my solemn vow." The English king yielded and gave Vigo the spear who then drove it into him with such force that he died shortly after. Vigo had paid his vow and died in peace with his conscience clear. But King Harold was not dead yet. They had been too busy until now to look into the pit and were surprised to find the king unharmed and then they noticed the leather suit; they removed it. It was not long until a serpent hooked its fangs into him right under his heart. He then identified himself by singing a little verse:

> If my ten Juniors could know
>   The anguish of their Senior
> They would rally to liberate me
>   From this anguish of my soul
> And set me free, and vanquish my foe

  And my identity will be known
That I am a King of might.

  Then they knew who the king was and they dispatched a delegation immediately to inform his sons of what had happened.

  And that was the beginning of the invasion by the Danes and Vigo representing Finland, and the evidence of that invasion is still evident today.

  And now, I will quote an eminent writer and historian, Mr. Matt Pelkonen, on the Finnish ancestry:

  "The Finns, or Ural Altaic people are a very ancient race and were at their height about the 6th century B. C. They dominated the great Eurasian, Europe-Asia continent, to the Pruth and Danube Rivers and north to the Baltic Shores, on to the Iranian Plateau, also Mesopotamia, Asia Minor, and Egypt and the islands of Crete and Cyprus. The boundaries between the Ural-Altaic Finno peoples, and Mongol languages are clearly traceable because of the racial differences. The Mongols belong to the yellow race, while the Finn Ural-Altaic people belong to the white race."

  "The Iranian Plateau was the center of Ural-Altaic civilization during the 7th century B. C. where the soil was first cultivated and animals domesticated. Metallurgy was developed, as well as the earliest syllabic cuneiform writing."

  "Mesopotamia became occupied by the Finno-Ural-Altaic peoples before the 7th century B. C., in the valley of the Tigris and Euphrates. Here in the lower valley, a nation of city states soon developed. The Finno-Ugrian name Sumer (in present day Finnish Suomas) indicates marshland or swampland. On ancient maps two marshy regions along the Tigres and Euphrates rivers were indicated as Suo-Paikka swamp. Suo in Finnish means marsh or swamps and 'paikka' means place, hence, Suo Paikka, marsh place or swamp place. Further up the river another is Suo Tila (here again suo means marsh or swamp and tila in Finnish means site of location)."

"Egypt, though not occupied by great numbers of Finno-Ural-Altaic peoples, owes much of its civilization to this race. At the time of the opening of King Tutankhamen's tomb, a researcher inquired into the hieroglyphs and found derivations and words of the same root as used in today's Finnish. The conjugation of verbs was also similar to Finnish."

"The modern discoveries in the sites of ancient Sumer and Elam, whose people were also Finno-Ural-Altaic people, indicate the earlier picture writing of Elam, Sumer, and Egypt was originally the same, as was the pottery. The early home of the ceramic arts might have been Elam. The earliest known name for Egypt was Kemi, the same as that of a river in Finland and another in Karelia. Later the country and river became known as Nile or Niili. This also is Finnish and means 'to creep'."

"In the book of Daniel, the inscription or handwriting on the wall appeared in Belshashazzar's warning, 'Meme, Meme, Tekee upharsin.' This is the Finnish meaning, 'Go, go in the making danger,' or literally translated, 'Go, go trouble in the making.'"

"The Finnish also lived in Hungary and the Hungarians today call the Finnish cousins. The Finnish also lived in Germany along the Pomerian coast. Even today some thirty-two towns in Germany, among the Gumbine, bear Finnish names as does the Nieman River."

"The Hittites (1400 B.C.) were Finno-Ural-Altaic people as were the Ludians and the Etruscans, the true founders of the Roman civilization. The name Venice (Venetsia) is derived from the Finnish. 'Venet' means boat and 'sia' means place of boats."

"Many textbooks and encyclopedias still use discarded theories on the ethnology of the Finnish people, claiming the Finns are related to the Mongols, which theory has been disproved by such noted anthropologists as Prof. P. Johansen of Denmark who says, 'The Finns in no way can be classed as Mongolians.' He concludes by saying, 'The Finns belong to the white race. The Baltic Finns, including the Finns in Finland, are racially almost pure and do not differ generally from their neighbors to the west.' Mr. Ray Basler, Research Director for the Library of Congress writes, 'Scientific research proves that the Finnish people in no way belong to the Mongolian race, they belong to the white or Indo-European race.' Mr. Basler refers to the writings of Prof. Carleton E. Coons, who has made a study of the Finnish people.

"The physical characteristics of the Finns are light complexioned, light hair, blue or gray-green eyes, and above average in height."

"In 1638, the first Finns settled in Delaware, eastern Maryland, New Jersey, and Pennsylvania. In July, 1640, Kalmer Nyckel arrived on the second expedition to America bearing many Finns who settled in Delaware in the city of Wilmington. The giant Dupont factories are located on the site of former Finnish farms. The first name for Philadelphia was Sauna (Finnish Steam Bath) and was so until William Penn changed it to the present name."

"John Morton, who cast the deciding vote in signing the Declaration of Independence was the grandson of Martin Marttinen (Morten Mortenson) who was born in Rautalampi, Finland. Presidents Theodore and Franklin D. Roosevelt also had some Finnish blood flowing through their veins.

Read *The Delaware Finns* by E. A. Louki and *Before William Penn* by Axel Rauanheimo."

I, Matt Pelkonen, hereby give my permission and right to print this letter or paragraph to Bennett A. Beck, and to include it in his History of Cromwell, and the Township of Red Clover and the Township of Eagle.

CHAPTER EIGHT

Brief History of the Genealogy and Biography of the Finnish People of Eagle Township and Their Accomplishments as Original Pioneers

In 1890, the township, as now organized, was part of the township of Moose Lake and later was included in the township of Red Clover when it was organized in 1893. In about 1898, they withdrew from Red Clover and organized the township of Eagle. The south boundary line of Eagle Township is the fifth correction line.

In 1890 there were no Finnish people living here except at Wright station where Mike Erkos, a Swede-Finn, had taken a homestead some two miles west on the Tamarack River, sometime in the 1880s. I believe Mr. Erkos had been a railroad man or worked on the railroad. There were other Finnish people that settled down there about the same time that Joe Larson and Isaac Maki located out in Eagle Township. A little later Abram Klavu, John Oberg, and H. Knuuttila settled on the shores of Eagle Lake.

About 1894, the Finnish immigrants started to colonize the south half of the township of Eagle. I do not know whether the Finnish people had organized a colonization company as the Danes, Norwegians, Swedes, and Germans had, or if they were just attracted to the lake region because of its similarity in climate and topography. Maybe the economic conditions had something to do with it. However, times were hard, not only in the United States, but all over the world, and the conditions were aggravated by Grover Cleveland's Single Gold Standard, whereby all silver was demonetized. Times were not good in Cleveland's first term from 1884 to 1888, nor in Ben Harrison's term from 1888 to 1892 and the panic was worldwide. It did not improve until after 1896 under McKinley. We had an unlimited influx of immigrants who had high hopes of establishing themselves on the land or in private business or enterprise after they worked and earned a little money.

Many of the immigrants had served four years without pay (apprenticeships) to learn a trade, craft, or some profession while many had a course in technology. All of them were well qualified to fit into the economy of this great new "Land of the Free."

Many responded to the invitation and the encouragement held forth by the United States government and the railroad companies who offered low rates of transportation. Many were disappointed when they came here, not being able to obtain employment in their vocation. Even a job at common labor was almost an impossibility to get, so they were forced to move into the woods to seek a homestead or to buy some wild, cut-over land and work in the woods to make a living.

The Finnish immigrants were well qualified. As pioneers they were the most excellent builders of log buildings. They would saw their own lumber by hand, make their own shingles by hand, and by helping one another they would soon have a good set of buildings. As soon as they would have a little land cleared with the stumps remaining, they would grub up the land between the stumps with a grub hoe. Here, they would plant potatoes and other garden vegetables. My, how these things would grow! They would seed winter rye so they could raise some bread grain. There were no grist mills here, so it was up to the mothers to grind the flour in the coffee mill. But the pioneers were resourceful, so it was not long before a pioneer, John Hakamki, built a windmill, similar to the Dutch windmills you have seen pictures of in books. He made the mill stones of flat field stones (blue stones) and so he started custom grinding feed and flour. He did so for several years.

There was another pioneer, John Perttula, who built a windmill for sawing timber, but was not so successful. However, he did some sawing when there was a high wind.

The first Finnish family to come was the Joseph Larson (Seppaanen) family. There was his wife, Eva (nee Moilanen), and four children—Maria, John, Eino, and Joseph. They came to Superior, Wisconsin, in 1889 from Suomus-salmi, Oulun Laani, Finland, where Mr. Larson was born. They moved to Eagle Township on a homestead, the NE1/4 of SE1/4 and SE1/4 of NE1/4 Sec. 26-48-40. His oldest daughter, Maria, worked in Carlton in the summer of 1893. She worked for Stanley Walker on the old J. M. Paine farm southwest of Carlton. Her father came there that summer and bought his first cow—the first cow to come to the town of Eagle. It was a young red cow and the price was about $18. Mr. Larson walked all the way from the farm about the first of July by way of Mahtowa and Park Lake on the old Mahtowa tote road on the Bean Dam. That fall someone mistook the cow for a moose and shot it. I do not know whether Mr. Larson was compensated for the loss. He worked in the lumber camp for a number of years, and became independent and lived to a ripe old age when his sons took over the farm. Three children were born to them here in Cromwell—Hedvi, Arvid, and Alina.

Matt Heikkila and his wife, Sophia (nee Lukkarinen), were the next family to homestead one hundred sixty acres, the NW1/4 Sec. 32. Matt was born in Kalajoki, Oulun Laani, Finland, in 1864 and Mrs. Heikkila was born in Rantsillassa, Oulun Laani. Matt came to this country as a young man to Marquette, Michigan, in 1882 and then worked for the Canadian Railway Company. He married and moved to Duluth in 1885 and came to the town of Eagle about 1893. They lived on their homestead for about ten years and cleared some land, but they did not farm much. They got some timber products and about 1903, the Heikkila family moved to Cromwell.

Matt Heikkila Family, summer 1915

Mr. Heikkila built a store building where the post office is now located, using the downstairs for a general store and the upstairs for living quarters. He did not succeed in this, so the family moved back on the homestead—poorer, but wiser. Mr. Heikkila was a highly educated man, who was a leader among his people, and was one of the organizers of school District #21 in 1896 and the town of Eagle in the same year. Mrs. Heikkila died in 1922 leaving her husband and eight children (two died in their youth): Ada, the first white child born in Eagle township, as it is now, John, Arthur, George, Otto, William, Hilda, and Hilja. Mr. Heikkila lived to be nearly ninety years old and served as fire insurance agent for the Carlton Mutual Fire Insurance Company until he died. Some of his sons and a daughter made the town of Eagle their permanent home. He was one of our first cooperators, to the extent that he and Peter Kaarkkainen were joint owners of one ox, and they did all of their hauling with that one. Often, I have seen them come to Cromwell for their provisions.

Antti Ainala, a widower, moved in 1893 to the SE1/4 of SE1/4 Sec. 34. Ainala was born in Oulun Laani, Lahespitaajaa in Finland.

That same year, 1893, Charles Saarela and wife, Sophie (nee Palm), settled in Sec. 34, S1/2 of SW1/4. Charles was born in Pihtipudas, Vaasan Laani, Finland, and his wife in Kokkola, where they were married. Two of their children died there; three are living—Anna, Henry and Emma—who all live here.

Isaac Maki and his wife, Serafina (nee Wallinmaki) were born in Ylistaro, married there and came to Superior, Wisconsin, in 1890. In 1893 they came to Eagle Township with their three children and located on a homestead of eighty acres, the S1/2 of NW1/4 Sec. 34. They made that their permanent home. A few years later, Mrs. Maki died, leaving her husband. Three daughters—Sophie (Mrs. Peurasaari), Marie (Mrs. Kuorikoski), and their youngest daughter, Helmi (Mrs. Joseph Larson), and a son, Jacob, , were born there. Mr. Maki was active and helped organize the Carlton County Telephone Association. Mr. Maki lived to be nearly 100 years old and his farm was left to his son, Jacob.

Marie Hellstrom, a sister of Mrs. Isaac Maki, homesteaded forty acres in Sec. 34 (NW1/4 of NW1/4) in the year 1894 and lived alone.

In the year 1893 Daniel Sangola and his wife, Brita, and son, Charles, bought eighty acres of wild land in Sec. 26 SE1/4 of SW1/4 and NE of SW of NE1/4. They came to Brainerd, Minnesota, in 1887 from Simon Pitaajaa, Oulun Laani, Finland, where they were born. They had worked in Brainerd until they moved to their land in Eagle, which they made their permanent home for the remainder of their days. Mr. Sangola was of a conservative disposition. He had served on the town board for a few years when Eagle was included in Red Clover township. Mr. Sangola died in 1922 and Mrs. Sangola in 1932. Their son, Charles, lived on the farm.

William Saarela was born in Pihipudas, Vaasan Laani, Finland, and came to Superior, Wisconsin, in 1888. He worked there and at Bean Dam in the logging operation in Kettle River. In 1892 he homesteaded eighty acres in S1/2 of SW1/4 Sec. 28. Mr. Saarela married a widow, Kristiina Granlund, who had one son from her previous marriage to Frank Granlund. Mr. Granlund had a homestead in Kalevala township. The Saarelas had one son, Matt.

Peter Kaarkkainen, born in Kiuruvesi, Kuopion Laani, Finland, came to the state of Montana in 1887 and in 1892 took a homestead of eighty acres, the E1/2 of SW1/4 Sec. 32, in Eagle township. In 1898 he married Erika Korpua, widow of John Muelun from Kalevala township. Erika was born Haarmaa, Vassan Laani, Finland, and was aunt to Marie Linjamaki, the wife of Charles A. Sangola. The Kaarkkainens had no children.

Arvid D. Neimi, born in Alkula, Vaasan Laani, Finland, came to Superior, Wisconsin, in 1890. He first took a homestead, NW1/4 of NW1/4 Sec. 34, from Kenneth McLeod in Eagle township. He married Henna Hiltunen in 1903. She was born in Sievi, Oulun Laani, Finland. They had five children—George, Arvid, Helmi, Vieno, and Ellen.

Gust Jussila and Evelina (nee Hiltunen), a childless couple, took a homestead, the NW1/4 Sec. 28, in 1893. Both were born in Sievi, Oulun Laani, Finland. The first schoolhouse in Eagle township was built on the northwest corner of Jussela's land. Jussila sold ten acres to Henry Krekula, a single man. Krekula let the school district have some of that land. Mr. Jussila was a shoemaker and worked at his trade, making Finnish shoes (shoe pacs). He would tan his own cowhides and he made some excellent boots and he was kept busy. They sold their farm to Maunu Jaakkola in 1913. They retired and had a little house on the corner of Sec. 20, the S1/2 SE1/4, where they lived their sunset days and I believe both died there.

William Peterson (Pulkkinen) and his wife, Fredicka, were born in Pihtipudas, Vaasan Laani, Finland. William came to Superior, Wisconsin, in 1890 and then in 1892 his wife and children came. The Peterson family took a homestead in E1/4 NE1/4 Sec. 28 in 1893. Three children—Onnie, Peter, and William were born in Finland. Richard, Ida, and Andrew were born here. Now all the children have moved away. Most of the Pulkkanens lived in Wisconsin. William's father, Peter, and brothers, Samuel and Andrew, and one sister, Miina, have worked somewhere in or around Superior.

Albert Johnson (Hietola) was born in Isojoki, Vaasan Laani, Finland, in 1868 and came to Superior, Wisconsin, in 1885. He was first employed in Superior and then came to work as a guard or watchman at Bean Dam on Kettle River here in Eagle township in 1890. He helped build a home on the homestead of Kreeta Peura on the W1/2 of SE1/4 Sec. 22 north of Bean Dam. The only way Miss Kreeta could get even with Albert was to marry him and so they married in 1895. Kreeta was born in Alkkula, Oulun Laani, Finland, in 1866 and came to Superior in 1887. She took a homestead in 1892. Kreeta's two brothers, Jacob and August, also made their home in Eagle township. Mr. and Mrs. Johnson have gone to their reward and left no children to mourn their passing.

Two young ladies, Bertha Lehto and Cornelia Olson, from Superior filed on homesteads. Bertha Lehto filed W1/2 of SE1/4 Sec. 30 and established her home there. She married Mike Mastola and they were getting along well for pioneers when Bertha had the misfortune to have her husband killed on the railroad track near Moose Lake when he was on his way there with their big black horse to get food supplies. He was killed by a St. Paul and Duluth train (now the Northern Pacific). Soon thereafter Bertha sold her land and moved back to Superior. The writer knew Mike and had worked with him and will say a word in memory of him. He was a big strong man with a very agreeable disposition and was always willing to do his share of work. I will say he was a good man and neighbor.

Cornelia Olson's homestead was the E1/4 of SE1/4 Sec. 10. She had a small house built on the land to hold her homestead and she did a little clearing. She married Andrew Korby before she proved up. When she had proven up, they sold the land and moved to Crosby, a new mining town.

An old couple, Elias Laasanen and his wife, Margaret, came here from Superior and bought eighty acres, S1/2 of SE1/4 Sec. 17 and moved here in 1894. They built a house and other small buildings and cleared nearly forty acres. They made this their permanent home until they retired at a ripe old age. In 1918 they sold their little farm to Waine Koskinen and built themselves a little house across the road from their farm in Sec. 16. They lived their last days here. They had no children.

John V. Sallman, his wife, two daughters, and one son came from Finland to Superior about 1895. About 1900 they came to Cromwell and bought N1/2 of SE1/4 Sec. 6-48-20. They built a house and other small buildings and cleared some land and made that their permanent home. They farmed there, raising chickens and dairying. I remember when Mr. Sallman used to come to Cromwell with his milk or cream and eggs on a wheelbarrow—a distance of two and a half miles on a poor road. He took all of his provisions home with him on the wheelbarrow—yes, those were the good old times. Some twenty years later, Mr. Sallman passed away and a few years later Mrs. Sallman passed away. Their daughter, Lydia, married John Cicorellia, an Italian immigrant who came to this country as a young man. They lived on the farm a few years. Mrs. Cicorellia became the victim of cancer of the bone in the arm and had several operations over seven or eight years. About 1940 she passed away and her husband lived for seven or eight years after that. He had retired from farming and moved to Superior where he died at the home of his son, John.

John Iru had left Finland in 1890 for Puerto Rico and lived there for a while. Longing for the brisk climate of the north country, he came to Minnesota and landed in Superior. He located on SW/14 of NW1/4 Sec. 21, town of Eagle. He built a home there in 1896 and later bought another forty acres. Mr. Iru was born in Alajarvi, Vaasan Laani, Finland, in 1856. In 1877 he married Margaret Lovissa Purimala. They had three children—Matt, born in 1878; Marie, in 1880; and Hannah, in 1887. Mrs. Iru came over to Eagle township in 1898 with the two girls and the son, Matt, came a few years later.

Erick Keskitalo was born in Kuolajarvi, Oulun Laani, Finland, in 1871 and came to Superior, in 1892. He settled in Cromwell in 1895 and that same year helped build a house for Henry Knuutila and later for John Iru. This was just before the arrival of Mrs. Iru and their two daughters, Marie and Hannah. Mr. Keskitalo met Marie at the depot and they were married at the home of Charles Morse. They made their home with Mr. and Mrs. Iru for some time and it is their home to this day. Mr. and Mrs. Iru moved to lived with their son, Matt, just south of their homestead. Mr. Keskitalo died in 1932 leaving his wife, Marie, and seven girls and two boys: Helga, Hannah, Anna, Ida, Julian, Mirian, Saima,

Bernhard, and Hjalmar.

Uriel Markkula was born in Sievi, Oulun Laani, Finland, in 1859. His wife, Hannah, was born in Toholampi, Vaasan Laani, Finland, in 1865. They were married in 1887. Mr. Markkula came to Superior in 1889 and worked there until his wife came over in 1896. They moved to Eagle township on the S1/2 of NW1/4 Sec. 28 which they bought from Gust Jussela and they made that their permanent home. Mr. and Mrs. Markkula had ten children: six girls—Saima, Henna, Lempi, Hilja, Jenny, and Aili; and four boys—Waino, Charles, Hugo, and John. Mrs. Markkula died young, shot to death accidentally in her own home sometime around 1913 or a little later. Mr. Markkula died about 1926 and the farm is now operated by one of his grandsons.

Henry Saukko was born in 1868 in Seivi, Oulun Laani, Finland, and came to Superior in 1890. In 1895 he took a homestead, SW1/4 of SE1/4 of SW1/4 Sec. 27, in Eagle township and built a home there. In 1907 he made a trip to Finland and married Katri Hautala; both returned here and made this their permanent home. Mr. Saukko had attended night school and learned English in Superior, Wisconsin. He was a well-educated man. After he came to Cromwell with Henry Knuutila and Matt Heikkila they organized School District #21 on January 13, 1896, and the first one-room school was built. Mr. Saukko served on the school board as clerk and treasurer for many years and on the township board of directors of Eagle township for many years. Mr. Saukko died in 1930 and none of the family remain. These pioneers, including Henry Knuutila, Matt Heikkila, Abram Klavu, and the Rev. John Oberg organized the School District #21 on January 13, 1896, and about the same time the township of Eagle and various churches were organized as their memorial to you and their posterity.

The first members of the school board were Matt Heikkila, Henry Knuutila and Gust Jussila. Maybe they were also the first town board members. The first pupils were Ada Heikkila, Jacob Maki, William Knuutila, and Tilda Klavu. Maybe the first teacher was Hulda Haroldson later Mrs. C. J. Dodge, who is now living in Moose Lake.

They also organized the Apostolic Lutheran Congregation Church with Rev. John Oberg as pastor. The church is still standing. They also organized the Evangelical (Suomi) Lutheran Congregation and one or two more congregations.

Abram Klavu was born in Tammela, Oulun Laani, Finland, about 1864. His wife, Anna Elizabeth (nee Kuivenen), was born in Kuusamassa, Oulun Laani, Finland, about the same year. The Klavus came to Superior as newlyweds in 1886 and moved on the land they had bought on the east shore of Eagle Lake in 1893, the NE1/4 of SW1/4 Sec. 17. They made that their permanent home, a very nice, good little farm. Mr. and Mrs. Klavu died in the late 1920s leaving four sons and five daughters to mourn their passing: August, Henry, Arthur, Charles, Tilda, Senja, Ida, Emma, and Ester. The Klavus were highly respected people and good neighbors.

Henry Knuutila and Mrs. Knuutila came from Kalajoki, Oulun Laani, Finland, about 1894 to Wisconsin near Brule. They took a homestead there and were engaged in the logging business. After Mr. Knuutila had proven up on his homestead there, he sold his land and moved to Superior, Wisconsin. They lived there for a while and in 1893 they came to Cromwell where he bought the W1/2 of SW1/4 Sec. 17 on the east shore of Eagle Lake. He built a house there and other buildings; about 1894 he moved his family there and they made this their permanent home. The Knuutilas had seven children: five boys and two girls—Henry, Jr., the oldest boy, and the daughter, Kristina, were born in Finland; Emma, Wilho, John, Elma, and one girl who died, were born in this country. Mr. Knuutila passed away in 1924 and Mrs. Knuutila in 1908. Mr. Knuutila had been educated in Finland where he had been a schoolteacher; he was well-versed in the English language and often served as an interpreter and as legal advisor. He helped in business transactions and his people held him in very high regard and referred to him as "Master" (meaning schoolmaster). He handled the legal matters of organizing the township of Eagle and served on the school board and the town board. He also served as land agent; he located people on their land and surveyed their section and subdivision lines so they were located on the right land. Mr. Knuutila was a highly respected man by all who knew him. Mr. and Mrs. Knuutila left to mourn their passing—their sons, Henry, Jr., living in Duluth, and John in Cloquet.

The Rev. John Oberg and his wife came to the copper country of Michigan in 1888 and moved to Eagle township in 1895. They bought Lot #3 Sec. 17 on the east shore of Eagle Lake. The Obergs had seven children—five girls, Hilja, Lempi, Olga, Anna, Siiri, and two boys, John F. and Emil. Mr. Oberg established their home on the land he had bought and made it a good farm. The

Rev. Oberg was not only a good preacher, but he was not afraid of working with his hands. He was a good mason and bricklayer—a good builder in general. A good deal of his work remains here to bear witness to his good workmanship. Mr. Oberg was a pastor of the old school—he did not hesitate to labor with his hands to advance the spiritual welfare of his people.

John Hakamaki was born in Jalasjarvi, Vaasan Laani, Finland, and came to this country as a small boy with his parents. They settled in New York Mills, Minnesota.

Grades Three and Four, Cromwell School, 1925.

CHAPTER NINE

Romance

It is said that romance is the spice of history, so I will here submit the following true story concerning two pioneers of the early 1890s. The names are fictitious.

In the little town of Sievisaa, Oulun Laani, Finland, there lived two small families, one of which had a son, Karl (our hero). The other family had a daughter, Lempi (our heroine). The parents of both Karl and Lempi were in limited financial circumstances so they were forced out on their own resources early in life. Their only resource was their ability to work on a farm. While they had been neighbors all their lives, as time went on their friendship grew. As they met from time to time, they found they had many things in common and so their friendship grew to courtship. Sometime later they became engaged to marry, and Karl gave Lempi a nice gold engagement ring—the best he could afford. Their financial circumstances did not permit them to marry immediately, so they agreed it would be best to postpone their marriage while Karl went to America to work, earn a little money and build a little nest for two. As both of them had been on the farm all their lives, it was natural for them to look for open country and for cheap land. After Karl had promised Lempi he would write her and send money for her ticket and other incidental expenses, he went to America. As soon as he had established himself on the land and built a home, Lempi would come over and they would be married.

Karl started for Superior, Wisconsin, as many of his countrymen had done before him. He came to Superior and there he met many of his countrymen—some of them from his own community. There were those who had learned a little English and they wanted to help all they could to make a good American. One of the first things they had to do was to change his name to Charlie. His last name was one of those long Finnish names that no American could pronounce. It was a combination of his great grandfather's name and his grandfather's name and his father's name along with the name of his birthplace. They told him he should cut off the excess—his great grandfather's and his grandfather's first names. Then he should cut off his umbilical, that is, the name of his birthplace, and when he had done that his name would come down to American vocabulary. After his name had been doctored, he made known his desire to locate on some land so he could establish a home. He did not say that he wanted to get married, but that was his privilege.

One of his new-found friends had a friend with a homestead out in Eagle township (as now organized) who could locate Charlie on a homestead for a fce of ten dollars. So he came to Cromwell, Minnesota, with the hopes of becoming a good American citizen. He had already taken the first step to becoming a citizen, in that he had taken out his first papers and had renounced his allegiance to the Czar of the Russian Empire and declared his intention to become a citizen of the United States so that he could file on a homestead. Charlie was located on a good 160 acre homestead covered mostly with hardwood. There was a ready market for all his timber, but at a low price. He was a young man and a hard worker so he not only got his land but also a permanent job cutting timber and clearing land. Here he made good use of his Finnish heritage. First he had to build a house and he built a very artistic log building, as only the Finnish people can do. He made nearly all of his furniture and bought such things as windows, hardware, a cook range or stove, and kitchen utensils. The other things he made on rainy days when he was unable to work outside. Although he was a very busy man, he never forgot his promises to write to his promised wife, whom he had left behind more than three years ago. He remembered her with a letter now and then and at last he sent her money so that she could come over and they could get married. However, he never heard from her.

Now, there was a young lady that came from Sweden some ten or twelve years earlier to Superior, Wisconsin. We will call her Anna. She was born in a little town of Malung in Kopparber, Sweden, and she had learned to speak good English. Of course, she had the Swedish accent and many words where "J" is used (such as job or John) it would be "yob" or "Yon." Nevertheless, she spoke very fluent English. She was a lady of good character, able-bodied, and in good health. She was fair to look at; in fact, she was a woman that would make any man a good companion. So it happened when she was working in Superior that she became acquainted with a Finnish lady and they became good friends. This Finnish lady had some friends or relatives that had settled out in the Finnish colony at Cromwell so she induced her friend, Anna, to come to Cromwell with her and file on a homestead in Eagle township. She became located right next to our hero, Karl.

Anna had worked hard and saved her money, and in the required six months she built herself a cozy little log house. She had to hire most of the work done. Charlie, as he is now called, did most of the work and while he could not speak English and Anna could not speak Finnish, they had to have the interpreter over at times. The interpreter lived more than two miles away and the only mode of transportation was the God-given way of walking (and that is one God-given gift that is not fully appreciated today). It was a little inconvenient, but it worked for Charlie who knew his business as a house builder. So Anna had her house built and established her home there. Well, now, here was a young man and young girl living next door to each other and seeing one another every day. Charlie was very sympathetic and always offered a helping hand whenever he saw that Anna needed some help.

As he could not speak English, he had to use his own judgment as to how Anna wanted the job done, and Anna always offered to pay him whenever he helped her. Charlie always refused to take payment with a smile all over his face. That was one thing Charlie could express in English and now his sympathetic attitude towards Anna (and she realized Charlie's attitude) was becoming more serious. She had noticed his admiration when he watched her swing the axe, chop wood, and use the cross-cut saw cutting cordwood. The only help she needed was to grind her axe and to file her cross-cut saw. As Anna became more and more independent, Charlie's admiration increased to the point where he would have approached Anna with the intention of courtship. We cannot blame him for wanting to live a normal life. When we consider Charlie's disappointment with his sweetheart, Lempi, after having written to her several times and having sent her his hard-earned money—he had not yet so much as received a "thank you" card. Now, he came to the "hour of decision."

Charlie went to his friend, the interpreter, and asked him to come with him to Anna's, and help him pop the vital question. Well, who would refuse a request like that, so they approached Anna, and Charlie asked her the plain question (through his interpreter) if she would become his helper, mate, and wife. That took her by surprise and her answer was a "No" that even Charlie understood. But, Charlie was persistent and did not give up. Anna, on the other hand, admired Charlie's nature and character.

However, Anna had a woman's intuition that told her or made her believe that Charlie had left a girl or maybe a wife back in his native Finland. That was her main reason for refusing Charlie's proposal. After two weeks Charlie returned with his friend and made another try. He would tell her all concerning his past life. When Charlie and the interpreter came, Anna met them with a smile for she was aware of their purpose in coming. Charlie spoke at length with his interpreter, who then spoke with Anna in English. He informed Anna that Charlie had been engaged to marry a girl in Finland and had written to her several times and had sent her money to come over here, but he had never heard from her and by now he had given up all hope of ever hearing from her. He said Charlie had come again to ask her to be his wife. After some consideration, she consented and the date was set for their marriage.

The morning train arrived at Cromwell about 6:45 a.m. They had more than six miles to walk through the woods to the depot, so they went to Cromwell the day before. Anna stayed there overnight in the section house with a Swedish family (the John Lindquist family) and Charlie, with his friend, stayed at the Morse Hotel.

The next morning they went to the depot and bought their tickets to Carlton. The morning train arrived a little ahead of time so they had plenty of time. They were all on the platform waiting for the passengers to get off the train first. Then, who do you suppose should get off the train, but Charlie's sweetheart, Lempi. Lempi recognized Charlie at first sight and embraced him to the embarrassment of Anna and the interpreter. It was Charlie's good fortune that the train was early so it gave him a little more time to talk and he had to speak rapidly, as only a Finlander can speak. Charlie went and bought another ticket to Carlton and Lempi boarded the train for Carlton too.

Now the interpreter had a dual job on his hands. He had to convince Lempi that no crime had been committed. Anna was now convinced that her womanly intuition was right and gladly gave Charlie up when he agreed to buy her claim (homestead). She would move back to Superior.

So the misunderstanding was cleared up. You see, Charlie had not informed Lempi of his new American name, so all of her letters had gone to the dead letter office.

By this time the train had arrived at Carlton and they all went to the hotel where Charlie and Lempi had their first breakfast together. After that Charlie and his friend, the interpreter, had to go to the courthouse and have his marriage license changed to "Charles Somebody and Lempi Mydear."

When this had been straightened out we find that Charles Somebody and Lempi Mydear were united in Holy Matrimony by the Reverend Squire, in the presence of our interpreter, and Anna, victim.

So they lived happily ever after.

CHAPTER TEN

The Second and Third Advent of Finnish People

Now, I will chronologically describe the advent of settlers, many of them second generation of immigrants from Finland who came here in the beginning of the twentieth century. This may be called the beginning of agriculture especially dairy, livestock, and potato farming. There were many carloads of potatoes shipped from here every fall and winter. Cream was shipped to Duluth until the creamery was built. There were roads, schools, churches, and other institutions of public welfare here.

Oat Stacks at the Morse Farm, Cromwell.
"7 Stacks from 25 Acres"

Charles Hill was born in Finland where he married the girl of his choice. He then left her behind and came to this country, landing first in Michigan in 1890 where he worked a short time. He came to Buhl on the Iron Range of Minnesota and worked in the iron mines. In 1895, Mrs. Hill came over to join her husband

and they established their home there. In 1904 he came to Cromwell and bought the S1/2 SE1/4 Sec. 20 from the Winona and St. Peter Land Company. The Hills moved to this land in 1905 and built a good house and barn. He cleared some land, did a little farming, and worked in the woods. In 1913, Mr. Hill built a house on his land for Gust Jussila who was retired and made this their home until they both died. Hill bought a portable sawmill in 1916 and operated that with the help of his sons for a number of years. In 1923 he bought a lot from John Pohl and built a garage. It was a large building and his son, John, an auto mechanic and machinist, was put in charge of the garage. Mr. Hill sold farm machinery. He moved off the farm in 1925 and a year later he sold the garage to Herbert Peterson. Later it was operated by Moline who had worked for Peterson—then Clarence Olson and later by Arnie Karppinen. They did not succeed and it was closed. Mr. Hill moved to the Range again for a while and a few years later returned to Cromwell. He returned to his first love and started a shoe repair shop. Mrs. Hill died, leaving her husband Charles, three sons, and one daughter to mourn her passing.

     Mr. and Mrs. Matt Hendrickson came to Cromwell about 1907 and bought the NW1/4 of the NW1/4 Sec. 21. They came from Finland about 1890 and had lived and worked in Wisconsin until they came to Cromwell to settle on their land. They built a log house and other buildings and cleared some land, but worked mostly in the woods around home. They lived there until about 1914 when they sold their land and went back to Finland. They sold the land to Charles Gulf, a building contractor from Cloquet, who had also come from Finland. He started building a house and other out-buildings and made other improvements. He built a good home and started a dairy with a herd of Guernsey cows, but lived here only a few years. He sold his little farm to the Westerlund brothers and moved to Flint, Michigan. The Westerlund brothers made this their permanent home. Mr. and Mrs. Gulf spoke good English and they were nice people and good neighbors. Mr. and Mrs. Gulf moved to Cromwell and bought a lot from J. H. Wright. They built a building and started a restaurant on the front part and lived in the back. They lived there about five years and then sold to Mr. Grover who converted it into a beer tavern. He later sold it to Nestor Mellin, who continued to sell liquor there until the village started a municipal liquor store and Mr. Mellin leased the building to the village to be used for a liquor store which it is to this day.

Mr. and Mrs. Mike Korpi came here from Sparta, Wisconsin, in 1903 where Mr. Korpi had been on the police force for some years. They bought Lot 2 on Eagle Lake and the NE1/4 of the NE1/4 Sec. 17. They established their home by building a log house and clearing some land. They were busy in the woods most of the time. Mrs. Korpi died in 1913 and Mr. Korpi in 1920, leaving two sons, Jack and John, and two daughters, Mrs. Emil Tuomi and Mrs. Airaksinen, to mourn their passing. Emil Tuomi and his wife are living on the old homestead. The other daughter, Mrs. Airaksinen, and her husband also built a home on the land and made it their home.

E. J. Hephmer, a non-Finnish man and single, had been an agricultural instructor at Floodwood and had also lectured on dairying and animal husbandry. He came to Cromwell and bought forty acres of land, SW1/4 of SW1/4 Sec. 16, that had little improvement on it. He wanted to put into practice what he had been preaching. He bought some cows and started dairying on a small scale. He kept at it for two or three years and then gave it up as a bad job, stating that he preferred to teach others how to do farming rather than practice it himself. So we lost a "book farmer" when he sold his farm to Maunu Jaakola.

Matt Parviainen came to Cromwell in 1917. He was born in Kaavi, Kuopion Laani, Finland, in 1897; his wife was born in the same place about 1882. He came from Finland in 1916 to Northome, Minnesota. The Parviainen's had nine children—four boys and five girls: Johan, Armas, William, Martin, Anna, Hilma, Elina, Tyyne, and Hilja. Mr. Parviainen passed away on October 21, 1944, at the age of sixty-five years.

Alex Wiherela was born in Finland in 1866 and came to this country in 1890, landing in upper Michigan where he made his home for three years. His father was a reindeer ranger (or farmer) so Alex also became a reindeer ranger with his father and later became a ranger himself, as was the custom. He moved from Michigan to Superior, Wisconsin, where he married Miss Cecelia Myllymaki in 1896. She died a year later and in 1899 he married again, this time to Mrs. Maria Sodervick who blessed him with two sons, Sanford and William. In the late 1800s he worked in the Superior shipyards and in the early 1900s he went out for himself, building small homes and working as a house-moving contractor. About 1905 he bought a small tract of land in Red Clover township north of Cromwell, but never did build on it. In 1907 he bought a piece of land in Eagle township south of Cromwell on the shores of Eagle Lake and built himself a home where he moved his family shortly afterward. His youngest son, William, was stricken with the dreaded disease, infantile paralysis or polio, as it is known today. The family moved back to Superior for a year and a half, operating a boarding house and trying to cure the son, William, who became a cripple for life. They moved back to Cromwell where they farmed and purchased cattle for slaughter on the side. In 1918 he purchased a small building in Cromwell from the Dottens and started a small business. In 1921 he sold his farm at Eagle Lake to the Boy Scouts who erected a beautiful camp on the shores. Then he moved to Cromwell where he purchased a home from E. W. Dotten on the main street. He also bought a lot from E. Maattala on which he erected a small place of business. Here, he conducted a grocery and meat market until 1934 when he retired. In February, 1940, Mrs. Wiherela died and was followed in death by Mr. Wiherela six weeks later. William died some years later on December 31, 1943.

  John Tuuri came to Jacksonville, Ohio, about 1900 where he met a young Finnish maid. They were married and he worked there in the coal mines until about 1908 when they moved to Cromwell and bought eighty acres of wild land, the S1/2 SE1/4 Section 20. They built a good log house and other out buildings and cleared forty or more acres of land. They operated a general farm but did mostly livestock farming. In the 1920s Mrs. Turi died. Mr. Tuuri kept up his farming operations with the help of his sons and daughters until he became a victim of cancer and passed away a year later. He left three boys and four girls to mourn his passing. The two older boys were born in Jacksonville, Ohio, while the younger boys and girls were born here on the farm. Two of the girls are married to Edward and Emil Heikkila, sons of Mike Heikkila, and the older son still operates the old home farm.

In 1882 John Stonelake came to Franklin, Minnesota, as a young man and lived and worked there. In 1902 he married a Finnish maiden, Ida Lampi, in Minneapolis. She may have come from Finland to Jacksonville, Ohio, and from there to Minneapolis about 1900. In 1904 Mr. Stonelake took a homestead in Marshall County. When he had proven up on his homestead in 1909, he bought eighty acres of wild land in Eagle township, the N1/2 of NE1/4 Sec. 29. He built a nice home and other buildings and cleared a good farm. The Stonelakes were blessed with twelve children—six boys, and six girls. Two boys and one girl died in youth. Four boys and five girls are living.

Andrew William (Uki) Paananen was born in Finland and came to Sault St. Marie, Michigan, in 1902. He came to Cromwell in 1914 and bought the S1/2NE1/4 Sec. 29 which he improved. H made this his permanent home until he passed away. William died in 1941, leaving two sons, John and Ernest, to mourn his passing. John took over the estate and made it his home. Ernest was a renowned violinist and had traveled all over this country and Europe, playing in orchestras, concerts and musicales. John was also a good musician and raised a family of eight—four boys and three girls, with one girl dying in infancy. Ernest did not maintain a home here.

Matt Paananen, Sr. (not related to William Paananen) came from Finland to Ohio in 1894. He might have settled in Sandusky, Ohio, first as there are many Finnish people there. He later came to Cromwell about 1898 and located on W1/2 SE1/4 and NW1/4 SE1/4 Sec. 29. He later bought the William Saarela homestead, the S1/2 SE1/4 Sec. 28, and was mostly engaged in getting out timber products. He died early in the 1900s. Mr.

Paananen, Sr. had one daughter and one son, Matt. One daughter died. Matt married Elizabeth Oberg and they were blessed with two daughters. Elizabeth died shortly after the youngest child was born but Matt kept his family together. With the help of the Oberg girls, the two children grew up to be highly respected young ladies. Matt, Jr. kept their old home. Jenny married Hannes Laine in 1925 and they made the old William Saarela homestead their home with their father, who died leaving the homestead to Jenny and Mr. Laine. Mr. Laine died in 1935 leaving his wife, two girls, Nina and Nancy, and one son, Norman, to mourn his passing.

Mr. and Mrs. Abraham Lampi, a son, Erick, a daughter, and maybe some other children, and a brother, Alex Lampi, came from Finland to Jacksonville, Ohio, in 1903. They worked in the coal mines there for two years and came to Cromwell in 1905 where he bought the S1/2 SW1/4 Sec. 21. Their son, Erick, helped them build a house. He also worked out to earn money and help his parents financially get established on the farm. In 1915 Erick married Lempi Heikkila and made their home with his mother. Abraham died in 1909 and Mrs. Lampi died in 1938 leaving her son, Erick, and daughter, Mrs. Stonelake, and other relatives to mourn her loss. Mr. and Mrs. Erick Lampi have two sons, Sulo and Deino, and one daughter, Siiri, living. They lost one son, Reino, in World War II in Italy.

Alex Lampi bought forty acres, the NE1/4 NW1/4 Sec. 16, and built some small log buildings but did not live there long. After about four or five years he sold to Victor Rajala, a single man who lived there a few years until his health failed him. He was taken to a hospital and did not return. Mr. and Mrs. Lampi had one son, Eino, who was a barber. He built a house in the village of Cromwell and maintained a barbershop there for a short time. He later sold the house. Edwin Kukkola now owns the house.

John F. Oberg, a nephew of the Rev. John Oberg, came to Cromwell where he married Matilda Klavu. He bought forty acres of cut-over land and built a small house which they made their home for a few years. Then they sold the land to John Heikkila and moved to New York City. They have one son, Sulo.

Jonas Heikkila (the brother of Mike and Emil Heikkila) bought the NW1/4 from John F. Oberg and built a good house and barn. He cleared some land and kept some milk cows. As Jonas was a good blacksmith, he also built a blacksmith shop and did some blacksmithing work. They have one son, John, who is a baker, and a daughter, Sally (Mrs. Donald Smith).

Jack Kauppinen came from Superior in 1908 and bought forty acres of wildland, the SE1/4 SW1/4 Sec. 16. He built some small buildings and lived there for a few years, selling out to Mike Mononen. Mr. Mononen married a daughter of Joseph Larson, the first Finnish settler, about 1916. He was a musician and played in the Cromwell band for some time. He died about 1935, leaving his wife, four daughters, and one son to mourn his passing. Mr. Mononen was a man of a very kind disposition.

John Paananen and his brother, Emil (not related to the other Paananens) were born in Finland about 1881. They first came to Canada, then to the United States and Cromwell in 1900 where they bought forty acres of wild land in Sec. 29, the SW1/4 SE1/4. In about 1927 John married Mrs. Amanda Laino and bought the SW1/4 SE1/4 Sec. 28 where he built a good home. He cleared a good deal of land and did some farming there, but worked mostly in the woods. He had bought this forty from John Maki, a brother of David Maki, in 1908. Mr. and Mrs. Paananen lived there until they retired about 1940 and sold their little farm to a party named Dormanen.

David Maki, brother of John Maki, came from Finland to the Iron Range of Minnesota and worked there a few years. He then came to Cloquet where he worked and met his bride. They were married in Cloquet and came to Cromwell about 1912 and bought the NW1/4 of NE1/4 Sec. 33. They built a good, up-to-date house and other out buildings. They cleared almost the entire forty and made a nice farm of it. This has been their permanent home ever since.

Matt Saarela (brother of William and Charles) was born in Pihtipudas, Vaasan Laani, Finland, and came to Superior, Wisconsin, about 1896. About 1898 he came to Cromwell and bought or homesteaded the NE1/4 of NE1/4 Sec. 32. He was married and was a road contractor and timber operator part of the time. About 1930 Edward Huhta bought the little farm and Mr. Saarala moved to Kettle River to live. They had a large family of seven children. Five boys are living: David in Kalevala, John in Esko, and Sulo, Waino, and Elmer on the Iron Range. One daughter, Lempi, is in Kalevala. One boy and one girl died some years ago of what is believed to be tuberculosis.

Edward Huhta came here about 1920 and married

Uriel Markkula's daughter. They first lived on the SE1/4 of NE1/4 Sec. 21. Then they moved on her father's farm and later bought Matt Saarela's farm and made that their permanent home. They have a large family of children.

Edward (Edvard) Huhta Family—l to r, Tony (Toivo), Kenny, Edward, Wayno, Charlie.

Emil Tauren came to Cromwell about 1930 and bought the William Paananen farm. He operated a dairy farm for some years there and sold the farm (the S1/2 NE1/4 Sec. 29) to Victor Heino in 1939. They bought the little farm of Mrs. Eino Selkomas, the old Angeline farm (the N1/2 NW1/4 of SE1/4 Sec. 30-20 acres) and lived there a short time. Tauren sold this farm to John Holmes and bought a farm in Sec. 27 of Charles Waris's eighty acres.

William Keiski and his wife were born in Finland and came to this country as young people to Cloquet, Minnesota. In 1900 they came to Cromwell and bought forty acres, the N1/4 of SW1/4 Sec. 33. They built a house and made other improvements and made that their home until they sold the land in 1910 to Henry Henrickson. They then bought forty acres, the SW1/4 of S1/4 Sec. 23. There they built a house and other buildings and cleared some land. They lived there a few years and then moved out west. They had three sons and four daughters. Uno Keiski makes it his home now.

Henry Hendrickson came from Duluth and moved on the little farm sometime in 1910 and started a country store that operated for twenty or more years. They had two sons, Henry and Arthur. John Larson (son of Joseph Larson) bought eighty acres, the W1/2 NW1/4 Sec. 25, and built his home there just across the road from his father's homestead.

Mr. and Mrs. Oscar Maki were born in Finland and came to Superior, Wisconsin, shortly after they were married in the 1890s. They worked in Superior and came to Cromwell about 1900 and bought the August Nyquist farm, the SE1/4 SE1/4 Sec. 9. They moved on the farm shortly thereafter and operated a general farm for a few years until Mr. Maki became the victim of tuberculosis. He was sick a long time before his death and so they had to have a hired man to help with the work. This hired man may be a relative of Mr. Maki as his name was Samuel Maki. Sometime after Amanda's husband died, she married Sam Maki.

John Rajala was born in Finland and came to Canada in the late 1890s and married there. They had one daughter, Ida. Rajala came to Cromwell as a widower with his daughter in 1920 or later and bought forty acres of land, the SW1/4 NE1/4 Sec. 21. They established their home there and in about 1930, Ida married Arthur Tammi and they made their home with her father. Mr. Tammi worked on the state highway for some time. They have a son, Roy.

Henry Ahola was born in Finland and came to

Fairport Harbor, Ohio, about 1898 and to Duluth in 1899. He worked there and was married in 1913. They came to Cromwell in 1916 and bought the NW1/4 SW1/4 Sec. 22 from Konstant Westerlund. They established their home there and cleared the forty before starting a dairy farm. Mr. Ahola became a victim of tuberculosis and was sick a long time before he died leaving his wife, one daughter, Rose, and one son to mourn his passing. Mrs. Ahola with the help of her daughter, Rose, and one son kept up the dairy farm for some time, until Rose married Arthur Jarvis and moved to Lawler. The farm has been vacant for some time.

Waino Koskinen bought Elia Laasonen's farm in 1918. He married Miss Emma Klavu and they established their home there. Mr. Koskinen carried on general farm operations but had mostly livestock and dairy. He also was a construction contractor, building roads and doing other jobs. He was considered a successful farmer until his health failed him and he suffered from a heart ailment which required him to have oxygen for a long time. He died in 1949 leaving his wife, Emma, and one son, Dale, to mourn his passing.

Waino Danski was born in Finland and came to South Dakota about 1900 as a young man. He met a Finnish maiden and married her there. They came to Cromwell about 1920 and bought the NE1/4 NW1/4 Sec. 21 from Jack Kaukonen. This was all wild, cut-over land. They built their home and other out buildings, cleared the forty, and made it their home for several years. About 1940 they moved to California to live, but still maintain their home here and may come back to live.

Andrew A. Parviainen came to this country in 1902 from Ishpeming, Michigan. He was born in Kaavi, Kuopion Laani, Finland, in 1877 and went to school in the same place. He came to Cromwell in 1903 and bought the S1/4 NW1/4 of SW1/4 and SW1/4 NW1/4 Sec. 36-160 which was all wild land. He established his home there by building a good house, barn, and other out-buildings. As a good deal of the land was river bottom, he cleared a large farm in a short time and operated a general farm with livestock and dairy farming.

Mr. Parviainen also contracted to build several miles of township road in Eagle township and engaged in lumbering. He operated a large stationery sawmill in Eagle for a number of years and he also operated a large threshing machine driven by a steam engine. We would now call it a large clumsy steam tractor (it had all it could do to pull the separator). For a few years, he went from farm to farm in the fall, threshing for the farmers. It was the first threshing machine in the township of Eagle. Mr. Parviainen was active in civic affairs and was always interested in the welfare of the township. He also spent much time and was a leader in organizing the Carlton County Co-op Telephone Association. He was an active leader in organizing the Farmer's Co-op Store and later was active in organizing the Carlton Power Association (REA) and served on the Board of Directors for a number of years. He at last retired from active labor and turned his farm over to his son-in-law and daughter, Mr. and Mrs. Waino Mikkola. He has one son, Aate, and one daughter, Mrs. Ailie Mikkola.

Nichkoulus Berg was born in Norway and Mrs. Berg was born in Denmark. They came to Chicago in 1895 and then to Minneapolis where they were married.

Mr. Berg was a turner by trade and specialized in making billiard balls. He worked in Minneapolis at his trade and in 1916 came to Cromwell where he bought forty acres, the SE1/4 NE1/4 Sec. 16. He built a house on the land and lived there a short time about a year or a year and a half, and then moved down on Tony Loufire's farm on the east shore of Island Lake in Sec. 3. They lived there four or five years and then bought forty acres from Mrs. Skramstead. The Bergs moved their house onto the Skramstead's forty about 1922 and sold their forty in Sec. 16 to Severt Johnson. Mr. Berg went to Minneapolis and worked at his trade while Mrs. Berg remained here in their new home. Mr. Berg would come home over the weekends. About 1929 he died from an infection (caused by a small pimple on his forehead), leaving his wife, Sophia, to mourn his passing. They had no children. Mrs. Berg remained here and passed away in 1934. Later the land was sold to E. W. Dotten and the house was again moved—this time to a lot in the lakeside addition. It is now the home of Mr. and Mrs. E. W. Dotten.

John H. Wright bought the NE1/4 SE1/4 Sec. 16 from the State of Minnesota. It was state school land and was sold on a long-term contract for deed with terms of 4% annual payments. He sold this forty to Gust Smith by assignment of contract.

Gust Smith came here about 1924 and built himself a small house. He established himself in a new house and then his wife took sick and died, leaving her husband and small children to mourn her passing. A short time later Mr. Smith married a daughter of Herman Carlson. One or two years later he let the land go back to the state and moved up near Grand Rapids.

About 1930 Werner Maki, a painter and paper hanger from Duluth, came out here and bought the Smith forty. There was little improvement on the land when Mr. Maki moved there and his wife remained in Duluth and operated a rooming house. She would come here on weekends to be with her husband. Mr. Maki would take odd jobs of painting and paper hanging. I do not know whether they have children.

E. M. Smitberg was born in Finland, came to Duluth in the 1890s, and married a sister of John Hakamaki about 1900. They filed on a homestead, NE1/4 SW1/4 Sec. 6, and lived there for a few years. Mr. Smitberg's health failed him and he died. I do not know whether they had any children. Mrs. Smitberg moved back to Duluth about 1912.

Nels Kristensen, a photographer from Minneapolis, came here about 1915 and bought the NW1/4 or Lots 3 and 4 in Sec. 18 (155 45/100 acres) on the shores of Eagle Lake (NW corner). Mr. Kristensen built a summer home there and his family would come there and live in the summer. Mr. Kristensen would come up and spend the weekends with his family.

R. E. Ilstrup, a civil engineer in Minneapolis, came here about 1908 and bought the SW1/4 of Lots 6,7,8, and 9 in Sec. 18 on the NE shore of Eagle Lake. He built a summer home on the lakeshore and his family lived there in the summer. Mr. Ilstrup would also spend a good deal of his time here with his family every summer.

S. Olson was born in Norway and came to South Dakota about 1884 or 1885 and filed on a homestead there about 1887. It was in the dry years of the late 1880s and early 1890s and the grasshoppers starved all, or nearly all, of the pioneers out. Many of them were immigrants and Mr. Olson and others came to Superior. It was the boom days of the infant West Superior of 1889 and 1890. Mr. Olson was a large man and entered the police force and became captain of the police. He remained so until he retired. He married in Superior and he bought Lots 1 and 2 in Sec. 9 (53 acres) and built himself a summer home. Mrs. Olson spent every summer here and he also spent his vacations here. The Olsons had no children, but had adopted a boy, William. This land was later bought by Mr. Berry and operated by Orin Kingsley.

Fred Anez came here from Stillwater about 1896 and worked for Sauntry Cain Logging Company as a cookee (second cook) in the logging camp. He bought or squatted on the SE1/4 NE1/4 Sec. 21 and had a small building where he "batched" for a short time. He left here, presumably going back to Stillwater, and in 1905 an elderly man by the name of Green with a little girl of about nine years old came here from Cour' de 'Alene, Idaho. He had received this land, or forty acres in exchange for ten or fifteen acres near the city of Cour' de 'Alene. When he saw this forty, all wild land, he was greatly disappointed. He stayed here eight or ten days and left for somewhere in Wisconsin where he had a son-in-law by the name of Bertly, who may have become the owner of this forty. However, Fred Anez returned some years later around 1903 and got out some cordwood which he sold to Charles Morse.

Severt or Sefrid Johnson came here from East Lake. He was born in this country, married at East Lake, and came to Cromwell where he bought the SE1/4

NE1/4 Sec. 16 from Nick Berg. They established their home there about 1928, built a house and barn and cleared some land. About 1934 Mr. Johnson became mail carrier on Star Route #1 from Cromwell and held that job for twelve years. He later sold his livestock and moved to Cloquet to work but still owned the farm. Mr. and Mrs. Johnson have one son.

John Winter came here in about 1898 and bought the homestead from Bertha Lehto, later Mrs. Mike Mustonen. Mr. and Mrs. Winter established their home there, farmed, and cleared some land, but Mr. Winter worked mostly getting out timber products. About 1915 Mr. Winters sold twenty acres, N1/4 NW1/4 of SE1/4 Sec. 30, to Victor Angeline who had sold his farm, the SE1/4 SE1/4 Sec. 19, in 1915 to Alex Ylinen which is now the Leroy Grogaard farm. In 1916, Mr. Winters sold the balance of his land to Samuel Maki, who had sold his farm to William Maki in 1914.

Sam Maki moved on the farm and made it his home for a number of years. He built a good house and barn and had a good start in making it a modern farm home. He was doing very well in every respect until he lost one of his sons by a tragic death. This unbalanced Mrs. Maki and she became a mental patient. Shortly thereafter Mr. Maki sold all of his stock and furniture and moved to Superior. Later he sold the farm to Ben Sleichter. Mr. and Mrs. Maki had two sons, John and Eino, and one daughter, Mrs. Ero Maki.

William Hill, born in Kalevala township the son of August Hill (a native son), bought the SE1/4 SE1/4 Sec. 16 in 1933, a year or two after he had married Miss Hulda Korpela. They established their home there and built a good house and other out buildings. They are operating a small livestock farm there now. Mr. Hill has worked as a truck driver and at one time he drove a cattle truck, hauling cattle to the stockyards in St. Paul and Duluth. He also worked at other odd jobs. Mr. and Mrs. Hill have one son, Norman, and two daughters, Karen and Lorraine (Mrs. Robert Beck).

A. V. Hoglund, born in Finland, was married there and came to Cloquet about 1900. He worked there and Mrs. Hoglund operated a Finnish bathhouse for a number of years. They came to Cromwell about 1915 and bought the S1/2 of SE1/4 or Lots 10-11 in Sec. 18, about seventy-seven acres on the south shore of Eagle Lake. They started a large chicken farm on this land and had a successful poultry business until Mr. Hoglund's health failed him. He, his son, and his daughter died, leaving Mrs. Hoglund and one son to mourn their passing. Soon thereafter Mrs. Hoglund went out of the chicken business, the son went out to work, and Mrs. Hoglund remained on the farm for the rest of her life, and so ended a happy beginning.

Kenneth McLeod, a woodsman of Canadian Scotch descent, came here when so many Canadians came here in the early days of logging operation—first in Thomson Township and later on the Kettle River. Mr. McLeod came here and worked for Sauntry Cain Logging Co. as a timber cruiser and surveyor, surveying lines and estimating pine timber for the company. He married a Finnish girl from Thomson and lived there for some years. He filed on a homestead in Eagle Township, the SE1/4 NE1/4 Sec. 34 (maybe 160 acres, I am not sure), in 1892 and sold the pine timber to the lumber company. After that McLeod sold and relinquished his homestead right to Arvid Neimi in 1898. McLeod lived in or near Thomson for some time and later he bought the SW1/4 SE1/4 Sec. 22 and built buildings there with the intention of making it his farm home and engaging in farming. But, Mr. McLeod was a woodsman who had spent all of his life in the woods and was accustomed to harvesting a crop upon which he had bestowed no labor, so he sold his prospective farm to Ivar Rajala and returned to his first love—the woods. McLeod went to work for the Boston and Duluth Land Co. estimating timber and locating land buyers.

Ivar Rajala and Mrs. Rajala came here from Michigan and bought the McLeod farm in Sec. 22 in 1920. There were some good buildings there. He made it a real attractive farm home and was a leader in improving Guernsey dairy cattle and had a good herd himself. Mr. and Mrs. Rajala have raised a nice family of children (I do not know how many). The oldest is a practicing medical doctor and surgeon.

A. Paajanen and his wife were born in Finland and came to Brainerd, Minnesota, as young people. They were married about 1900 and came to Cromwell about 1926 where they bought SE1/4 SE1/4 Sec. 26. and started farming there. This land was part of the old homestead of the Albert Johnsons (Greta Peura became Mrs. Johnson) About 1927 Mrs. Paajanen was killed in an auto accident. After that Mr. Paajanen did not farm very much, but he lived on the place. They have one son, Waino, who is a co-operative store manager.

Otto Vilonen was born in Finland and came to Chicago as a young man. He married a Finnish maid and worked there for many years. They came to

Cromwell about 1920 and bought forty acres, NE1/4 SE1/4 Sec. 19. After building a cozy little home, they retired from active labor but kept a cow or two and raised a good garden.

Arthur Klavu, almost a native son, is the son of the late Abraham Klavu. Mr. Klavu tried to be a merchant and a salesman for a little while but then entered the army in World War I and so is a war veteran. He had bought the S1/2 NE1/4 Sec. 20 from Thomas McCausland, but it appears that Mr. Klavu had bought this land before entering the army and had sold or made an assignment to Mr. McCausland on a loan. When he returned from the war, he bought it back. After he married, he established his home on this land and has farmed some and worked in the woods when his health permitted. He is one of many whose health was impaired by shellshock so that he has not prospered as well as could be expected. Mr. and Mrs. Klavu have raised a nice family of children—two sons and two daughters.

Victor Angeline bought the SE1/4 SE1/4 Sec. 19 in 1915. He built a small house on this land, cleared some of the forty, and in 1919 sold the land to Alex Ylinen.

Alex Ylinen and Mrs. Ylinen came from Superior, Wisconsin, and they moved on the land and built a good house and barn. They cleared the forty and operated a dairy farm for some years until Mr. Ylinen's health failed and he died in 1929. Mrs. Ylinen moved off the farm and rented the place to Arvo Maki, son of William Maki. At last the farm was sold to Mr. and Mrs. Leroy Grogaard who are operating a dairy farm there now.

Abel Laine, who was born in Finland, came to this country about 1908 as a young man and came to Cromwell about 1910. He bought the NW1/4 SW1/4 Sec. 16 and built a log house and other small log buildings. He cleared some land and worked in the woods around here. In 1914 he sent to Finland for his sweetheart. They were married in Cromwell and then established their home on this land. Mr. Laine worked in the woods and kept a few cows until his health failed him and he died in 1935 leaving his wife, Ida, three sons, and one daughter.

Jack Hjerppi was born in Finland and came to Superior, Wisconsin, about 1900 where he worked for a few years and married there. They lived in Superior until 1914 when they came to Cromwell and bought the S1/2 SE1/4 Sec. 20, all wild land. There they built a house, other buildings, and cleared some land for dairy farming. In a few years they moved back to Superior to work and their son remained on the farm for some time. In 1932 the farm was sold to Fred Salo, an old friend who came over from Finland with Jack but had gone to Duluth and worked there. In 1918, Mr. Salo was married in Superior to a Finnish girl and about fourteen years later they moved to Cromwell where they bought this farm. Mrs. Salo had poor health and died a few years later leaving her husband and two sons to mourn her passing. Mr. Salo continued to farm with the help of his sons, and made some improvements on the farm.

Frank Niemi was born in Finland and it is believed he came to Superior about 1900 and to Cromwell about 1920 where he bought forty acres from Konstant W. Westerlund, the NW1/4 NW1/4 Sec. 22. Mr. Westerlund had built a good house and cleared some land. Mr. Niemi moved onto the farm and started to operate a small dairy farm. Shortly after he became a victim of tuberculosis and was confined to the TB sanitarium for a long time. He did recover partly and came home, but could not do any hard work. They sold the little farm in 1935 to Toivo Heikkila who lived there a short time and then sold the farm to Sydney Christenson, the present owner. Frank Niemi and his wife moved to his brother Isaac's place across the road from their former house.

Isaac Niemi, a single man, came here with his brother, Frank, and bought the S1/2 SE1/4 of SE1/4 Sec. 21 (twenty acres), but Isaac died while Frank was in the sanitarium.

Santen Rentola was born in Finland and came to Superior as a young man about 1900 where he worked and met the girl he married in 1911. About 1915 they came to Cromwell and bought S1/2 NW1/4 Sec. 20, where they moved, built a good house and barn, and cleared forty or more acres of land. They made it a very attractive dairy farm and as time went on, Mr. and Mrs. Rentola built a little cottage on the NE corner of Eagle Lake. They retired there to live and have turned their farm over to their son. They have two daughters and one son.

Ivar Maki was born in Finland and came to Pine River north of Cloquet about 1908 where he worked and owned some land. Shortly after, he was married in Cloquet and they made their home in Pine River where they lived at the time of the 1918 fire. Mrs. Maki died as a result of that fire and left her son, Ero, and daughter, Ellen, besides her husband. About 1919 Ivar came to

Cromwell where he bought the NW1/4 and the W1/2 NE1/4 Sec. 19 from K. Lindgren. He also acquired the title to or contracted for the W1/2 of the NW1/4 and W1/2 of NW1/4 and SE1/4 NE1/4 Sec. 19 from Olag Raski. Mr. Maki sold the land to Kino Kahara, his son-in-law.

William Maki was born in Finland and came to Cloquet in 1909 where he worked for a few years and married Ida Saukko. In 1914 they came to Cromwell and bought the improved farm from Sam Maki where they moved to make their home. They have greatly improved the farm, and Mr. Maki has been a successful dairy farmer. Mr. and Mrs. Maki have been good and helpful neighbors and had thirteen children—six sons and seven daughters. The boys are Arnold, Arvo, John, Arthur, Waino, and Tauno. The girls are Irene, Lila, Irja, Elma, Sylvia, Hilda, and Ilene. They are all highly respected and the youngest daughter will soon graduate from high school.

Waino Kiiskila was born in Finland and came to Duluth about 1900. It is believed he married in Duluth and worked in and around there until they came to Cromwell about 1920. They bought the NE1/4 NW1/4 Sec. 26, built a good house and barn, and cleared a nice little farm home. They made that their home and operated a small dairy farm. Mrs. Kiiskila was a paralytic for a number of years and was wholly incapacitated. About 1929 Mr. Kiiskila sold his farm to Walter Tamminen and he moved to Duluth and lived there for a short time. He came back and bought forty acres from Charles Sangola. There was a small house on it and some of the land was cleared. Mr. Kiiskila repaired the house and established their home there. Mrs. Kiiskila died a year or two later, leaving her husband and two daughters to mourn her passing. Mr. Kiiskila continues to make it his home.

John Niemi was born in Finland and came to Superior about 1905 and was married to Lizzie Niemi in 1912. They came to Cromwell in 1914 and bought the NW1/4 NW1/4 Sec. 29 and built a house and other buildings and cleared some land. They started a small dairy farm. Mr. Niemi died in 1918 a victim of influenza, leaving his wife and two daughters to mourn his passing. In 1926 Lizzie Niemi sold this land to Thomas Goodnow who moved on the land and established his home there. He lived there about five years or until the house burned down. About 1932 they sold the land to Emil Pehkonen, a barber from Minneapolis. Mr. and Mrs. Pehkonen moved onto the land after having built a new, attractive home. Mrs. Pehkonen had very poor health, which was one reason for them moving here. She died in 1942, leaving her husband Emil. In 1944, Mr. Pehkonen married Selma Jokinen of Minneapolis and they are now operating a small dairy farm.

After John's widow, Mrs. Lizzie Niemi, sold her little farm to Goodnow, she married Joseph Pihjala who had bought the SE1/4 NW1/4 and NE1/4 SW1/4 Sec. 29. They established their home on this land and built some good buildings on it. They lived there a few years and moved to Duluth where they had lived before and started a rooming house in 1940.

Aadi Lahti was born in Finland and came to Superior 1907 with his wife. They came to Cromwell in 1911 and bought the NE1/4 NW Sec. 29 and built a good house and other buildings. They cleared the forty and started a good dairy farm. In 1937 Mr. Lahti died leaving his wife; one son, Dauno; and one daughter, Mayme, surviving. Mrs. Lahti followed him in death in 1939 and the farm has been occupied and operated by Uno Koivisto since 1946 and may be owned by him now.

Alex Koivisto was born and married in Finland and came to Superior with his wife. They left three children behind there. He came to Cromwell in 1910 where he bought the SW1/4 NW1/4 Sec. 29 from Waino Koskinen. Matt Mattson had built the first small house on this land; however, Mr. and Mrs. Koivisto established their home there about 1910, built a good house and some out buildings, and cleared thirty or more acres of land. They had three sons two daughters here. and They were getting a good start on a little dairy farm when Mr. Koivisto was killed by a car on Hwy 210 near Four Corners in 1935, leaving his wife and three sons. The little farm was heavily mortgaged. Sometime later Mrs. Koivisto married John Kummala, a fish peddler from New York Mills or Brainerd. He was a widower and had some children. After they were married they lived on the farm a short time, but Mr. Kummala bought forty acres, the NE1/4 NE1/4 Sec. 28, from F. Ronkainen and built a little home there. Their old farm was sold to Crawford, a blacksmith who came from Wright where he had lived a number of years.

A. Kinnunen was born in Finland and came to Minneapolis as a young man and later to Brainerd and worked there in the NP shops. He came to Cromwell where he bought a little farm from John Tammi who returned to Finland and remained there. It had a little building and some cleared land (E1/2 SE1/4 Sec. 23). In 1923, and Mr. Kinnunen moved on this land with his wife and sons. They built a good house, barn, and other out buildings and cleared a good farm. In 1923 Mrs. Kinnunen moved to Cromwell and rented the little Thomas Chaput store from Bennett Benson where she started a restaurant which she operated for three years. She then rented the Emil Graves' building for one year. This building later became property of Eli Kinnunen and her son. Then Mr. and Mrs. Kinnunen rented the Violett Hotel after Christ Nelson gave up the hotel business and they operated that for three years. Then Mr. Kinnunen moved to Kettle River and later sold the farm to William Hill. The Kinnunen brothers owned a good deal of real estate in the village.

Nickolas Salenuis bought the NE1/4 NE1/4 Sec. 26 from Fred A. Haish in about 1928 and made some improvements on the land. About 1933, he sold the land to Andrew Hill, who came from North Dakota and later married a widow, Mrs. Erickson. They established their home there. Mrs. Hill had some children and one is married and living in this community.

Abraham Saari was born in Finland and came to Superior in 1889 and to Cromwell in 1893. He took a homestead of eighty acres, E1/2 NE1/4 Sec. 30, and married Sophia Maki, daughter of Isaac Maki. He proved up on his homestead in 1900 and maintained their home there and raised a family of one son, Hjalmer, and daughters, Helmi, Mamie, and Sigrid. None of the daughters are living here. But Hjalmer bought the SE1/4 NE1/4 from Ivar Rajala and established his home there. He was married to a daughter of John Kummala in or about 1935 and cleared the land with the intention of starting a dairy farm.

John Salo was born in Finland and came to

Duluth about 1905 and came to Cromwell in 1908 where he bought the NE1/4 NE1/4 Sec. 33 from a brother of Toivo Heikkila. He had married in Duluth and his family was left living here when he died in 1933 leaving his wife and one daughter, Mayme, to mourn his loss. Mrs. Salo married Jacob Maki, the son of Isaac Maki. Salos sold their farm to Kalle and Selma Jarvi in 1933.

  Matt Hiettikko and his wife were born in Finland. They were married there and came to Superior at an early age. Later they came to Cromwell in 1914 and bought land and from August Hill (not Bill Hill's father). They improved the farm and made it a nice home and operated a dairy farm until Mr. Hiettikko died in 1940. Then his wife operated the farm with the help of her son, Leonard, until 1949 when she died. They had two sons, Leonard and George, who later sold the farm to William Nyberg.

  John Johnson was born in Finland and married there before coming to Hurley, Wisconsin, in 1900. He came to Cromwell in 1908 where he bought the S1/2 SE1/4 Sec. 33 and built some good farm buildings. He cleared fifty acres or more and operated a dairy farm there and made it an attractive farm. When his wife became ill, he cut down on his farming, sold his livestock, and retired from active labor. His wife died in 1942 but Mr. Johnson maintained his home on the farm and a few years later married an elderly widow. Mr. Johnson has four boys—Walter, a banker; Edward, an ordained minister and mechanical draftsman; Tauno, and John; and one daughter, Vieno.

  Mr. and Mrs. Rantala were born in Finland and came to this country in 1903 and lived in Wisconsin before coming to Cromwell. They bought the S1/2 SW1/4 Sec. 9 in 1909. Mr. Rantala died a few years later, leaving his wife, Maria, and two sons. A short time later she married Mr. Bertrun Harvala but this marriage did not last for more than five years. Maria Rantala Harvala married Joseph Anderson who came to Cromwell in 1919. Mr. Anderson had a shoe shop and then a restaurant and was financially independent. He died a few years later.

Otto Tossavainen was born in Finland and came over here in 1900 after being married in Finland. He and his wife came directly to Cromwell and lived with Isaac Maki for more than one year. They bought the NW1/4 SE1/4 Sec. 32 from Peter Karkkainen and Mr. Tossavainen built some log buildings. They made this their permanent home and operated a dairy farm.

Mr. and Mrs. John Kahara were born in Finland and came to Duluth about 1900 and came to Cromwell in 1914 and bought the SW1/4 NE1/4 Sec. 32 where they built some log buildings, cleared the land, and started a small dairy farm. Mr. Kahara died in 1930 leaving his wife, Kaino, sons, Elmer and Unto, and one daughter, Irene. The daughter remains at home.

Matt Tianen was born in Finland and he and his wife came to Superior, around 1898. They came to Cromwell in 1904 to Kalevala township. They bought ten acres from Charles Saarala in the NW corner of SW1/4 SW1/4 Sec. 32 in Eagle and established a home there and remained there the rest of their lives. Mr. Tianen died in 1935, leaving his wife and two sons to mourn his passing. Mrs. Maria Tianen died in 1948.

Arthur Lehto was born in Finland and was married in Brainerd where they came in the late 1890s. They came to Cromwell in the late 1920s and bought the N1/2 SW1/4 Sec. 23 from Jack Johnson. They built a good house and other buildings and made an attractive farm home. About 1940 they sold the farm to Eli Lehti, the present owner.

August Lehto (brother of Arthur Lehto) and his wife, Hilda, came from Poplar, Wisconsin, and bought the SE1/4 of NW1/4 Sec. 23 and built a small house and some small out-buildings. Mr. Lehto left his wife here and contracted to work on the lakes. With the help of her two sons, his wife kept eight or ten milk cows for a few years. When Mr. Lehto died, she sold out. Her son Sidney married and bought his own farm and William went to Brainerd to work.

Frank Grandlund, a native son born in Kalavala in 1892, married Anna Saarela about 1912 and lived with his father-in-law, Charles Saarela, for about a year. Then he bought SE1/4 NE1/4 Sec. 33 and built a good house and barn and cleared some land. He made it into a nice farm home. Mr. Grandlund was a good electrician and was kept busy nearly all the time. About 1941 or 1942, he met with a serious accident, suffering a broken back. He was paralyzed for several months before he died, leaving his wife, Anna, five sons—Ernest, Edward, Elmer, Walter, Eugene—and two daughters, Esther and Edith. He was a good neighbor and always ready to help.

Konstan W. Westerlund was born in Laptrask, Finland, and came to Duluth in 1910. Ellen was born in Merikarva, Finland, and came to Jersey City, New Jersey, about 1906 and then to Duluth in 1912. Mr. Westerlund worked in the car shops in Superior for three years and came to Cromwell in 1916 and bought the SW1/4 of SW1/4, Sec. 22—all wild land. He built a good house and other out-buildings and cleared some land. In 1920 he sold this little farm home to Frank Niemi and moved to Superior. He worked eight months in the car shops there and then moved to Cleveland, Ohio, and worked at construction work until 1923. He then came back to Cromwell and bought the NW1/4 of NW1/4 Sec. 21 from Charles Gulf (the old Matt Hendrickson farm) and built a very attractive farm home and operated a small dairy farm. Then after selling the north half of this forty to his brother, he bought additional land nearby. Mr. and Mrs. Westerlund have two sons, Leo and George, and one daughter, Margaret. They are good neighbors and highly respected citizens.

Charles Theo. Westola, a brother of Konstan Westerlund, was born in Laptrask, Finland, and came to Duluth, Minnesota, in 1913 and worked there for about three years. In 1916 he moved to Cleveland, Ohio, where he worked at building construction. There he met the magic maiden whose attraction had brought him to Cleveland and they were married in 1917. She was born in Laptrask and came to America in 1913. About 1919 they came to Cromwell and bought the SE1/4 of NE1/4 Sec. 21 and built a house and made other improvements with the intention of establishing their permanent home. But in 1920 they sold this land to one Koski, who later sold the land to Andrew Beck, the present owner. They returned to Cleveland and worked there until 1923 when they moved back to Cromwell and bought twenty acres, the N1/2 of NE1/4, Sec. 21. They built a very attractive farm home, cleared all the land, and now operate a small dairy farm. Mr. and Mrs. Westola have no children; they are good neighbors and Mr. Westola is of a very conservative disposition.

Ony Nyberg was born in Saarijarvi, Vaasan Laani, Finland, in 1882. He came to America in 1902 to Ironwood, Michigan, and worked there and around Superior and Maple, Wisconsin, where he met and married Hilma Peura in 1911. She was born in Ylitornio, Oulun Laani, Finland, in 1892 and came to America as an infant with her parents to Superior. They moved to Maple, Wisconsin, and she went to public school there. They came to Cromwell shortly after they were married and bought forty acres of wild land, the NE1/4 of NW1/4 Sec. 27, and established an attractive farm home and operated a small dairy farm. Mr. and Mrs. Nyberg are good neighbors and they have two sons, William, who is married and has bought the Kinnunen farm in Sec. 23, and Charles, who is single and has worked in the Co-op store for many years. Their daughter, Edna (Mrs. Engen Stick), lives in Duluth, and Ellen (Mrs. Walter Muttonen), lives on a farm at Brule, Wisconsin.

S. Jarvinen was born in Finland and came to America in about 1895 and landed at the head of the lakes and worked around Duluth and Superior and Cloquet. He came to Cromwell about 1912 and bought the old Frank Nord farm from Frank Nord and lived there a number of years. About 1930 they sold the farm to Konstan Nyman, who lived there for some years, and then sold the farm to Fred O. Alberg. S. Jarvinen moved to Cloquet and later to Michigan. They had two sons. Mr. Jarvinen and his sons were not satisfied with the economic conditions here in the land of the free and they were looking for greener pastures in the realm of a new political philosophy, so they emigrated to Russia where they were promised equality and freedom from want and internal fear. But, they were not there very long before they wanted to return home and after much strife and effort did return home as the Prodigal Son of Old.

An early Finnish family near Cromwell in front of a typical Finnish farmhouse.

CHAPTER ELEVEN

Origin and History of the Christian Church in Eagle

I will quote from the church history concerning the advent of the introduction of the Christian Church in the North Country. The background of the Church and the Christian civilization in Finland is, in part, identical with that of Denmark, Sweden, and Norway.

The first missionary was a monk of Corpie, named Anscair or Ansgius, a young fearless enthusiast, ardent for the toils of a missionary and the glory of a martyr. His first exertion was made in Denmark about 820. Later, in 830, he advanced into Sweden (Finland at this time was a part of Sweden until the year 1710 when Russia took the Baltic States from Sweden and the rest of Finland in 1809) where such promises of success attended him that Louis, the Meek, determined to establish an Archepiscopal See in Hamburg. The account of Anscair's successful expedition into Sweden in the year 854 and his arrival in the capital, he communicated to King Olef, the object of his mission. The King replied, "I would willingly consent to your desire, but I can accord nothing until I have our god by the lot, and 'til I know the will of the people who have more influence in public than I have." Olef first consulted his nobles and after the customary probation by lot, the gods were ascertained to be favorable to the proposal. The general assembly of the people was then invoked and the King caused a herald to proclaim the object of the Imperial Embassy. The people murmured loudly, and while they were yet divided in their opinions with regard to the reception of the religion of Christ, an old man rose up among them and said, "King and people, listen to me. We are already acquainted with the service of that God and He has been found of great assistance to those who invoke

Him. There are many among us who have experienced it in perils by sea and on other occasions. Why then should we reject Him now? Formerly, there were some who traveled to Dorstad for the sake of embracing the religion of which they well knew the utility. Why then should we now refuse that blessing when it is here proposed and presented to us?" The people were convinced by this discourse and unanimously consented to the Christian religion and the residence of its ministers among them. Anscair died ten years afterwards and it is claimed that he was buried at Ribe, so tradition has it (and this old man might have been a Finn). Ribe is located on the west coast of Jutland.

The first Christian King of Denmark was Hareld Klak, who was converted to the Christian faith when he sailed up the Rhine River to Ingelheim and received baptism in 826. It was he who gave Anscair a letter of introduction to King Olef or Olova, King of Sweden. Now it is well to remember that the Christian faith was not forced upon the people by this decree of the kings of Denmark and Sweden, that all of their people *had* to accept the Christian faith, but the Christian missionaries or evangelists, as we call them today, had the legal right to proclaim the gospel of the Christian faith and to convert the people to the Christian way of life. So in the time the Christian Church was firmly established there and was a part of the Catholic Church of Rome.

Now I will quote church history about the early "reformers." The first was John Wycliff. He was born in Yorkshire, England, in 1324 and educated at Oxford and was known as the Evangelic or the Gospel Doctor. He died in 1415. He was a forerunner of John Huss or Hoisenezt, the Bohemian Reformer and Instructor in theology in the University of Prague. Huss was executed in July, 1415, for his testimony of the "truth." His disciple was Jerome of Prague, a young Master in theology at the University of Prague. It is said that he was a very eloquent speaker and a lay preacher of the Gospel. For his testimony, he was also convicted and executed three or four years later They were burnt alive at the stake (at this time Church members were under the influence of the Hapsburg rulers of Austria).

Then we come to the history of one Weisselucs of Gronengen. He was a very eminent, ingenious man of learning. He died in peace in his native city in 1489 and has been designated The Light of the World and the forerunner of Martin Luther. We read of one named Erasmus, a great writer, who published the first translation of the New Testament. It is thus recorded that "he laid the egg which Martin Luther hatched."

The reformation was begun. Martin Luther (1483-1546), the son of a Thurengian peasant miner, became the leader. He was not opposed to Catholicity of Catholicism (the Universal Body of the Church) but wanted to correct their "errors" and apply the "truth" of the New Testament, salvation by faith.

About the same time, a Swiss reformer, Hubreick Zuigly (1484-1531), who was killed in battle early in life, was the forerunner of John Calvin, a French reformer. They were all highly learned men in theology and since they had their instruction in different schools, they were not in agreement on many interpretations of the Bible. So we find that Luther accepted all the teachings of the Church of Rome that was not forbidden in the Bible, whereas John Calvin rejected all the teachings of the Church of Rome that was not commanded in the Bible. So we have two dissenting forces in the Protestant Church today, but they were temporarily united during the Thirty Years' War, starting in 1618 and continuing to 1648, one century after Martin Luther posted his thesis at Wittenberg.

The signal for the struggle was an attempt of Protestant Bohemia to make itself independent of the Catholic Hapsburg Empire. Her independence lasted only a few weeks, but this was long enough to place all of Germany into two armed camps. The Protestant German princes had never shown themselves disunited, timid, and incapable, and had the war been left to Germany, an Austrian victory would soon have been assured. All over Europe, earnest Protestants felt the chance must not be lost to break, what seemed to them, the dangerous power of the Hapsburg rulers. First Denmark and then Sweden, with a well trained army (45,000 men of which there were about 25,000 Finnish soldiers), entered the field in behalf of the Protestant cause and in 1635 for more selfish reasons. Catholic France, under Richelieu also threw its weight also against the Hapsburgs who had long surrounded France with hostile arms.

The war was marked by the careers of four great generals: Tille and Wallenstein on the Catholic side, Gustavus Adolphus of Sweden (The Lion of the North) and Mansfeld on the side of the Protestants. Gustavus was immediately great and admirable, but he fell at the Battle of Lutzen (1632) in the moment of victory for his mighty army of the North. It is written they were giants and they did not live by plunder or by robbing the people of the land. His army was supported by a regular Commissariat, but after Gustavus was killed, his Christian discipline was discarded. His successors, Mansfeld and Wallenstein, from the first deliberately adopted the policy of making war pay by supporting their armies upon the country. The armies became ruthless free booters until 1648 when peace was made at Westphalia (then they robbed Germany of all her substance). They left the Romans and the south of Europe Catholic, and the Teutonic North, that is northwest Germany, Denmark, Sweden, and Finland became Protestant.

Their enemies called them Lutherans and they were established as state churches, (The Evangelical Church) meaning the Gospel Church and the followers of John Calvin were in the west and Scotland. Several denominations sprang from them. And so we find the Imperial Army was defeated and the integrity of the Protestant states had been preserved in Northern Europe. Germany was divided into many states and each state had its own prince or king to rule over it and who became the Spiritual Head of the Church in their domain. In time they became national groups and their animosity was so great that they even made war on one another. All the evidence of Christian brotherhood was lost. We find in the 17th century there was a beginning of a spiritual awakening among the Christians in the state churches. They called themselves "Converted" or "Born-Again Christians," and "Haugennets" in Norway. In Denmark and Sweden they were called "Free Mission," but in history, however, it is called the "Spontaneous Piety" or "Evangelical Holiness." In Norway they were influenced by some of John Wycliff's writings. They were not all in agreement but in Denmark, Sweden, and Finland, they were strictly influenced by Luther's writings. There were also some influences from the Church of England.

As time went on the state church became static and more concerned about nationalism and commercialism, for the church affects the present day economy and our standard of living and we are all prone to forget the spiritual value of the church in our moral life and its influence on our governments and our courts of justice. The Evangelical Church continued to be supported by the state, but in Finland it was influenced some by the Orthodox Church of Russia since it came under the Russian rule. The church was free to exercise her independence of Russia but three or four groups grew—the state church, independent groups, the Evangelists, and maybe two or three groups of the Apostolic congregations.

I have quoted this from various sources to show that the Finnish people have done their share in establishing the church and Christian civilization in Northwestern Europe. So when they migrated to this country and this community they brought their church with them, along with their know-how, industry, and a reputation for honesty.

I will now record the spiritual activity in the Town of Eagle, but first a little poem.

Beautiful Words of Truth

Keep a watch on your words, my darling,
For words are wonderful things.
They are sweet like bees' fresh honey,
Like the bees, they have terrible stings.
They can bless like warm glad sunshine
And brighten a lonely life,
They can cut in the strife of anger
Like an open two-edged knife.

Let them pass through your lips unchallenged
If their errand is true and kind,
If they come to support the weary,
To comfort and help the blind.
If a bitter, revengeful spirit

Prompt the words-let them be unsaid
They may flash through a brain like lightning
Or fall on a heart like lead.

Keep them back, if cold and cruel
Under bar, lock, and seal.
The wounds they make, my darling,
Are always hard to heal.
May peace guard your life and ever
From the time of your early youth,
May the words that you daily utter
Be the words of Beautiful Truth.

    Now that I have laid the background of the Christian faith and Christian civilization in Finland, I will record their activities in the town of Eagle. I find that the first Lutheran denomination to be incorporated was the Apostolic Lutheran Church on the 15th day of January, 1905, at the residence of Abram Klavu in said town and said place being a usual place of worship. Daniel Sangola was elected the President; C. A. Sangola and Matt Ranuva as Secretaries; Erik Jokimaki, Treasurer; and John Oberg, Sr., Vice-president and Pastor (priest).
Abram Klavu and John Heikkila   three-year term.
Lars Johnson and John Renko   two-year term.
Gust Jussila and Mikko Neimala   one year term.
There were twenty men present and the number of ladies present was not reported or recorded. The incorporation was notarized by John E. Green in the presence of August R. Norman on the 17th day of January, 1905.

    Then we have the Incorporation of the Finnish Evangelist Lutheran Church of the Town of Eagle at a meeting held in the school house in School District 21 in the said Town of Eagle on 20th day of February, 1905 and the following officers were elected:

Matt Hendrickson	Chairman of the meeting
Jack Karpi	Secretary of the meeting
Matt Hendrickson	elected as President
Erick Keskitalo	elected as Vice-president
Jack Karppi	elected Secretary
Peter Karkainen	elected Treasurer
John Koski, trustee	three years
Otto Tossava, trustee	two years
Henry Grekula, trustee	one year

Their first pastor was Rev. L. V. Niemi and incorporation was notarized by John E. Green in the presence of Peter Erk and John E. Green on the 3rd day of March, 1905.

Then we have some settlers that came later and brought the Evangelical Lutheran Church with them and were organized August 31, 1912, and are members of the (Suomi) Synod of the United States with headquarters at Hancock, Michigan.
First officers werc:
John Johnson, President
Jacob Pohoto, Secretary (they were old friends)
Trustees   Joseph Larson, Sr.
             Alex Weherila
             Matt Tianen
The Articles of Incorporation were notarized in September, 1912, by I. E. Morse.

I wonder if this division in the Christian church among the Finnish people is not the cause for so many of the third and fourth generations of the Finnish people looking for succor and salvation in our modern political philosophy. It is self-evident that there is a lack of Christian brotherly love.

CHAPTER TWELVE

Introduction to the Commercial Life of Cromwell

    In the beginning (in the 1880s) there were only logging operations here but tradition has it that there was a headquarter lumber camp about where the Morse house now stands and that one Peter Grapau kept a wanagan or store house where the camp supplies and provisions, such as men's clothing, tobacco, matches, sugar, and flour were stored. There were also sleeping bunks for anyone stranded here for the night, such as timber cruisers and surveyors. There was also a log barn (hovel) where horse or ox teams could be put up, but it burned down before 1892, as it was not here when I came in that year. There was a rough board building here when I came that was occupied by the Morse family. They were living in it at the time of the Hinckley Fire. Other than that, there was the section house which served as the only hotel here. It was a large, two-family house and was built to provide for railroad men principally, but would accommodate strangers when there was a room to spare. There were no provisions, except cigars and tobacco to be had, so anyone needing provisions had to go to N. P. Junction (Carlton) or Aitkin or send an order and have things sent by freight.

    Most of the early settlers went to Aitkin and did business with D. L. Young. In 1894, Mr. Young had a contract with a firm in Detroit (now Detroit Lakes) to furnish railroad ties. He bought ties from anyone who could get them out. He had an open and loose contract that would allow the ties to be landed anywhere along the railway track. The railway company would send an inspector once a month to accept the ties. Mr. Young would advance supplies to anyone who would get ties, but in February, 1894, the railway canceled their contract and would not take any more ties. This left Mr. Young with ties on the tracks and in the woods for which he could find no market. He offered to take all the ties providing we would take his promissory note for one year, which we did.

Mr. Morse, who had a contract with the firm Brown and Wood at Detroit, was not affected by the cancellation of the Young contract. So he and Edward P. Duffy, who was the depot agent, took up many of the notes with the understanding that we would take them out in trade. They in turn sold the notes at par to the Stone Ordean Wells Co. in Duluth for merchandise. They built a building about ten by twelve and stocked it with merchandise. This was the first store in Cromwell. It had a paid capital of $100 and was located just north of the railway depot on land owned by Morse (it was called Morse and Duffy Mercantile Co.). When the Hinckley fire swept through here on the first day of September, 1894, it burned everything except the little green schoolhouse. Morse and Duffy lost the store in addition to their homes and all their belongings.

Four months later Mr. Duffy leased a lot south of the railway from George Wright, Sr. and built a small building and started a general store which was operated under the name of his brother Andrew. It was known as Andrew Duffy and Co. This store was operated for a little more than two years with John Pohl doing the clerking. This was where John Pohl got his start. When Mr. Duffy was transferred to Aitkin on January 1, 1897, where he remained as depot agent for many years, he closed out the store and sold the building to Frank Lemire, who moved it west of town onto some land which he had bought from Ole Benson. This property is now owned by Joseph Holecek.

Early view of Cromwell Main Street with the Co-op Store, Chaput Store, John Hill Store, and Morse Store

About this time Mr. Morse built a fairly large building north of the railway on the lakeshore, stocked it with merchandise, and opened a general store. There was now a market demand for timber products and this gave the merchants an opportunity to expand and increase their business by extending credit to the settlers. There was no cash money in circulation in those days. The pioneers could get no cash unless they could get a job on the railway. Most of the men needed were shipped in by the road master from Brainerd or some other place; a local man could get work only when they were short of help.

At this time the railway men were paid twice a month. The section men received $6.60 a week for sixty hours. The telegraph operator earned $40 per month, the pump man about $40, and the depot agent about $60. These people had cash and also passes on the railroad so they could go to Carlton or Aitkin or even as far as

Superior or Duluth to buy provisions or visit friends. These people knew the value of a dollar and were looking for bargains and as they had cash, they could buy to better advantage.

As for the settlers, many were homesteaders who had only a crop of forest products to sell once a year. Later on when they had a cow or a few chickens, they would sell a few eggs and a few pounds of butter to the merchant and get merchandise in return. Eggs at this time were five to ten cents a dozen and butter sold about the same price per pound. The butter was usually dumped into a barrel and sold to Bridgeman Russell Creamery Co. as grease. They worked it over and sold it in the winter time as renovated butter at forty cents a pound or even more at times. There were a few wives who made good butter and who could sell all their butter at a better price. As the settlers got more land cleared, there were also some potatoes to sell for which there was no market, but the merchant would do his best to take these products and credit the settlers' account with them. This was a very general practice. The accounts were usually about twelve months short on the credit side, but if a family was in need and had no cash, the merchants would advance some, just so they got by.

When a customer established his credit with a merchant, generally by agreeing to cut and get out railway ties, fenceposts, cedar posts, cordwood, or other products, the customer would get a little book, very similar to a bank book. All goods bought or cash advanced would be on the left side and all credits would be on the right side. The books would be balanced once in a while and if the debit side was greater or more than twelve months behind, there would be a reminder to try to get more on the credit side. It was the duty of the salesman to watch out for the merchants' accounts and the merchants' credit depended on his accounts receivable. This applied quite generally to all the merchants of these days, so much so that nearly all of their liquid assets were tied up in their accounts receivable.

Mr. Morse operated his first store for about ten years, a few years of which it was the only store. In the meantime, a few roads had been built, one of which was the main street of Cromwell.

Up to this time the depot had served as the community center of Cromwell where even the local elections had to be held. Mr. Morse, seeing the need for a community center, built a two-story brick building with a full basement south of the depot on the main street. The first floor was used as his general store and the second story was used as a hall or community center. Here, during his lifetime, Mr. Morse conducted a prosperous

Morse Mercantile Co. opened with a dance on March 17, 1909. Later, movies were also shown on the second floor.

Interior view of the Morse Mercantile Co.

business known as The Morse Mercantile Co. which Mrs. Morse continued as long as she lived.

I will record a little story of what happened in the old credit days:

There was a man who had enjoyed the credit given him at the store and on this day he had enjoyed too many drinks and was in good spirits and enjoyed living, or so he wanted to make you believe—but not with the Morse's approval as Mr. Morse was a teetotaler. (Mr. Morse being a teetotaler is a story in itself. Mr. Morse was just married and on a warm September day he had been out in the woods about five miles looking over some timber with the intention of buying it. When he came back to Frazee he was very thirsty so he entered a saloon and ordered a beer. The bartender knowing he was buying some timber thought he had the money in his pocket. Mr. Morse drank his beer and that was the last he remembered until he awoke the next morning in the back room. That was the last drink Mr. Morse drank of any strong liquors and it made him a teetotaler for the rest of his life). The man came to the store to tell Mr. and Mrs. Morse how much he appreciated, and how thankful he was, for the credit he and his family had had at the store and that every cent would be paid in full. And so he held out his hand to Mr. and Mrs. Morse and tearfully said, "If it were not for you, my family and I would have gone hungry many times." "Well," said Mr. Morse, putting his hand on Mrs. Morse's midriff with Mr. and Mrs. Morse both laughing, "It does not look as if we have been starved."

Louis Larson was born in Finland and came to this country as a young man and worked in Michigan as a molder in the foundries and also in the copper mine. He later worked in the car shops at Brainerd until his health failed him so he could not endure working in the dust as a molder. He first engaged in a little business at Brainerd and came to Cromwell in 1897 or about that time, and started a little store on the east shore of Eagle Lake on his brother's land. He operated the store at that location for two or three years and then he leased a house from A. Dotton and put in a stock of merchandise in the front part of the house and "batched" there, making that his living quarters. He did fairly well and he operated the store there for four years when he bought eight acres of land from J. M. Paine Lumber Company at Carlton (the N1/2 of NW1/4 Sec. 3-48-20). He platted the lake addition to Cromwell and built a two-story frame and brick siding store building. Now he had ample store space and stocked it with merchandise. He finished the upstairs for living quarters and he employed a housekeeper.

Having moved away from the center of town, it

was hard for Mr. Larson to hold his trade, and so he kept only those that he had to carry on his books. As the timber supply diminished, his trade also fell off and it also meant that many of his accounts receivable became worthless and had to be charged off his books and this made it hard for him to survive. A few years later he married a young girl and she presented him with one son and five daughters and it was a very nice family of which any father could be proud. That did not make it easier for Mr. Larson, but added to his responsibility. He had not received much schooling and he was a man with strong likes and dislikes. If any customer could captivate his fancy, it would not be necessary for him or her to be very scrupulous about their accounts. If he disliked a customer, he would sometimes refuse credit when it would have been to his interest to have given it. He had one customer whom he liked above all others and the customer approached him on a business proposition—Mr. Customer wanted to buy a sawmill. (That was one of the first portable sawmills out). He also wanted a threshing machine and an old-time gasoline tractor. He could buy it on time payment, but he had to have someone like Mr. Larson to go surety for him, and he asked Mr. Larson to do so. Mr. Larson knew that Mr. Customer had plenty of support in his own family to finance the sawmill, and also knew that none of his sons had any experience in operating a sawmill or threshing machine, but Mr. Larson signed on the dotted line with the understanding that Mr. Customer would saw logs or lumber for him—that was the bargain. In due time, the mill, threshing machine, and tractor came, shipped in on a flat car, and were moved out in the woods where the logs were. They worked there all summer and sawed very little lumber as they had one breakdown after another and had nothing but trouble as the result of inexperience. When autumn came and the first payment was due, they said to Mr. Larson, "The outfit is yours." What could Mr. Larson do about it? He had no written contract. It was an oral agreement, so Mr. Larson was stuck with this outfit and with a plaster on it upwards of $3,000. For good measure they brought a lawsuit against Mr. Larson for wages and they demanded that he pay the three or four of them wages for all summer and got a judgment against him. Mr. Larson had to mortgage all his property. He hung on for a few years by the grace of his creditors and at last they had to foreclose to protect their interests. Mr. Larson was an old man now and partially lost his memory. Mr. Larson was a good citizen and a good neighbor and after many years of hard struggle, he passed away leaving his wife and children to mourn his passing. None of them remained in this community.

James Violett

James Violett was born in the state of Maine and was of French descent. He came to Wright Station as it was then called and married a young girl there. He filed on a homestead about one mile north of Wright and they established their home there about 1895. They cleared a small farm, proved up on their claim, and lived there about ten years in all. They were blessed with a large family but several of them died in an epidemic of diphtheria about 1897. A year later Mr. Violett sold his farm to the Dotten family and moved to Cromwell to build the Violett hotel. It was a two-story frame building with the upstairs as a hotel and the downstairs for a general store. By this time Mr. and Mrs. Morse had retired from the hotel business which gave Mr. Violett a monopoly on the transient trade.

Mr. Violett was aggressive and conservative which were common characteristics and a heritage forced on them by the meager economy of their colonial forefathers. They were the second and third generation and they knew they had to depend on their own initiative for their daily bread. Mr. Violett was very active in drumming up business and seemed to prosper for about six years when he met with a misfortune as he was helping to unload timber in the railroad yard to be shipped. A horse kicked him in the head. He was taken to the hospital and never regained consciousness. He died two or three weeks later. That was a death blow to the mercantile establishment. Mrs. Violett closed the store and remodeled the store space into a reception room in the front part and in the center a dining room with a good-sized kitchen in the back part. All the upstairs became sleeping quarters. She operated the hotel herself for some years until she was taken ill and was hospitalized a long time before she died. The hotel was leased to various parties for some years until U. S. 210 was completed in 1932 which made it unnecessary for many traveling people to stop overnight here and so the hotel was closed. Mrs. Violett left three sons and four daughters to mourn her loss and none of them remained in the community.

Now we come to the fourth venture in the field of merchandising. Matt Heikkila had formerly lived in the town of Eagle on a homestead and had made a nice farm there but had not farmed it much. He had made his living and supported his large family on the income from the sale of forest products. He had cut most of his timber and was looking for other means to support his wife and eight children.

Now many of the pioneer farmers were starting dairying with a few cows and most of the Finnish people were good livestock farmers. The Bridgeman Russell Creamery of Duluth wanted to buy cream, shipped by express to them in Duluth. They shipped back the empty cans deadhead (that is free of charge) and sent the check for payment for the cream in the next mail. This gave a little cash income, but the farmer had to buy hard separators in order to sell cream. The merchant soon realized that their customers became more independent and they led many adventurers to believe anyone could start a store and make it a successful business. Mr. Heikkila was one of them. He moved his family to town and built a good-sized, two-story frame building with living quarters upstairs and used the downstairs for a general store. He did not attract the amount of trade needed to make it a success, but he hung on for about two years and then had to quit. He was poorer but he was also wiser.

Oscar Isaacson also had the idea that all you had to do to prosper was to start a general store so he put up a building the same as Mr. Heikkila. He had enough trade to keep on for three years and then he sold out to a Mr. Korhonen, a sick man, who kept the business for two years, then sold his merchandise and did not live long after that. He left his wife and one son to mourn his passing. Mrs. Korhonen served as the first telephone operator and then moved to Kettle River. Mr. Isaacson moved to Sawyer and became a successful merchant there.

Soon after two young men, John Knuutila and Arthur Klavu, bought the building and started a general store and they also failed. They operated the store for about two years and had to close. This ended their glorious expectations.

I will now record the history of those who also believed in the infallibility of a tradesman and the mystic pot of gold at the end of the rainbow. That end was in a small store.

Jack Mace
Jack Mace built a little store which was also his home on the north side of the street. He put in a stock of merchandise and sold a little of this, a little of that. He and his wife lived there a number of years. Mr. Mace worked some in the woods, but they finally sold out and moved away. Mr. Mace came back to his first love every fall in the hunting season. Mr. and Mrs. Mace had two children—a boy and a girl.

We will now return to the south side of the street. There is something peculiar about the south side (jinx). Everyone who has attempted a merchandising business has failed not because they lacked the know-how, as some of them were trained and well educated. So there must be a jinx involved. On the other hand, strong liquor dispensary seemed to prosper on the south side.

Axel Wherela (Weherela or Wheeler)
Yet one more tried his luck. Mr. and Mrs. Axel Wherela sold their home on Eagle Lake and moved to town and operated a meat market and light grocery store. They operated it until his health failed him in 1940 and then his two sons took over. William and Sanford

did not operate it as a meat and grocery store very long, but converted it into a beer tavern, a pool hall, and a bowling alley. William was a cripple and died in 1943 while still young. Sanford has continued the business and has added a good supply of magazines and newspapers.

John Oberg

In about 1906, a young man by the name of John Oberg formed a partnership with Markkanen of Duluth (I believe). They built a fairly large store building now occupied by Bushey Bros. Department Store. They started a general store and were successful for a few years. Then Mr. Oberg became a victim of tuberculosis and had to retire. He sold out the stock of merchandise about 1912. He hoped to regain his health and made some improvements and started to work a little as bookkeeper in the bank. He then suffered a set-back and did not survive. He left his father and several sisters to mourn him. Mr. Oberg was a man that everybody liked.

John Hill and Victor Ylen

The next enterprise in merchandising was with two brothers, Victor Ylen and John Hill. They came to Cromwell about 1910 or so. They built where the Farmers Co-operative building is now located and operated a general store there a few years and built up a good trade. (You will note this is on the north side of the main street). In 1914 they sold out to the Farmers Co-op Co. John Hill left this community and Victor retired for a year or so and then came back in partnership with his brother, Hjalmar Ylen, and opened a small store just east of the Co-op store. Victor was a single man, but Hjalmar was married and had one son and one sickly daughter. Hjalmar built himself a home across the street from the store. Now the business was good, but they were unfortunate. Hjalmar's wife and daughter died. His brother Victor contracted tuberculosis and died shortly afterwards.

Thomas Chaput

About 1919 when Victor Ylen took sick, they sold the little store to Raymond Cook who had just returned from the army and he operated the store two years when he sold the store to Thomas Chaput. Mr. and Mrs. Chaput operated the store in that location for a few years and then bought a lot east of their present store near the back. They built a large brick building (now occupied by the Gamble store) and stocked it with up-to-date merchandise. Later Mr. Chaput also engaged in the sale of farm machinery and continued the business as long as he lived. Mr. Chaput was stricken with a stomach ailment and was rushed to the hospital but did not survive and died a day or two later leaving his wife and foster daughter to mourn his loss. Mrs. Chaput continued the business as a general store until sometime around 1945 when she sold the store to be operated as a Gamble store.

John Hill

Sometime in the early 1920s Mr. and Mrs. John Hill and his big family of one son and three daughters returned to Cromwell and bought the store building from the John Oberg estate. They started a general store and conducted that business for a number of years and he was considered a successful business man. Mr. Hill was also active in public affairs but his health failed him. He was suffering from a heart ailment so he closed out his stock of merchandise. He had the intention of starting a strictly flour and feed store as there was a big demand now for dairy and poultry feed. One morning he died suddenly as he went across the street to the store to work. He left his wife, one son, and three daughters to mourn his loss. Mrs. Hill opened the store again with a stock of light groceries for a short time but sold out to Bushey Bros. of Wright who made a Fairway store (called a semi-chain department store) and they are doing a large business.

John Hill Family: Lillian, John, Kenneth, Marie, and Marcella. Photo from their store calendar, ca. 1920s.

Chronology of the Liquor Dispensary

There was a Williams, who in partnership with John H. Wright, had a saloon south of the section and the side track. It was started in the early 1880s or maybe in the 1870s and remained in business. They may have done some gambling also, such as poker games and other gambling devices for money, until about 1891 when, by an act of legislation, a law was passed requiring all liquor dispensers to pay a minimum license fee of $500 dollars. Only an incorporated village could grant such a license. So the saloon was closed in the year of 1891 and the building was sold to Jerry Royer. He tore the building down and moved it over on his homestead about one half mile east of Cromwell.

So now we have a period of about sixteen years

when there was no legal liquor to be bought at any price. When people went to town to buy provisions they would bring their one-gallon jug with them and have it filled with whiskey or brandy. Some Swedish, Irish, and German people would buy alcohol and bring it home with them in the little brown jug. We have a communities with alcohol roads and alleys but not so in Cromwell, but the little brown jug was here. We could have provided the basis for the lyric "The Little Brown Jug and Me."

Later when we had a grocery store on the south side they would sell some patent medicines as a cure for catarrh—most people had catarrh (now called sinus infection). There was Peruna that may have had more than 90% alcohol or brandy and one patent medicine called Rock and Rye that was mostly Scotch, but American made, at one dollar per pint.

Now a little story of a man and wife—we will call him Joe. Joe had been to town to buy provisions, and of course, had his little brown jug with him. He came with his provisions and he had not only his jug full, but he himself was full too. When he came into the house he fell and broke his little brown jug. His wife was there to help him up and he was very tearful and sad. His wife was very sympathetic and appeared as tearful and sorrowful as he was. Seeing his wife so sad, he made a resolution and declared that he would never take another drink as long as she lived and he lived up to his promise.

Now we come to the year 1903. The village of Cromwell was incorporated and a liquor dispensary could legally be established.

The Duluth Brewing Company built a double house, one part to be used for a hotel and the other part for the saloon. May Jager opened the first saloon under the local option law and she operated only a few months when she sold her interest to John H. Wright who operated it very successfully and without any rowdyism. One would not know on the street that there was a saloon there and it was conducted as respectably as was possible. Mrs. Wright was a capable manager of the hotel and they conducted a successful business until the time of prohibition when the saloon was closed, but Mr. and Mrs. Wright continued to operate the hotel until the building burned and was a total loss. Mr. Wright built himself a new home where the little green schoolhouse used to stand in the middle 1920s. He was suffering from a heart ailment and only lived a few years after he had moved into his new home.

Prohibition gave birth to many taverns and roadside inns serving all kinds of beverages and in some, food was served. They are too numerous to mention except that I must mention the Trolley Inn operated by Ivar Dahlquist as a most respectable place and the only place in Cromwell where complete meals are served.

The Beginning of Limited Industrial Activities

In the 1880s or maybe about 1884, the Grant Brothers built a sawmill at the north end of Cromwell Lake. I do not know how many seasons they operated, but not more than two summers. They had to raft their lumber across the lake, floating and piling their lumber along the railroad track to dry before shipping. It must have been a tedious job and involved much labor.

Wages were from $26 per month plus board and on up. Lumber was cheap in those days, as low as $7 per 1,000 feet, FOB. It can easily be seen why it was a very profitable business.

The spring of 1894 brought several homesteaders here and Mr. Morse had bought his land and established his permanent home here. Altogether we had nearly 100,000 feet of lumber to be sawed in the summer of 1894. We induced a Mr. Olson at Tamarack to move his sawmill here to Cromwell to saw our logs at $3 per 1,000 feet. So he moved his stationary mill here which involved a good deal of money and labor. Mr. Olson erected the sawmill some eight rods north of the Morse house on the west shore of the lake. There was heavy timber there so he had to clear the land first and he worked more than two months before he could start sawing. His total reward for all of this work was $300 after he had sawed the logs. Of course, it was a permanent structure and Mr. Olson expected to remain here and cut more logs next winter, but not so.

On September 1, 1894, the Hinckley fire burned everything and Mr. Olson and his family lost all they had, but saved their lives by being near the lake. The lumber they had sawed burned and a good deal of the lumber belonged to Mr. Olson as many of the homesteaders had no money. Mr. Olson took his lumber for sawing so after the fire there was only little more than 2,000 feet left and that went into the west part of the Morse's house.

The town of Red Clover was organized and some roads were legally established so the county surveyor, William Meyers, was employed to survey the town line road starting about one and one half miles east of Cromwell, then west, north of Wright station to the Carlton County west line. After that it was a big job to clear the right of way which amounted to about three acres per mile. There was heavy timber on most of the line and some of the way had to be corduroyed and ditched on both sides when the surveying was done. They served as our first roads. Money for grading the roads was short and it was hard to get from place to place.

Now since this synopsis concerns the village of Cromwell only, I will limit my remarks to this area.

Our only source of revenue was a tax. You have all heard about the political football that the southerners have been playing with the northerners the last few years. The poll tax (head tax), an old system of taxation, was an exclusive road tax. It was levied by the town board and could be levied not to exceed two days labor per year on each able-bodied man between the ages of twenty-one and fifty years and payment could be enforced by law. Any citizen had the right to challenge the vote of anyone who had not worked his poll tax. It was a work tax, but one could commute by paying one dollar and a half per day assessed at least one day before he was to appear to work. The town also levied a five mill property tax. The taxpayer could "work out" the tax if he wanted to; if not, it would be collected by the county treasurer and returned to the town treasurer with other taxes collected. The town also levied an additional road and bridge tax, not to exceed fifteen mills, so we proceeded with our limited means.

In 1897 the town of Red Clover voted to sell

bonds. I do not remember the exact amount, but it was something like four hundred dollars to build three bridges—one across the lake east of Cromwell more than 200 feet long and one across the Tamarack River at Wright Station. A contract was let to a Minneapolis contractor who built the bridges in the spring of 1897. The town board had to build the approach to these bridges which were four feet above lake level and the swamp at both ends was the low water mark. It was necessary to corduroy about sixty rods from the west end of the bridge to the highland so the town board sold a contract to John Pohl at one dollar per rod. (Jobs were auctioned off or sold to the lowest bidder). That same spring the corduroy and the approach were completed with fire-kilned, sixteen-foot poles. We could drive across with horses and a lumber wagon, but not with a buggy.

At the town election that spring, B. A. Beck was elected as road overseer of this district, including the north half of Cromwell. Albert Johnson was overseer for the south half. Now the overseer was a law unto himself. His duties were to maintain the public roads and to construct new legally established roads. It was also his duty to collect the poll tax and the five mill tax. B. A. Beck proposed constructing a turnpike road beginning at the west end of the corduroy and west as far as the work and money he collected permitted.

Mr. Johnson turned over all his poll and land taxes to Beck to collect as far as three miles south and so work was started. When the local people saw that Beck meant business they all gave him loyal support by not only working their poll tax and their property tax, but some of them also donated labor. Land owners in Superior and Duluth sent in their land tax to Beck to be worked out. Nearly one half mile of turnpike road was built which was one of the first in the northwestern part of Carlton County from all the way east to Carlton and south to within three or four miles of Moose Lake. There were no real public roads, only tote roads built by the lumber men and the old stage road that connected with the military road east of Barnum and then on to Aitkin and Anoka and North Minneapolis by the Mississippi.

Now we will return to the industrial aspect again.

In the winter of 1897 two men from West Duluth came here to see if there was an opportunity for operating a sawmill. They were assured there was plenty of timber to keep a sawmill busy. So they shipped a sawmill in from Duluth and got permission from J. M. Paine of Carlton (Paine Lumber Co.) to erect the sawmill on the east side of the lake just north of the highway. They worked all winter and were unable to make it run, so when spring came they had to give it up. There were a good many logs put in the lake to be sawed so Mr. Morse got a sawmill man from Frazee to lease the mill and saw the logs—about two months of sawing. Then the mill stood idle until the next winter when a Mr. Smith from Duluth leased or bought the mill and converted it into a shingle mill. He operated it for about one year and then sold the mill to Arthur Dotten who was a logger and who had operated logging camps for a number of years. Mr. Dotten logged in the winter and operated the sawmill, sawing his own logs and doing some custom sawing for several years. Mr. Dotten had to haul all of his lumber from the mill over the lake to the railroad siding and pile it there. He built a tramway on the side of the bridge and the road from the mill over into the yard which used wooden rails (he covered the corduroy with sawdust) and a four wheel truck generally used in lumber yards. He could haul several thousand feet on one load with one horse. He continued until about 1903 and then moved to Louisiana.

About 1905, Mr. Morse, seeing the need for a sawmill on the west shore of Cromwell Lake, set one up and operated a planing mill and conducted a lumber and building supply business in connection with his mercantile business. In 1916 or 1917, when Mr. Morse closed down his lumber business, a commercial coal and lumber company established a lumber yard here and carried a complete line of building material, hardware, and coal. It was operated under the ownership of various lumber companies and as a branch lumber yard under the able and courteous management of John A. Holmes until they sold out to Farmers Co-op.

Mr. Frank Wilcox came here with his family from Oelwein, Iowa, with the intention of starting in the real estate business. Mr. and Mrs. Wilcox had two children— a son and a daughter. They had lived in Nebraska and several other states. Mr. Wilcox had been admitted to the bar as an attorney in the state of Tennessee and had been in the sawmill business there until he was washed out or flooded out of that business. He then moved to Oelwein, Iowa, for a short time before coming to Cromwell. He opened a real estate office and sold some timber. This lasted about six years when Mr. Wilcox became a victim of tuberculosis in 1910. He moved to Oklahoma or New Mexico for his health and lived only a few years. The Wilcox family was highly respected by all who knew them.

About 1912, Raymond Barstow of Barnum,

together with Charles Morse and John H. Wright, organized the State Bank of Cromwell. They built the bank building and opened the bank in 1912 with Ray Barstow as cashier. It seemed to have a very promising future and I believe it would have had under the leadership of Mr. Barstow, but he sold out his interest to Leif Illstrup who had no experience in the banking business and later sold his interest to Norman Houck. The bank closed in 1929 because of a shortage of funds. It was too bad, as a good bank is an invaluable asset to any community, whether there is a need for cash or a surplus of cash to invest in bonds or savings accounts where our own surplus cash would help to develop our community.

    Mr. Marenius Markusen was born in Denmark and had come over to this country as a small boy with his parents to establish their home in Minneapolis. About 1906 Marenius had bought eighty acres of land in Sec. 24-49-20 and was here one winter getting out timber and doing some carpentry work. He then left, presumably on a hunting trip. He was not heard from for many years, but about 1920 he returned with a planing mill and that was not all. He also brought with him a wife and two sons, so his hunting trip was successful. Mr. Markusen established a planing mill and manufactured all kinds of moldings, flooring, and other building material. Mr. Markusen was a first class carpenter and cabinetmaker and conducted a successful business for some years until he became the victim of tuberculosis and was bedridden for more than five years. Mrs. Markusen returned to teaching in order to support her husband and two sons. Before her husband recovered, her youngest son, Sidney, also became a victim of the dreadful disease and was bedridden for more than five or six years. Mr. Markusen recovered sufficiently and by careful attention to his health became very active as a carpenter. In the meantime, Mrs. Markusen continued to teach in the English department of our high school. She was a faithful teacher, very highly respected and loved by her students. She became the victim of the most dreadful of all diseases: cancer. She could not survive and left her husband, Marenius, and two sons, Sidney and David, to mourn her passing. Her younger son recovered sufficiently to engage in light work and exercise.

Ruth Lee Markusen (1888-1948)

Now we will go back to the horse-and-buggy days of 1890 when there were plenty of horses, but no buggies as yet. In every little burgh or village you would find a blacksmith shop. They were busy nearly all year round—shoeing horses, making sleds, and repairing wagons and all types of farm equipment. But blacksmithing is becoming a lost art.

The first blacksmith shop in Cromwell was operated by John Derosier, who first started his shop south of town on his farm, but when he sold his farm to Otto Lust he came to Cromwell and built a shop just west of the Co-op store (where it is now) and operated it for three or four years. Andrew Korby and Edward Ekstrom bought the next lot west of John Derosier and built a blacksmith shop identical to his—so they could be called twins.

So A. Korby and Ed Ekstrom started blacksmithing in competition with John Derozeer, but it was not long before A. Korby quit the blacksmith business and moved to Crosby where he remained. Ekstrom continued the shop and later bought out John Derozeer's shop and moved into it. He sold the other building to James McDermot. Mr. Ekstrom operated a very successful shop there for a few years until he lost all by fire. Mr. Ekstrom rebuilt his shop and operated it until he retired and sold his property to the Farmer's Co-op.

About 1912 Gust and Ernest Forslund bought forty acres of land in Sec. 27-49-20. They never did build any building, but cleared a little land and may have had a garden and raised some potatoes. Otherwise they made no improvements. They later sold the land to Emil Sparing who moved on the land about 1916. He established his home there and made a small farm of it and lived there a number of years. Later he sold it to Kenneth Mann. The Forslunds were blacksmiths and started a shop in Cromwell but it was not successful, so the family moved away—Gust to Kimberly and Ernest to Washington.

Now we come to the transition from horsepower to motorized farming, and the horse-and-buggy stage to motorcars and trucks for transportation. The blacksmith shops have given way to the auto repair shops and many service stations have been started and some have failed. Some people have small shops on their home places and even on small farms. The main service stations in Cromwell are one operated by Ivar Dahlquist and Ray's Service Station, which is a complete repair garage. The Farmers Co-op also operates a complete service station and most of the time they also have machinists there to do a complete job of repair work. The Farmers Co-op Garage is the successor to Edward T. Walker and Son who built the garage in the early days of the automobile industry, but failed. Also Gunnard Skramstad operates a garage over on the east side of Cromwell Lake. Mr. Skramstad is an auto mechanic and worked as such some years in Duluth and then came home and built a garage on his old home place and is making repairs on all makes of cars.

Earl Dotten with his horse and buggy.

The Cromwell Contracting Company was organized by E. W. Dotten. His principal operation was well-drilling all over northeastern Minnesota and he has put in many wells in and around Cromwell and Carlton.

Introduction to the Co-operative Movement in Cromwell

In 1910 there was a public meeting held at the home of B. A. Beck for the purpose of organizing some form of a co-operative. There are two types of co-operatives—one is the producers' co-operative, which is considered capitalistic and a defender of individual ownership of property and private enterprise and the other is the school of consumer co-operatives which is strongly influenced by the political philosophy of socialism and is considered a stepping stone to national socialism.

It was quite evident the intent of those who called the meeting was to organize a co-operative store. After surveying the experiences of many communities in various parts of northeastern Minnesota, we found all had failed who had undertaken the organizing of co-operatives, such as stores and creameries. I will mention a few: the Mahtowa Creamery, which bought the machinery but never got started, one at Barnum failed after a few months, and another at Moose Lake which failed shortly after it started. Tamarack, Floodwood, and Cloquet all failed with the same story in the undertaking of co-operatives. In all cases, the people, mostly farmers, organized the co-operatives and lost all they had put into the organization. In the case of one creamery they lost two or three months' income payment and some of them had sold wood for fuel and lost the payment for that also. Failure must not be attributed to dishonesty on the part of those whom members elected to office nor on the part of the men they hired as managers of their business. As a rule, the members refused to grant the board they elected and the people they hired, the authority to exercise their best judgment without coming into conflict with the membership. That was also true regarding the change of the school district to an independent school district. Under common school district law, the school board had no authority whatsoever, only what a majority would give them at the election. But when they voted to become an independent school district, they invested or gave the school board full authority to manage the school with only some legal limitations.

I am recording this as I have stated before that our schools are only big co-operatives in governing the school system and there was no improvement in our common school education from the early days until now.

So, by a legislative act, a representative form of government was created. The Board of Education, who are the representatives of the people with the full authority to manage the school system as they think best according to law and the standard of the school, depends on the people who elect them. This is a lesson that the co-operatives had to learn: they had to put aside all personalities and elect officers whose character was without reproach, who possessed sound judgment, and could subdue malice. So the success of the co-operatives depended on their loyalty and the good judgment the members exercised in choosing their officers.

The failure of the creamery was due to lack of sufficient volume of cream, low quality cream, lack of capital, and lack of markets. There was also a lack of coordination in management and that applies to all co-operatives in their undertakings. The early co-operative stores failed for lack of capital and lack of experience in the field of merchandising.

Now we will return to our first meeting in 1910. After considering all of these things stated above, we decided to go slow as we lacked all of the requirements needed for the successful operation of any co-operative enterprise. We organized a farmers' club for the purpose of learning how to work together (Co-operative) in a small way and to improve our farming by uniting our efforts in producing the same kinds of potatoes and other products and taking advantage of all the information we could get from the Extension Service of which Mr. A. D. Wilson was director. Whenever we had an important question for our meeting we were always favored with a speaker who was a specialist in the problem up for our consideration.

A Champion Guernsey Butter-Fat Producer. Photo from the U. S. Department of Agriculture Yearbook, 1922.

We also organized a breeding association and agreed to promote Guernsey dairy cattle. There was opposition to this and the contention became very heated, even to the extent of splitting the club into two groups. One group wanted the club, as a whole, to buy a sire and the other group wanted to organize a breeding association. The first group bought their club sire, but as a group did not last long. The second group organized the Red Clover Guernsey Breeding Association and kept one sire and later they incorporated because of the danger involved in handling the sire.

At last we have five purebred Guernsey sires and

have greatly improved our dairy cattle. This was the first dairy improvement program here and second only to Barnum, by not more than two years, to be the first in Carlton County.

There were several small herds of dairy cows so mill feed then became a question. We tried pooling orders for feed and to buy by the carload. We bought two or three carloads, but it was not satisfactory. We had to pay cash when the car arrived and no one had any money, so the committee that was in charge of ordering the car of feed had to pay cash before they could open the car. Sometimes we were stuck with several tons of feed and no place to store it. Others would get their feed on a promise to pay. The first thing we knew, we had a book with accounts receivable and we had no capital. It took some time before we got our accounts collected. No one lost anything, but the members who had charge of the distribution and collection had plenty of grief as their reward for their time and labor.

It was self-evident that if we wanted to have the benefit of wholesale and bulk buying we would have to have a warehouse. So we organized a warehouse association and sold shares. All members had to be shareholders and we raised enough money to buy a lot and nearly enough to build the warehouse. We then borrowed six or seven hundred dollars on a joint promissory note bearing 6% per annum. All decisions were made and all the rules were adopted at membership meetings and the secretary was instructed to order carloads of mill feeds when he could get the best price on terms and that always was cash. He was also instructed to keep the warehouse open one-half day a week and to add five cents per sack to price cost as margin. It was expected this five cents per sack would pay all the costs of operation, to say nothing of retiring the loan. You can readily see most members were there to receive and not to give and were motivated by expectation of personal gain at the expense of a few. I wonder if that is the spirit that is the cause of all of our troubles today right here in the United States.

We continued in the warehouse business for about two years and by this time we had nearly one-half of our borrowed capital on our books as receivables. At a membership meeting where all rules and regulations were formulated, it was decided to close the warehouse and sell it.

This left the members who had signed the promissory note holding the bag. Four of them assumed the responsibility of paying the note and interest by having the members transferring all rights and title of the warehouse to them. They in return leased it to different parties for a blacksmith shop. They at last sold it at a loss of more than four hundred dollars and the members lost their five dollar membership fee. That was our first experience in co-operative merchandising.

The Farmers' Club continued and held meetings from time to time and in 1910 there was considerable farming but no market. There was some livestock and potatoes to sell in car lots, but no buyers at five cents a pound for veal calves, ten to fifteen dollars for a cow, and as low as sixteen cents per bushel for potatoes FOB Duluth. Under these circumstances we organized the Producer's Co-operative Market Association of Duluth and we were incorporated under the laws of Minnesota. (As yet, we had no co-operative law in Minnesota). We had no capital but we had the full support of the Commercial Club of Duluth. The Commercial Club advanced us $5,000 as working capital without interest. Now, you may wonder why. Well, the banks and trust companies in Duluth were vitally interested in the successful transition from a timber and lumbering industry to agriculture, as they were the owners of large acreages of cutover lands. This sum was used as advertising to people in the older farming communities to come here to buy land and establish permanent homes which were most desirable. However, many came and bought land for speculation purposes only.

Now we will return to the organizing of the marketing association.

There were Farmers' Clubs organized in many farm communities, just as we had in Cromwell. This fact was known to the Commercial Club who sent invitations to these clubs to send representatives to a meeting to be held in the Commercial Club rooms in Duluth. The problem of finding a market for the increasing supply of farm produce and finding ways and means to improve the marketing conditions of farm produce would be discussed. There were representatives from many communities of northeastern Minnesota, northern Wisconsin, and upper Michigan. It was a large meeting and it was realized that we could not expect much relief from the commission houses of Michigan Street. I do not remember who presided over the meeting, but the secretary was John Stone Pardee. There were various forms of organization suggested with B. A. Beck suggesting that we had a good foundation for a central organization by uniting or federating farm clubs.

The meeting was adjourned and a few of the delegates who had spoken were invited to a banquet. There were two from Carlton County—L. H. Bugbee of Wrenshall and B. A. Beck of Cromwell. After discussion, the plan suggested by Beck was adopted and a committee was appointed to draw up articles of incorporation to be adopted. The names of the charter members were as follows: J. H. Bugbee, Wrenshall; A. J. McGuire, Grand Rapids; Ludvig Masbeck, Askov; Louis Christenson, Sandstone; B. A. Beck, Cromwell; C. L. Goodell, Barnum; Adolph Solem, Nea; J. H. Peterson, Meadowlands—all from Minnesota. The first Board of Directors consisted of the following: L. H. Bugbee, chairman; A. B. Hostetter; B. A. Beck; Ludvig Mosbeck; C. L. Goodell; C. P. Craig; A. Solem; J. H. Peterson. We leased a building on Michigan Street in commission row and hired a manager—a good man, but not a commission man—and a part-time bookkeeper. The manager resigned after four months so we employed a manager who had been in the commission business in Cleveland, Ohio. Business seemed to go very well, with only one hitch; namely, we could not supply our own commission house with enough produce to meet the demand so the manager was forced to go out into the open market and buy in competition with the old commission houses. They objected, protesting to the Commercial Club for financing us to do business in the open market and in open competition with them, so the Commercial Club withdrew their advancement of $5,000 and that let us down flat as we had no other working capital.

We accomplished something; we had two years of experience in the commission business. We also created a demand for our produce by convincing buyers that our products were equal or better than what they had shipped in from southern Minnesota and southern Wisconsin. A big question was raised for the Board of Directors. Should we try to raise the needed capital to keep going or close up? The membership had not lost anything except the membership fee of ten dollars, but the Board of Directors were out about one hundred dollars cash for expenses. So the board had a kind of farewell party and by motion dissolved the meeting. That last meeting may well have been the beginning of the Land O' Lakes Creamery, for a few of us who remained there that afternoon agreed if we would have had ten or more creameries with a steady supply of products to sell, we could have raised the capital and continued in business. Those were the parting words of Beck, and the idea hatched in McGuire's head. He soon started to organize the creameries down in central Minnesota which are now the Land O' Lakes Creamery, Inc.

About 1914 we organized the Carlton County Telephone Association under the leadership of Andrew Parviainen and Edward Benson. B. A. Beck acted as secretary. We built some sixteen miles of telephone line in Eagle and Red Clover townships and installed a switchboard and established a co-operative telephone exchange—the first of its kind in all of northeastern Minnesota. There was a rural telephone line in the western part of Eagle township which combined with the Carlton County Co-op Telephone Association to get telephone service through our exchange. We served as a toll station for the Bell Telephone System and they paid us a commission of five cents per out-going call which paid part of our operating expense.

The Finnish people had also organized a group

similar to our Farmers' club about the same time, but not with the same objective in mind. Their leaders were strictly consumer co-operative minded and they solicited subscriptions for shares to be bought when they were incorporated in June 19, 1917, as the Farmers Co-operative Company. They bought the store operated by John Hill and his brother, Victor, and they entered the commercial field. The next problem was to employ a manager. There were no trained co-operative managers to employ at any price. Also required was a complete new system of accounting that had to be worked out, tried, and tested. It had to be efficacious and at the same time simple enough to be understood by the average member. So I want to give thanks and express gratitude to of all the officers and managers for their loyalty and patronage given in support of their businesses. The had the responsibility of steering us through the trying period when we traveled in the pains of growing to our present stage of maturity. And thanks also for the harmonious and friendly attitude of all private businesses in Cromwell.

Cromwell Co-operative Creamery Association

Sometime in July, 1910, there was a mass meeting called by a self-appointed committee to consider the possibility of organizing a co-operative creamery. There was a large attendance and a permanent creamery organization committee was setup. B. A. Beck was elected permanent chairman and John H. Wright was elected secretary. The meeting was called to order and the purpose of the meeting was stated by the chairman. It was then opened for free discussion of the question of organizing and operating a creamery. There was no one present that had the least idea as to the amount of butterfat or the volume of cream we had here. No one knew how much cream and butterfat we needed as a minimum in order to operate a creamery profitably and competitively. These were important questions for us to decide. Realizing our need for more information concerning the operation of a creamery, the chairman and the secretary were instructed to obtain information for the next meeting to be held in two weeks. The meeting was then adjourned.

The chairman wrote to Mr. A. D. Wilson, director of the Extension Service (there was no county agent then), setting forth the purpose of our meeting and the object to be obtained. We asked him if he could favor us with a speaker for our next meeting—one who had the experience of organizing and managing a creamery. In response to our request, Mr. Charles Nilsen of the extension force came here on the morning train from Albert Lea, Minnesota. The first thing he did was check at the N.P. express office to see how much cream was shipped out per month for the last twelve months. He came up with the answer of 40,000 pounds of butterfat for the last twelve months, only a little more than one-half of what we needed to operate a creamery, even with just one man. So the group decided not to organize at this time and the meeting adjourned.

On May 1, 1912, there was a special meeting of farmers and others held on the invitation of a committee of citizens for the purpose of considering the organizing of a creamery at Cromwell. It was presided over by Mr. M. J. Cort, a representative of the Creamery Package Manufacturing Company, an organizer, and machinery salesman—his only object was to sell machinery.

He was an able and convincing speaker (well, that

is how he made his living). He prevailed on all his audience that it would be profitable to organize and build a Farmers' Co-operative Creamery at Cromwell. His only evidence was based on a list of papers he circulated there asking the people to give the number of cows they would keep if there was a creamery (not the number they had). The list included more than 200, but less than 300 milk cows here. He used this number of milk cows as an argument favoring the organization of a creamery. With his eloquence and his assurance that a Farmers' Co-operative Creamery never would go broke, the minutes of the meeting show that he was successful and convincing, for a vote was taken for organizing a creamery and only one vote was in opposition. They elected a board of directors right then and there. It was as follows: Edward Benson, president; Sulo Vasanoja, vice president; E. T. Walker, secretary; Edward Ekstrom, treasurer; and Mike Heikkila, John Johnson, and C. M. Peterson, directors. Mr. Cort had them sign a contract (an unconditional contract at that) that said, for $1.365 they would get machinery. This was before they actually were incorporated. I would call that high-powered salesmanship, wouldn't you say? The company takes no risk. The farmers who signed the contract were responsible for the full amount of the contract. That was also the experience of the farmers and businessmen of Barnum.

    The board proceeded to sell shares, to choose a site for a creamery building, and also to agree on the size of the building and to contract for the building of it. This is a big order for six or seven men to carry out without money, plus they could be held responsible personally for all the indebtedness. There was no co-operative law as yet in Minnesota limiting the liability of the officers in a co-operative association. The creamery was completed at a cost of $3,252.76.

Finally the creamery was built and the machinery was installed and we opened for the receiving of cream on April 1, 1913, with George Houghton as buttermaker until August 15, 1913. He was replaced by H. F. Beckmark who stayed with us for more than one year. While we suffered such grief and disappointment, we kept moving forward. In October, 1920, we paid the mortgage in full and also paid the first interest on the shares.

Cromwell Creamery, 1914.

We were then in the clear. In the last days of October, 1923, our creamery burned with almost a total loss, but we survived. We had some insurance and a little reserve. We had good demand for our butter and we were blessed with an abundance of goodwill which is invaluable in all businesses whether they be small or large.

We built the present brick structure and moved in the spring of 1924. A few years later, we had to enlarge the building with an addition. During World War II the creamery was converted into a whole milk creamery and that required an investment of several thousand dollars. From our meager beginning, the shareholders and patrons have accumulated total assets of more than $30,000 in the Cromwell Creamery Co-operative Association.

Listed are the names of the buttermakers and managers in the order and the duration of service:

George Houghton	Dec., 1912 to Aug. 15, 1913
H. F. Beckmark	Aug. 15, 1913 to Oct. 15, 1913
Soren Carlson	Oct 15, 1913 to Mar. 1, 1915
Oscar Johnson	Mar. 1, 1915 to Mar. 15, 1917
R. S. Rodgers	Mar. 15, 1917 to June 7, 1917
Oscar Kauppi	June 7, 1917 to June 25, 1918
Johnson	July 1, 1918 to June 1, 1919
William Amundson	June 1, 1919 to April 1, 1922

Amundson was made manager March 1, 1920, and given full control over the operation of the creamery and remained with us until he resigned in March, 1922, to take effect April 1, 1922. Mr. Amundson had given us a very able and judicious management which established us on a solid and firm financial foundation. The board of directors realized this and offered Mr. Amundson $250 per month if he would stay with us. Mr. Amundson declined the offer and moved to his hometown in Wisconsin. We then employed a local boy who had worked in the creamery as a part-time helper for some years. This was Bennett A. Benson. He continued the able and successful operation of the creamery for upwards of thirty years and then he retired.

In May, 1918, the creamery started to market eggs for the farmers and it required nearly the full time of one extra helper to handle the eggs. The creamery continued to handle eggs some twenty years until the creamery was converted into a whole milk creamery and the handling of eggs was discontinued for lack of room.

```
Cromwell Co-operative Creamery
            Association
      Manufacturers and dealers in
  HIGH GRADE CREAMERY BUTTER AND
          FRESH COUNTRY EGGS
    B. A. Benson, Buttermaker and Mgr.

  C. M. Peterson, Pres.    Directors:
  C. A. Sangola, V.-Pres.     Carl Brandt
  A. E. Vigness, Sec'y        John Reimer
  B. A. Beck, Treas.          Jacob Pohto
  CROMWELL      -      -    MINNESOTA
```

Co-op Creamery advertisement, 1927.

Introduction to the Fraternal Activities from the Beginning of Cromwell

A question arose in the mind of the writer.

What is the motivating spirit that causes people to fraternize? People of different backgrounds and different conceptions of the future, of the Creator and of the Christian church somehow bind themselves together much closer than the members of the Christian church who have the promise of eternal life. Can it be that the spirit of Lucianism prevails in the fraternal associations or is it just their appeal to the humanitarianism and benevolence that holds forth and unites them into a fraternal brotherhood?

In the spring of 1896 there came an organizer of a fraternal order, The Modern Samaritans, one of the so-called fraternal orders which also offered some life insurance. He organized a group of about twenty members and they met in the little green school house once a month. Some of them came from Wright and had to walk the distance to attend meetings in the evenings. They could take the train back. The group lasted about two years. Many of the members had to go somewhere else to get employment and some did not return. It died a painless death.

There were no fraternal orders organized here for many years. About 1901 there were some families who moved here from Duluth and Superior, Wisconsin, who were members of the Modern Woodsmen of America. About 1902 there was a camp organized with the following charter members: John Krakora, Edward Estrom, Louis Knutson, Josef Wavern, Emil Rypka, William Rypka, Oscar Homstad, George Wright, John Shie, and John A. Johnson (Old Soldier Johnson). Until 1923 growth was at a standstill. Since that time there has been a steady growth and an increase in its membership to more than 250 members in good standing in Cromwell. The junior members under the age of sixteen years have their own club with a party every month. Martin Stoner has been the secretary since 1926—is more than twenty-five years.

Then about 1920 the Independent Order of Odd Fellows was organized here. They flourished for some years, even to the extent of building the Odd Fellows

Hall. After a few years of seeming prosperity, they fell apart and dissolved. At last they sold the Odd Fellow Hall to the American Legion which operated it as a Legion Club bar room.

The Rebekas, a ladies auxiliary order of the Odd Fellows, had a large membership and were very active in social activities for a number of years. When their parent order became inactive and finally dissolved, it meant the dissolution of the Rebekas also.

Cora Ilstrup when she was District President of the Rebekas in 1924.

There was one very impressive organization that seemed, judging from its activities, to prosper in the 1920s. That was the Ku-Klux-Klan. This was Many a cross burned at their festivals on Skunk Island and elsewhere. When a national headman (the dragon) was convicted of a crime and sentenced to prison for life, their organization dissolved. Yet there may be those imbued with the spirit of intolerance still around.

Now, I will record the names of the earliest citizens. They were mostly railroad men, depot agents, depot personnel, and section men. I have not been able to get the names of the agents before 1883 as there is no record kept before that date.

The station was established in 1870 and was named Island Lake station. The name was changed in 1883 to Cromwell to agree with the post office that was established at that time in honor of James L. Cromwell of Duluth, Minnesota. He was identified with the West Duluth Land Company and also the Carlton Lumber Company located east of Wrenshall near the state line.

The first agents of record were the following:

E. A. Woodard	1883 to 1887
John H. Wright	1887 to 1892
Edward P. Duffy	1892 to 1897
John H. Wright	1897 to 1904
S. A. Hage	1904 to 1906
H. O. Mannes	1906 to 1907
E. A. Keer	1907 for a few months.
Martin H. Duffy	1907 to 1910
Geo. W. Callahan	1910 to 1919
J. S. Spurrier	July 1919 to 1920
A. F. Moen	1920 to 1922
W. J. Soshea	1922 to 1925
F. W. Hoffman	1925 to 1927
W. J. Soshea	1927 to 1929
H. F. Olson	1929 to 1930
W. J. Soshea	1930 to 1935
C. L. Wallace	1935 to 1947
Walter E. Johnson	1947 to 1954

Many of the agents and their families were very active in community affairs—some more than others, but they all were a valuable asset to the community. Very important elements of our early citizenry were the section foreman and his section crew which in the early days consisted of fifteen to twenty men in the summertime.

From 1870 to 1894 inclusive, there were two section crews stationed at Cromwell and each crew had six miles of track to maintain—one beginning at the depot east to the center of the side track at Corona and the other west to the center of the side track at Wright Station. Wright was named in honor of John H. Wright. It was mandatory that the section foreman and one section man go over their section of track each day. To make sure they had done so, each foreman had a switch light at each end of his section to keep in good order. Lard oil was used in the switch lamps and had to be replaced each day (or nearly so) and the switch lamp had to be cleaned as well. You know how smoky your oil lamp chimney becomes, especially when exposed to the winds. Well, you just try lard oil for the fun of it. Lard oil was also used in the switchman's lantern. There were no dry cell batteries then to use in lanterns as there are now.

     I have not been able to get the names of all the section foremen as the railway company has no record of them. So I will do the best I can from information at hand. It appears that Enoch Arden and Peter Parson were the first section foremen here. I have known both of them personally. Enoch Arden had charge of the extra gang in the summer and the gravel train and tie loading train in the spring when I was first here. Peter Parson retired from the railroad and entered the saloon business in partnership with his brother in Carlton. He later returned to his first love, the railway company and the section foremanship at Cromwell for a short time. Then he was transferred to Brainerd to have charge of the railroad yards and he remained there until he died a few years later.

     In 1892 when I came here, Gust Johnson and Joe

Bissen were the section foremen. In the spring of 1893 Gust Johnson was transferred to Tamarack and John Lindquist was promoted to foreman and took over Johnson's section. And so John Lindquist and Joe Bissen were section foremen until the spring of 1895 when a Mr. Tyler became roadmaster. He increased the length of the sections from six to nine miles per section leaving only one section crew at Cromwell. The other section crew was moved to Wright and the first section foreman on the rearranged section was Peter Parson (but for a short time only). He was replaced by Mr. Alstad who remained here until Mr. Tyler was transferred to the Montana division and he took Mr. Alstad with him. John Eastman took over the section.

Now I will record the names of the section foremen and the approximate time they served here to the best of my information: Peter Parson for perhaps six months in 1895; then John Eastman to about 1897; Alstad to 1899; John Herman to 1901; Joe Peterson to 1904; and Louis Knutson, 1904 to 1908. Then there were no permanent foremen here until Otto Swanson came in about 1908. He remained here until he retired around 1941.

Now I will record the names of all the people that have made their home in Cromwell for two years or more. Please pardon me if I fail to record the names of some who may read this and have lived in Cromwell at sometime in the past. I am writing this from memory and from information I have been able to gather.

Mrs. Erickson, a sister of Louis Lungren, moved up here from Lake City to keep house for her brother, a bachelor. But that did not last long and she they moved into town and rented the Morse house on Main Street.

She had two sons and two daughters. Fred was the oldest (about twenty) and he worked on the section and supported the family. They lived here about three or four years and then moved to Fargo, North Dakota.

John Allen, a carpenter, came here in about 1900 or earlier and made his home at the Alex Bellanger home when he was working. Otherwise he lived in Cloquet.

John Brackett came here about 1897 from the western part of Minnesota and worked for Charles Morse for a year and then he and his family moved to Moorhead or Fargo, North Dakota. They lived there about two years and came back to Cromwell and worked again for Charles Morse and then after two years moved out west again. They had one daughter.

Then we have the Smith Collinson family, he was a brother-in-law of Samuel Elliot, who came out from Ontario, Canada. They lived in Cromwell and bought eighty acres of land, the S1/2 of the NW1/4 Sec. 9-48-20, and cleared about four acres of it. Then they sold the land that now belongs to Carl and Gust Brandt and moved to Winnipeg, Canada, about 1903.

About 1902 Mr. and Mrs. August Greschell and their two daughters came here from central Minnesota. They were Germans. Mr. Greschell had contracted to buy 160 acres of land from the Boston and Duluth Land Co. of Duluth and got a contract for the deed for a small down payment. He moved up here in the following spring with his family, five or six cows, three horses, and some farm machinery. He called on the company to send out a man to show him the land and locate him on the land he had been shown in the fall. According to his contract for the deed, he had contracted to buy 160 acres of all open swampland in Sec. 5-49-20. He had not seen it before so he dropped the contract and bought a lot in Louis Larson's Lakeside addition to Cromwell and built a house and barn. He rented pasture and hay land from Louis Larson and lived there for about three years. Then they moved to Stearns County in Minnesota.

In 1904 Mr. and Mrs. Herman Farness came here from South Dakota and bought eighty acres of wild land in Sec. 25, S1/2 NW1/4 49-20. They built a house and small barn but made no permanent improvements. They lived here about two years and moved back to South Dakota. I do not know if they had any children.

In 1860 John H. Jackson was born in the state of Tennessee, migrated to the state of Michigan in 1870, and came to Northeastern Minnesota in the 1880s. He came to Wright, Minnesota, in about 1895 with John Brennick, who had bought the Solomon Moronzee farm from three miles east of Wright. Then Mr. Jackson took a homestead nearby, improved it, and made it his home until he sold it about 1907. His neighbor, Philip Dennie, also sold his home farm and they moved to Cromwell and bought a lot from Louis Larson in Lakeside addition. Mr. Jackson was a carpenter and built a house there and they made that their home. A few years later Mr. Dennie died and Mr. Jackson worked some as a carpenter and continued to live there for a few years until he sold the house about 1929 to Otto Swanson. He then retired from active labor. He made his home with Mr. and Mrs. Everret Anderson on their farm during the declining years of his life. He must have been nearly ninety-four years of age at his departure. Mr. Jackson was a man blessed with a kind and conservative disposition.

Mr. and Mrs. Weslee Schonover went from Pennsylvania to Missouri and from there to Oelwein, Iowa, and then came to Cromwell in 1903 with the Frank Wilcox family. He worked with or for Mr. Wilcox in the woods three miles north of Corona for three years and then moved into Cromwell and bought a lot from Charles Morse and built a small house. The first telephone exchange was installed in their house and Mrs. Schonover served as telephone operator until they sold the house to William Martwig who is the present owner. Mrs. Martwig is the present telephone operator.

Edward Wolf came here in 1904 and worked for Charles Morse as a millwright. He built the sawmill and operated it for about two years and then he was replaced by Jacob Haubner, a blacksmith and steam engineer, who worked until Mr. Morse finished sawing his timber.

Mrs. Sarah Wilson came here from Iowa in 1904 and became the housekeeper for Amasa Dotton. She had two sons, Harry and Edward, and a daughter, Grace. Harry worked for Charles Morse as a teamster and Ed worked at odd jobs. The boys moved to the Iron Range and Mrs. Wilson and Grace followed them soon after. Mr. Dotton married a widow from Iowa and lived in Iowa for some time; however, in a year Mr. and Mrs. Dotton returned to Cromwell and lived here until he died in the 1920s. He was laid to rest by his first wife in Carlton and his second wife moved back to Iowa.

Mr. and Mrs. M. S. Allshire and his brother, William, came from Todd County in 1899 and operated a cedar camp four miles north of Corona. We had very little snow that winter so very little timber was hauled out to the railroad track. The timber belonged to the Cloquet

Lumber Co. We had green grass the first of April that spring. Mr. and Mrs. Allshire moved to Cromwell into Ben Pepin's house on the shore of Island Lake. Mr. Allshire's brother, William, went back to Todd county and M. S. Allshire lived here two years and then moved to Washington.

Claude Wilson came here with the AIlshires in 1899. He had been separated from his wife who remained in Todd County. They had one son, Clarence, who came here with his father and lived here with the Bellanger family until his father married again, and then he moved back to Long Prairie. He lived there until Mr. Wilson became ill with diabetes a year or two later. They came back to Cromwell and lived here three years and after that they made their home in Larson's lakeside addition to Cromwell. There Mr. Wilson died, leaving his wife and son to mourn his passing. Clarence, married Mary Frost. Shortly after, he was electrocuted, leaving his wife and, I believe, two sons to mourn his departure.

In 1904 Mr. and Mrs. John Crosley and his brother, Guy Crosley, came from Superior, Iowa. They drove two horse teams (and I believe covered wagons). John Crosley sold one team to Oscar Homstad and Guy sold his one team to Arthur Dotton. Guy worked for Dotten that winter hauling logs with four horses to the sawmill on the east side of the lake, right in front of what is now Dotton's house. In the spring he drove up to the Iron Range with a team of horses. He later married and made Stevenson his permanent home for the rest of his life. John Crosley remained here at Cromwell for three years and lived in a log house built by Joe Gravelle in the northwest corner of Ben Pepin's land where John Hill's house now stands. He bought eighty acres of land in Sec. 10 E1/2 NE1/4 48-20 plus a lot of a half an acre—he lot now owned by Ray Langevin. He built a small house on the lot and later sold the house to Frank Wilcox who moved it across the road (now owned by George Frost). Then he built himself a small log house on his land in Sec. 10 living there and clearing some land. He then moved to the range by his brother, Guy, and worked there a few years. Then he came back with his family and lived here a few years until his health failed him. Then Mr. and Mrs. Crosley moved to the Iron Range again to live with a son and daughter. He died there some time later, leaving his wife and two sons and two daughters to mourn his passing. Mr. Crosley was a very mild-mannered man of a reserved disposition and well liked by all who learned to know him. Mr. and Mrs. Crosley had one son and one daughter when they came here and some twenty years later, they were blessed with another son and a daughter.

With the Crosleys came Mr. and Mrs. Harvey Walters. He was a brother-in-law of the Crosleys. Walters took a homestead, the SE1/4 of SW1/4 Sec. 2-48-20, cut the timber from it, and made sufficient improvements to prove up. He sold the land to O. Sodowick from Duluth who moved onto the land but kept working in Duluth. The Walters family moved to the Iron Range. The E. H. Fowler family also came with the Crosleys from Spencer, Iowa. They lived in Cromwell until they took a homestead in Sec. 14 and then they also moved to the Iron Range. In addition, Mr. and Mrs. A. Davidson came with the Crosley's and lived here for a short time, possibly a year or two.

Scott Mingus came to Cromwell with Harry Wilson about 1900—both as young boys. Scott worked

Scott Mingus with Agnes Donahue and Olive Clifton at the teacherage south of Cromwell.

for E. T. Walker and Harry for Charles Morse. Sometime later his mother; two younger brothers, Albert and Ernie; a sister, Maud; and his brother-in-law, John Tayler, and Mrs. Tayler, an elder sister of Scott's, came from Iowa and made Cromwell their permanent home. Scott and his brothers bought four acres of land from Louis Larson and built a house on it for their mother, father, younger sister, brothers. His father did not live here very much as he worked away from home most of the time as a stone mason, but he came home from time to time for short periods. About 1908 his brother Albert died and his mother died in 1910, leaving her husband, Windfield C. Mingus, and eight children to mourn her loss. Her daughter, Mrs. Tayler, hadalso passed on before her. Mrs. Mingus was a good and kind neighbor and an active worker in the Methodist church.

Shortly thereafter the Mingus family sold their

home to the Harry B. Paine family and Scott went back to Iowa in 1911 to work with his brothers who were bricklayers and have followed that profession ever since. Scott met and married Myrtly McLaughlin, but she did not live long. She died in 1913, leaving her husband, one son, Robert, and one daughter, Gertrude, to mourn her passing. In 1919 Mr. Mingus met and married Bessie Dougal and they lived in Iowa for some time before moving to California and living there until 1932. They moved back to Cromwell and bought the old Bellanger farm and have made that their permanent home since and have greatly improved it. They cleared a good deal of land and built a most artistic house out of native cobblestones. Mr. and Mrs. Mingus have four sons—Truman, Vance, Douglas, and John.

Mr. Mingus is a descendant of old pioneer stock. His grandfather Mingus emigrated from Ireland in the eighteenth century. He settled in North Carolina and lived there sometime, and later moved to Iowa in a covered wagon drawn by an ox team. He and his wife settled on a homestead about the time land was opened for settlement by the federal government. When they started farming they had to transport their farm produce sixty miles to Des Moines and it took three days to make the trip by ox team. That was the only "locomotive power" in those days. There Scott's father was born and in due time he married Elizabeth Von Guilder (of Dutch descent) and lived in Iowa until about 1900 when they moved to Cromwell.

(Thank you Scott, for this information)

John Clark and Jesse Lee were both natives of Wisconsin and when they were not working in the woods they made their home with the Harry Paine family. Clark came here possibly around 1888. In 1896 Jesse Lee came here and then moved up north to Cook, Minnesota where he ran a little store there.

Ernest Forslund and his brothers, Gust and John, came from Superior. Ernest had just been married in Superior and came to Cromwell and rented the Co-op Farmers' warehouse (not the present Farmers Co-op Co.) starting a blacksmith shop and operating it for about two years. Then he moved to Washington state and his brother, Gust, took over the blacksmith shop and operated it for some time until he moved to Kimberly. The building was sold to John Juntanen and he operated the blacksmith shop for a few years until he sold out to Roy Baski, who is now the owner.

Some sixty-five years ago our area was still covered by heavy green forests, but here and there a homesteader had cleared a small living space. The paths of wild animals were the only roads besides the tote roads which could be used to bring home the needed commodities in a pack sack. In the evening we could listen to the concerts of wolves and musical beasts. If one wanted to visit a neighbor he had to take care so as not to get lost. At times a person started from his cabin or camp with the intent of calling on a neighbor and found himself right back at the starting point.

How things have changed! Roads crisscross the area from north to south and east to west. Even the smallest distance is traveled by car and planes fly overhead. Electric lights and telephones are in nearly every home and many have television. The times have changed, but people are less content than ever before.

Children who used to walk up to two miles to school and bring their lunch with them are now hauled by bus from their home and back and are served hot lunch at noon. What more do they want?

The first airplane in Cromwell on July 4, 1928. The plane was a 1927 Travel Air used for barnstorming.

In 1920 there was no barber shop here when Mr. Franzen started one, but he failed. There were too many men wearing a full beard (the King George style) as it was still the age of whiskers. The long, well-kept hair was the glory of the ladies so there was not much for the barber to do. Well, it was too bad and a real loss as Mr. Franzen was a good manager of one of our baseball teams. We had two teams for some years—one was the Morse team and the other the John Wright team. We also

Cromwell baseball team, 1913.

l to r. Horace Morse—batboy, George Callahan, Fred Larson, unknown, Wilson Wright, Irving Debolt, Bill Felgen, Oscar Benson, George Wright, the others are unidendified.

had a good band or orchestra with Mr. John Pannanen as leader.

Another man tried to continue in the barber business. His name was Lampi and he was a local boy but he had to quit for lack of patrons. By this time an old barber from Brainerd, Gust Raymond by name, came here in about 1925. He was a graduate of the old school that was represented by the barber's tricolored sign. He had been given a course in trichology which meant shaving the beard and cutting and dressing the hair. He also could extract teeth and do manicuring—taking care of the nails of both hands and feet. In those days the barber served the people as barber, dentist, and manicurist. He would even make house calls, the same as a medical doctor would. He was always at your service at your home, applying his trade. Those were the good old days. Mr. Raymond was born in Joplin, Missouri, and had served six years as an apprentice. He came here about 1925 after he lost all he had in a fire at Brainerd. He remained here until he retired in the year 1953 at the age of eighty-two.

In the 1920s we had also a medical doctor located here by the name of Arents. There were so many of the old pioneers here yet and they were not used to calling in a doctor every time they had a little ache or pain. The same was true of the mothers and grandmothers of the present generation. They were satisfied to let the stork deliver the precious little bundle with only the help of a good neighbor woman, so they rarely needed the help of a medical doctor. That was not because they liked it that way but because of the general economic circumstances at the time.

Following Dr. Arents, Dr. Kloves located here and remained for about one year. He then moved to Wright and lived there a year and then moved to Minneapolis. There has not been a doctor here since. It could be because of the good roads and the present modes of transportation. Another cause may be the highly specialized medical profession of the younger doctors who prefer to practice in a hospital.

Another modern improvement is a modern sewer system in the village proper. We also have an up-to-date volunteer fire department that gives fire protection to the town of Eagle and Red Clover and in case of an emergency they will give protection to more distant points.

And now I have cleaned my attic—the store house of my memory. I want to thank those, especially Andrew Parviainen, who have given me information of any kind and any other help in gathering the material recorded herein.

Sawmill near Cromwell, 1916.

CHAPTER THIRTEEN

The Introduction of Christian Civilization and Spiritual Life in the Area of Cromwell, Minnesota

The first white men to visit Minnesota were some French traders in 1659. Father Hennepin reached St. Anthony Falls in 1680 and it is possible Father Hennepin was acquainted with the French traders so that he was not all together a stranger to the surrounding area. He and his crew and companions may have explored the Mississippi River for some distance north and some of its tributaries and streams. They could have come up the Mississippi to where Portage is now located at the mouth of Sandy River and up the river to Prairie Lake and up Hasty Brook to just four miles north of Cromwell. They could also have come up from Big Sandy Lake on the Tamarack River to its headwater at Cromwell. It is known that there was a line of communication between Fond du Lac and Big Lake and between Fond du Lac and Sandy Lake, but now that is hidden history to me.

It is known history that Father Hennepin or some of his missionaries came here at an early date and introduced Christian civilization long before Colonel Leavenworth built Fort Snelling in 1819. They worked among the Indians and suffered great hardship and privation. They had sacrificed the enjoyment of remaining in the Old Country enjoying the standard of life which was maintained in those days, but they believed and were obedient to the call of the Lord (St. Matthew, Chapter 28, V. 19) and who questioned their sincerity?

They labored hard among the Indians, gained their confidence, and established mission homes at central points, such as Sandy Lake and Fond du Lac and then branched out and established small chapels. They were not just for church services as we maintain churches today, but were the very first institutions of learning —instructing the Indians in the simple Christian way of living and the Christian white man's art of home life. The chief admonished his people to treat kindly the visitors who had come so far. The first missions and church in Minnesota were built at Crow Wing near Brainerd by the Reverend Francis Pirz (or Pirec), a native of Austria. He was the only missionary in Minnesota in 1852 and his successor was the Reverend Joseph Francis Buh, also a native of Austria. Belle Prairie became his headquarters and the Reverend Buh had a gathering of thirty brave men as his assistants who willingly sacrificed all the comforts of life and lived laborious days on a very meager subsistence such as wild rice, potatoes, hard tack, tea, and sometimes a little wild mutton given to them by the Indians.

The Indians traveled hundreds of miles in the winter on snowshoes and in the summertime in Indian birch bark canoes which they could carry on their backs for miles from one stream to another. Missions were started at Little Falls, Brockway, Rich Prairie, Long Prairie, and other places, and finally at Sandy Lake in the early 1860s. The mission was served by one or more of Father Buh's helpers and many of the Indians may have been ministered to by Father Buh and Father Genins, also a native of Austria. It was possible for them to travel by canoe in the summer and snowshoes in winter up the Tamarack River to Cromwell from Sandy Lake, and also up Prairie River to Prairie Lake, and then up Hasty Brook, three miles north of Cromwell, or Island Lake and five or six miles east to work at Stoney Brook in those days. By the time the railroads were built through this area, the Indians, or many of them, were converted to the Christian religion and they had all heard about the white man's God. Many were anxious to learn about the Christian religion so in many instances they would send their chief long distances that took many moons to travel, to beg the missionaries to come to their villages or settlements, as they were convinced that the white men were more successful than the red men because the white man's God was a more powerful God. Therefore, the white man held the confidence of the Indians and also enjoyed their hospitality for more than one hundred years or until the advance of the white traders. There were unscrupulous white traders who took advantage of their simplicity. The confidence that had been gained by many years of hard labor was now endangered by the tactics of those unscrupulous traders, so that many of the Indians began to doubt the sincerity of the white man's religion. But there is no doubt, however, that many of the early fathers had given them warning that all white men were not angels and could not all be trusted.

When the white traders introduced commercialism to the Indians one of their stocks in trade was "fire water" (as the Indians called alcoholic drink). Other immoral practices, such as disrespect of their moral standard of monogamy, were introduced so that we found many fatherless half-breeds as far back as one hundred years ago. The red man had no legal recourse. We also find the federal government failed to fulfill its promises to the red man which led to uprisings and open rebellion. History refers to them as Indian uprisings and yet we find these Christian ambassadors laboring faithfully among the Indians and sometimes pleading their cause before United States' officials together with their own chiefs; this is what distinguishes the missionaries from their accusers.

Now we come down the years to about 1870 when the railroad was built and the first white people started to make permanent settlement here. They were for the most part railroad men and some hunters and trappers, who were mostly Irish people who followed the railroad in the early 1870s. It was not until about 1885 that an attempt was made to establish a real community here and we find the first people to make a permanent settlement here were Canadian French and other Eastern Christians. Most of them were Roman Catholics and they brought their church with them. Likewise when other nationalities came some twenty years later and settled here, they brought their native churches with them—maybe not in a material sense like the Israelites bringing the Ark with them out of the land of Egypt, but rather symbolic reminders of their covenant with God.

So when those people came here, not with a material church, but with the spirit of the church and the covenant of God planted in their hearts, they could be ministered to in their own language by their own nationalities. We find that the Irish, the first pronounced and confirmed Christians here, had the service of an Irish priest from Brainerd and later when the French came here about 1886 they too were serviced by an Irish priest, Father Dugal (1886-89). He held meetings in the homes maybe one or two times a month. (There were only two homes where meetings were held—John Wright's and Alex Bellanger's). Father Dugal was replaced by a French priest, Father Giraux, in 1889 when there was only one Irish family left here and the majority of the people were French, so they could enjoy fellowship with the priest in their own language. Father Giraux came here periodically until 1891 and was then replaced by Father Newl (1891-94). However, Father Giraux returned here and ministered to his people and also at Wright Station from 1894-1906. Father Giraux resided in Cloquet in a French settlement they called Little Canada.

The first church in Cromwell was built in approximately 1902 under the leadership and guidance of Father Giraux. The funds for the construction of the church came from parishioners and visitors to the young community. Contributions of lumber and labor were received from the members of the parish. The lot on which the church was located was donated by John H. Wright. The first church was not incorporated into the Diocese of Duluth. Mass was celebrated in this church until about May, 1917, when the church was struck by lightning and burned.

Following the destruction of their church in 1917, Mass and other religious services were conducted in the homes of the parishioners of the area by the priest sent by the Bishop from Duluth. Later the Board of Red Clover Township granted the use of their hall for services. This hall was the old Morse store and leased by the town of Red Clover for public meetings. It was located on the southwest corner of Cromwell Lake and at the end of and just north of the road that runs by the depot and in front of Morse's house.

When it was decided to build a new church in Cromwell in the latter part of 1921 or early part of 1922, a delegation consisting of Mrs. Chupat, Mrs. J. H. Wright, and Mr. Patrick Maher contacted Bishop

McNicols relative to getting the church incorporated within the Diocese of Duluth. It was incorporated and recorded in Carlton on July 11, 1922, in Book 69 of Deeds, page 171.

In the summer of 1924 the present church, the Immaculate Conception Church, was built under the direction of Father Gilfoile. The funds for the construction came from the following: $500 from the Extension Society, $500 from the insurance on the church destroyed by fire in 1917, and the remainder from the members of the parish. The second church was built on the same grounds the first church had occupied and an additional lot just south of the first church was purchased at this time. Construction started with Brother Burthum from Duluth, a carpenter by trade, in charge of construction. He donated his time and labor and all other labor was donated or paid for by the members of the parish.

A large number of priests in the present Diocese of Duluth have at one time or another celebrated Mass in the Cromwell parish. The Reverend Father A. Bernard Roy is the present pastor and has served the parish for the past several years and under his guidance many improvements have been made.

Introduction to Protestantism

Now we come to the advent of other nationalities who brought their religious convictions and their conception (nativism) of true Christian worship with them. Some came here for the purpose of proselytizing and establishing their own denominational church at Cromwell as this was considered a free mission field by all Protestant denominations.

First, we had a missionary in the fall of 1896 who was sponsored by William Hill of New York, a railway official and financier, who supplied him with a railway coach with living quarters in one end and a chapel in the main coach. This was transported free of charge by the railway company from a stop on sidings (or side tracks), remaining in each place a week or more—as long as he would have an interested audience. About four people made a confession of faith and he concluded his mission here by organizing a Sunday school with Amasa Dotten as leader. However, it did not last long as there were not many children at that time. Only Mr. Dotten continued and became a member of the Methodist Church some years later when it was organized.

Mr. Gravelle was a member of the Brethren who called themselves "Bible Christians." After Mr. Gravelle had been here some time and established his home, he had a friend in Chicago, a Mr. Patriquea (or Patriquean), who came here as an able Gospel preacher. They held meetings in the little green schoolhouse and in various homes and in the course of two weeks he established an assembly. He believed and taught that there is only one Church which includes all Christian believers, and the subdivisions of the Church are assemblies or gatherings of Christian Brethren and not a Church in itself, but a part of the one and only Church of Christ. So they were opposed to sectarianism. He continued to hold meetings in the homes and rented a room in the Section House for about two years.

Then came two "go preachers," as they called themselves, but they were Erwinites from a movement started in Ireland in the 1880s by one man named Erwin, who anathematized Catholicism and Protestant

Clericalism and started out to proselytize the whole world by starting new churches the "Jesus way" as they called it. They traveled in pairs and walked from place to place or nearly so. The two who came here had one bicycle and one would ride a mile or so on the railroad track and then leave the bicycle and walk along the track and the other man left behind would come up to the bicycle and take it and ride for about two miles and then leave it for the other man, and so on, until they got to their destination. When they came to Cromwell, they saw the Methodist church and they got permission to hold meetings there with the Brethren. But they were both condemned which split them apart so there were no more meetings and the brotherly love vanished.

The Beginning of the Methodist Church in Cromwell

The summer of 1898 brought Reverend Williams, who was building a Methodist Church in Carlton, to Cromwell to explore the possibility of organizing a Methodist congregation here. He held meetings in the

The Methodist Church in Cromwell. little schoolhouse a few times and there officiated at the marriage of Mr. and Mrs. John Bohl, the fourth couple to be united in marriage in Cromwell. The first couple was Mr. and Mrs. H. Wright in 1888, the second was Mr. and Mrs. John Lindquist, section foreman, in the fall of 1892. The third was Mr. and Mrs. Daniel Frazer, also in the fall of 1892. There may have been one other marriage—that of Mr. and Mrs. Gifford. She was the sister to Mr. Charles Morse; they were married in the spring of 1894 and made their home in Montana. Reverend Williams also held funeral services for Mrs. Amasa Dotten in 1899.

On May 7, 1903, the Methodist Church was incorporated by Reverend A. McKinzee; Robert Forbes, D.D., District Superintendent; and Charles Morse, who gave them a building lot of one-half acre of land he had just purchased from B. A. Beck. He may also have given some lumber. I do not know all who were charter members but as far as I know Mr. Elwood E. Bolles and his wife, Effie, were the first professed Methodists. They had moved here from North Dakota and worked hard to get a Methodist Church built here; however, the most progress was made when the Rev. Norman Batdorf was their leader in 1904. He was also principal of our school and during his summer vacation time he worked hard on the church building—giving his labor, material, and money.

The Reverend McKinzee lived at Aitkin and would ride on the morning train to Tamarack, hold meetings there, then walk or ride on the section handcar to Wright, hold meetings there, and then walk to Cromwell. Well, that is only six miles and sometimes he had to wear rubber boots to get there to hold meetings. He returned to Aitkin on the evening train.

The Methodist Church has no record of the Reverend McKinzee here but the records in the court house at Carlton have him as one of the incorporators and I know that he came here and held meetings for at least two years, in 1901-02, for a promised salary of $200 a year. The meetings were first held in the schoolhouse. The church could not have been built before 1905 as Mr. Morse did not buy the lot or land until early in the summer of 1903. It appears in the Methodist Church records that Rev. John Parrish was their pastor until 1904. Here are their pastors' names as they have them recorded:

Rev. Norman Batdorf, 1904-06; Rev. G. H. LaVag, 1909-1912; Rev. F.B. Luce, 1912-13; Rev. J. J. Wittrup, 1913-16; Rev. Harry Paynter, 1916-17; Claude Spicer, 1917-18; Rev. Rev. John Roper, 1918-1921; L. A. Jenson, 1921-22; Rev. John Clark, 1922-25; Rev. Paul Hendricks, 1926-28; Rev. Henry Aud, 1928-29; Rev. S. S. Olafson, 1929-30; Rev. U. E. Dahle, 1930-33; Rev. A. J. Parks, 1933-36; Rev. Elmer Kind, 1936-37; Rev. L. A. Brattam and Franklin Miskiff, 1940; Rev. J. P. Hart, 1940-46; Rev. Homer D. Munson, 1946-1950; Rev. Louis Allen Sunner, 1950-51; Rev. Harold Larson, 1950-1951; and Rev. Paul Langer, 1951-52.

About 1900 the Presbyterians sent their Superintendent of Sunday School here to see if he could organize a Sunday School, but he failed.

Also in the early 1900s the Seventh Day Adventists also tried to win some converts here and did gain a few. The Pentecostal Church also tried and won some converts—how many, I do not know.

The International Bible Student Association got a

few converts. They sometimes were called "Russellites" and later became known as Jehovah's Witnesses. They made some sincere converts and many "quasi" converts. They teach that Jesus Christ has come to his Temple as said He would, and that the Christian Dispensation is over, so they believe they are justified in renouncing the church, the clergy, and all organization of the church.

The Beginning of the Evangelical Lutheran Church in Cromwell

In 1902 when several Norwegian families came here from Superior, Wisconsin, they were members of the United Lutheran Church (the Concordia; Harmonious Church in Superior) which is now a part of the Evangelical Lutheran Synod of America. They would call on their former pastor, the Reverend Lium, to come here to visit the sick, hold some public meetings in the schoolhouse, and conduct a few funeral services and likewise. Reverend Lium's successor, the Reverend Lockrum, also was called here to visit the sick and conduct funeral services, but this was outside of their field of labor. So the Reverend Lockrum advised the people to get in contact with a mission pastor or some lay pastor. In 1908 they contacted the Reverend J. N. Thomasberg who lived in Aitkin. He agreed to come once a month and hold services in the homes. The first thing he did was organize a Lutheran Ladies Aid Society and hold services jointly with the Ladies Aid monthly meeting. Their goal was to begin a building fund so they could build a church home.

The Reverend Thomasberg labored hard and faithfully for some years. He held Bible School in the schoolhouse for two weeks every summer for six or seven years and confirmed many of the older boys and girls who are now married and have their own families and children. Reverend Thomasberg was afflicted with a throat ailment (called Preacher's Sore Throat) that forced him into retirement. He organized the Ladies Aid in 1914 and the first officers were the following: Mrs. Julia Skramstad, secretary; Mrs. Edward Benson, treasurer; and J. J. Thomasberg, chairman. Later, Mrs. John Shie was elected treasurer and she held that office for many years, in fact for all the days of her life. However, when the Reverend Thomasberg retired, that left the Ladies Aid without a leader and no pastor here to hold services for some years.

Bethany Lutheran Ladies Aid of Cromwell. l to r standing: Rev. Thomasburg, Mrs. Schei, Mrs. Morse, Mrs. Ed Benson, Mrs. Johnson, Mrs. Dalen, Mrs. Lindquist, Mrs. Lust, Mrs. Axel Swanson, Mrs. Mace, Mrs. Ahlstad, Bessie Lum, Mrs. Fred Johnson, Ida Morse, Charles Morse, Mrs. Ole Benson, Mrs. Coty, unknown, Frank Nord, Ole Benson, John Stoner, Oscar Benson, Arthur Skramstad, Helmer Stoner, Otto Lust, the rest are unidentified.

About 1918, Mrs. Shie was sent to Superior to see if the Reverend Lockrum could help in getting a mission pastor to come to Cromwell to organize a Lutheran congregation. (Mrs. Shie may have been sent or she acted on her own initiative, I do not know. She was a very active personality). In 1918 they sent the Reverend A. T. Juvland.

    The Ladies Aid had a building fund of about $1,000 or more. The Rev. Juvland and Mr. Ole Benson were selected as a committee of two at a meeting held at the home of Mr. and Mrs. Shie in 1919 where it had been decided that a church home was needed. Mr. Benson and Rev. Juvland went out in horse-and-buggy to see the people in the community to get subscriptions for the building fund, and they had a very successful drive. They received some $100 and some $50 pledges so the total subscriptions for the building fund in cash was $1,400 or more. Some promised to give lumber and others to donate labor that amounted to several hundred dollars. This, together with the Ladies Aid's $1,000 or more, gave them a potential building fund of more than $3,000.

    They were encouraged and wanted to start building at once, but first they needed to organize and incorporate, which they did, under the name of Bethany English Lutheran Church of Cromwell at a meeting sometime in the early part of 1920. The incorporation was recorded in the court house in Carlton on May 1, 1920. The first officers were Reverend Juvland, chairman; Ole M. Holm, secretary; John Lindquist, Edward Benson, and Otto Lust, trustees. Now they were ready to start planning a building program.

    The Rev. Juvland secured the services of an architect in Duluth who donated his services and the actual building of the church started with Mr. M. Markusen in charge. The basement and superstructure were built but only the basement was finished. With an obligation of $500 loaned from Rev. Juvland on a note, it was a long time before it was repaid. But at last the money was raised and deposited in the Bank of Cromwell and a check was drawn on the bank to pay Rev. Juvland the $500 with interest. But before the check was presented for payment, the bank was closed by the State Bank Examiner in 1927, so it took some time before Rev. Juvland got his money back. But by the time the Rev. Juvland retired the note was finally paid. He had given about twelve years of untiring labor and faithful service until 1930.

The people then wished to have a permanent pastor. As this was a young congregation and not able to support a pastor itself, a movement was started to unite with Floodwood, as they were also a small congregation which was served by a pastor from Proctor. So after many meetings it was agreed to unite with Floodwood to form one parish, and call a pastor. They extended a call to the Reverend O. P. Sheggeby and he accepted the call and was installed as pastor of the two congregations in 1930. Until this time only the church basement was finished, and, under the leadership of Reverend Sheggeby, the superstructure was finished and on October 25th the church was dedicated. The congregation had a mortgage of $2,500 and some other small amounts to pay. The church was under the leadership of the Reverend Sheggeby for five years until 1935; under the leadership of the Reverend L. A. Wagen for three years from 1935 to 1938; under the leadership of the Rev. Harold M. Rye from 1938-1941: and under that of Reverend M. G. Halverson for four years—1941-45.

In a few years the Ladies Aid reduced the indebtedness to about $600. Mrs. Julienne Skramstad wanted to help clear up the mortgage by donating most of the money to be applied to the mortgage. One member of the congregation went out to some of the members and raised a little more than was required to pay the mortgage in full. A very impressive mortgage burning ceremony was held in the fall of 1943 with many of the former pastors and their wives and many friends of the congregation present from out of town. The Reverend Halverson resigned after serving faithfully for four years and was replaced by the Reverend T. G. Sandeno, who was an elderly pastor, but still very active. Under his leadership, Bethlehem Evangelical Lutheran Church of Wright united with Cromwell and Floodwood. Reverend Sandeno gave the congregation able leadership for four years, from 1945 to 1949, and was replaced by Reverend John A. McDermid, the present pastor, in 1949.

Ed. note: We can only speculate as to why B. A. Beck ended his manuscript so abruptly, without any conclusion or summation. Perhaps he had just reached the end of his available information and energy.

We are appreciative of Bennett Beck's making this volume of local information his final contribution to his beloved home place.

Carlton County, ca. 1930s.

State of Minnesota showing Carlton County

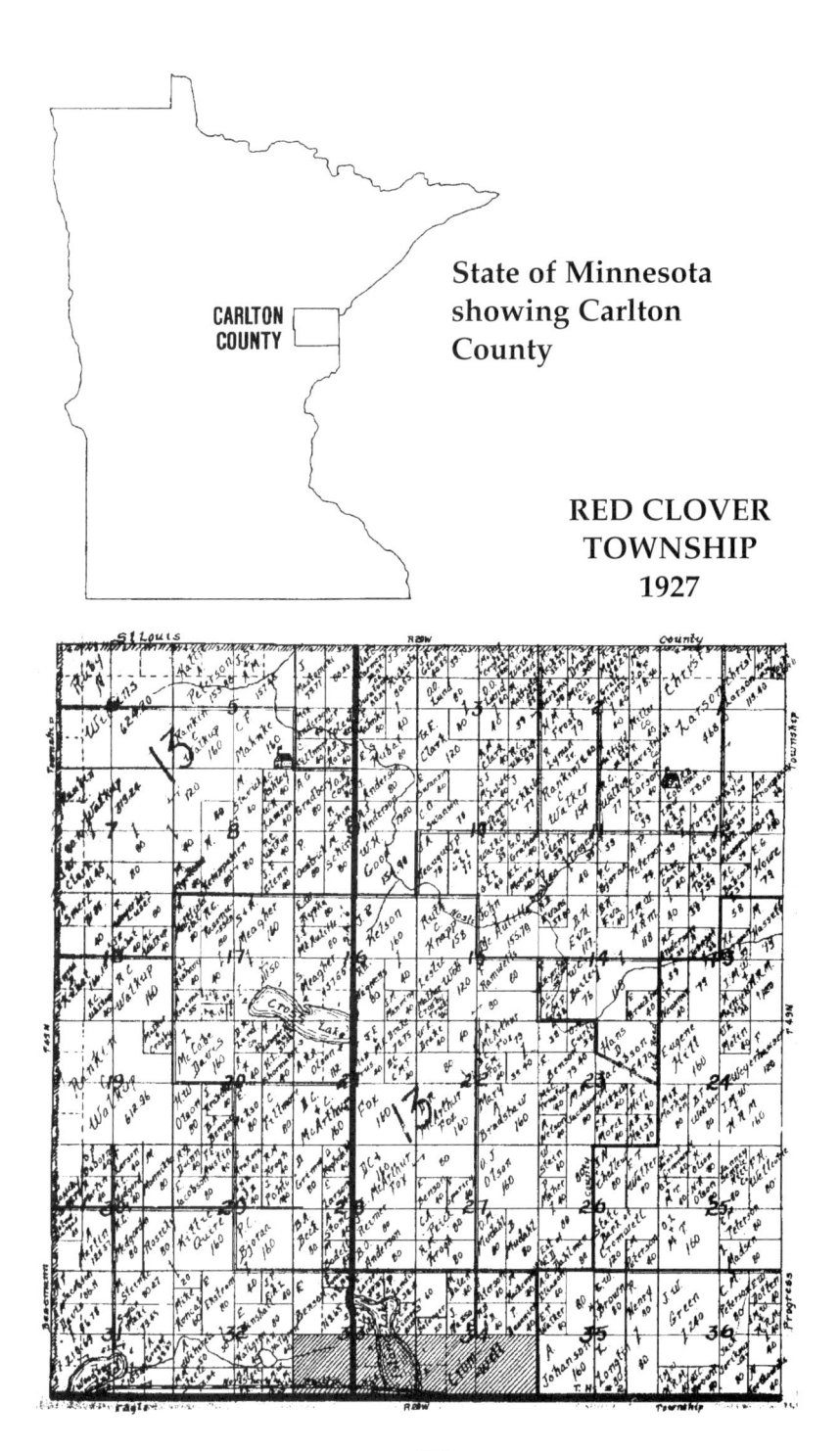

RED CLOVER TOWNSHIP 1927

EAGLE TOWNSHIP
1927

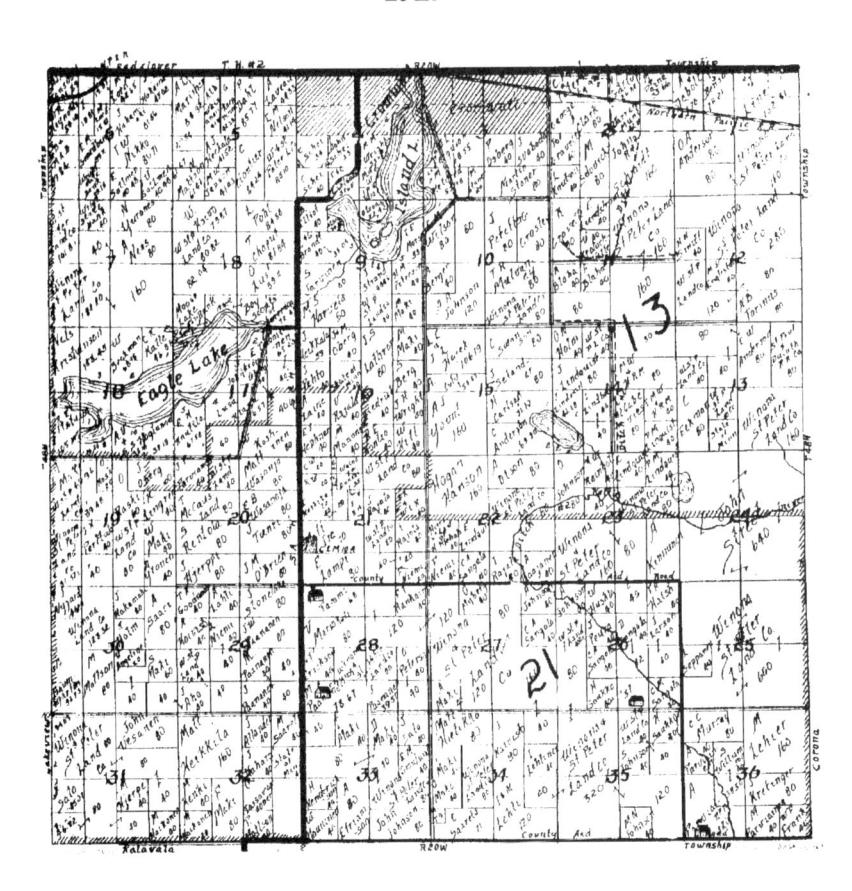

CROMWELL

Pop. 230. A village on the N P Ry 21 miles w of Carlton. It has a well established state bank, several general stores, a co-operative creamery, and the lines of business needed to meet the farmer trade. Cordwood and timber products are shipped out. W W Wright, P M.

Village Council—Jno Hill, pres; C H Martwig, clk; Matt Schin, treas; C E Gulf, assessor; E A Bolles, justice; R F Bodway, constable; W G Martwig, Jacob Pohto, Bennett Benson, members.

Cromwell entry in the 1927 Carlton County Directory.

INDEX of CROMWELL AREA SETTLERS

Adelgruber, Otto, 131, 132
Ahola, Henry, 178, 179
Ainala, Antti, 152
Allen, John, 253
Allshire, Mr. & Mrs. M. S., 255, 256
Ambau, George, 55
Anderson, Andrew, 108
Anderson, Mr. & Mrs. Charles, 125
Anderson, James, 108
Anderson, Mr. & Mrs. Joseph, 91
Anderson, Peter V., 129
Anderson, Thomas, 68
Anez, Fred, 183
Angeline, Victor, 187
Arden, Enoch, 24
Arents, Dr., 262
Balsness, Andrew, 82
Barstow, Raymond, 229, 230
Beck, Bennett A., 72, 73
Bellanger, Alex, 52, 53
Benson, Bennett, 247
Benson, Mr. & Mrs. Ed., 86, 87
Benson, Ole B., 74
Berg, Nichkoulus, 180, 181
Billeveau, John, 54
Blaha, Mr. & Mrs. Albert, 130, 131
Bodell, George H., 106
Brackett, John, 253
Brandt, Carl, 121
Brandt, Gust, 121
Cain, Martin, 29
Carlson, Mr. & Mrs. Herman, 123
Chaput, Thomas, 221
Clark, John, 259, 260
Cody, Dan, 79
Cool, Willis, 69

Crosley, Guy, 256, 257
Crosley, Mr. & Mrs. John, 256, 257
Dahlman, Edward, 59, 60
Dakken, Ole, 94
Dalen, Mr. & Mrs. John P., 89, 90
Danski, Waino, 179
Davidson, Mr. & Mrs. A., 257
Davis, Mr. & Mrs. Oscar D., 134, 135
Debolt, William, 133
Dennie, Philip, 254
Derosier, John, 58, 231
Dotten, Amasa, 56, 57
Dotten, Arthur, 55, 56
Dotten, Earl W., 233
Duffy, Edward, 64, 65, 209
Eastman, John, 76
Ekstrom, Edward, 71, 72, 231, 232
Elliot, Samuel, 65
Emerson, David, 68
Engelin, Ray, 134
Erickson, Mrs., 252, 253
Erkkila, John, 59
Erkos, Mike, 148
Farness, Mr. & Mrs. Herman, 254
Finberg, Arne, 98
Finn (or Finch), Thomas, 33
Finnila, Mr. & Mrs. Oscar, 90, 91
Flaugher, George, 49
Forslund, Ernest, 232, 260
Forslund, Gust, 232, 260
Franzen, Mr., 261
Frazer, Dan, 54
Gill, Jack, 70
Giraux, Father, 267, 268
Good, William, 119, 120
Gradberg, Andrew, 111, 112
Granlund, Frank, 196

Gravelle, Clement, 113
Gravelle, Mr. & Mrs. Henry, 89
Gravelle, Mr. & Mrs. Joseph, 88
Graves, Emil, 98
Gregor, Mr. & Mrs. Anton, 98
Greschell, Mr. & Mrs. August, 253, 254
Gulf, Charles, 169, 170
Hakamaki, Felix, 76, 115
Hakamaki, Frank, 76
Hakamaki, John, 75, 76, 161
Hakkala, Victor, 91
Hanson, Hogan, 70, 71
Hedman, Mr. & Mrs. John, 124
Hendrickson, John, 74
Hendrickson, Henry, 178
Hendrickson, Mr. & Mrs. Matt, 169
Heikkila, Emil, 116
Heikkila, Mr. & Mrs. John, 91
Heikkila, Jonas, 175
Heikkila, Matt & Sophia, 151, 152, 217, 218
Heikkila, Mike, 92
Heikkila, Mike, 91
Hellstrom, Marie, 153
Hephmer, E. J. , 170
Herrick, Mr. & Mrs. Rex, 135
Herrick, Ronald, 135
Hiettikko, Matt, 194
Hill, Charles, 168, 169
Hill, John, 220-222
Hill, William, 184, 185
Hjerppi, Jack, 188
Hoglund, Andrew V., 185
Holecek, Joseph, 86
Holm, Mr. & Mrs. Ole M., 128
Homstad, Oscar, 67, 68
Houck, Norman, 230
Hougland, Ole, 79
Huhta, Edward, 176, 177
Ilstrup, Cora, 249

Ilstrup, Leif, 230
Ilstrup, R. E., 182
Iru, Mr. & Mrs. John, 157
Isaacson, Oscar, 72, 218
Jacobson, Lars, 100
Jackson, John H., 254
Jager, May, 224
Jarvinen, Sakri, 198
Jensen, Olaf, 84
Jerecovsky, Mr. & Mrs. Nick, 132, 133
Johnson, Albert, 124
Johnson, Mr. & Mrs. Albert, 155
Johnson, Alfred (Fred), 78
Johnson, John, 194
Johnson, Mr. & Mrs. Olaf, 125
Johnson, Sefrid, 183, 184
Jussila, Evelina & Gust, 154
Kaarkkainen, Peter & Erika, 154
Kahara, Mr. & Mrs. John, 195
Karppinen, Erick, 115
Kauppinen, Jack, 175
Keiski, Mr. & Mrs. William, 177
Keskitalo, Erick, 157
Kiel, George, 97
Kiiskila, Waino, 190
Kinnunen, Mr. & Mrs. A., 192, 193
Klavu, Mr. & Mrs. Abram, 92, 159
Klavu, Arthur, 187
Kloves, Dr., 262
Knuutila, Mr. & Mrs. Henry, Sr., 93, 160
Knutson, Mr. & Mrs. Louis, 128
Koivisto, Alex, 192
Koncal, Mike, 98
Korby, Andrew, 231, 232
Korpi, Mr. & Mrs. Mike, 170
Koskinen, Waino, 179
Krakora, Mr. & Mrs. Frank, 87
Krakora, Mr. & Mrs. Mike, 87, 88

Kristensen, Nels, 182
Krogh, Mr. & Mrs. Richard, 90
Krotovel, James, 132
Kubat, Mr. & Mrs. Joseph, 84, 85
Kubat, Milo, 85
Kubista, Frank, 112
Kubista, John, 112
Kubista, Joseph, 112
Laasanen, Mr. & Mrs. Elias, 156
LaGou, Peter, 46
Lahti, Aadi (Ade), 191
Laine, Abel, 188
LaMier (Lemir), Frank, 55
Lampi, Mr. & Mrs. Abraham, 174
Lampi, Alex, 174
Larson, Edward, 73, 74
Larson(Seppanen), Joseph, 150
Larson, Louis, 92, 93, 214-216
Lee, Jesse, 259, 260
Lehto, Arthur, 196
Lehto, August & Hilda, 196
Lehto, Bertha, 155
Lindholm, Mr. & Mrs. Martin, 125
Lindquist, John, 122
Line, Jack, 99
Lines, Jaster, 133, 134
Lipa, Charles, 86
Lundstrom, Alfred, 132
Lust, Otto, 58
Lynne, Ivar, 136
Mace, Jack, 219
Maki, David, 176
Maki, Isaac & Serafina, 152
Maki, Ivar, 189
Maki, John, 176
Maki, Mr. & Mrs. Oscar, 178
Maki, Sam, 184
Maki, Werner, 182
Maki, William, 190
Mannikka, Matt, 75
Mann, Kenneth, 117
Markkula, Uriel, 158
Markusen, Marinus & Ruth, 230, 231
Martwig, Charles, 110
Martwig, William, 110, 111
Masten, Niels, 68
Mastomaki, Jack, 90
McArthur, Mr., 103, 105
McDermot, James, 71
McLeod, Kenneth, 185, 186
Meagher, S. , 121
Melvold, Mr. & Mrs. S., 126, 127
Mendenhall, Mr., 116, 117
Merwin, George, 52
Mingus, Scott, 257-259
Morrison, Peter, 57, 58
Morse, Charles, 61-63, 209, 210, 212-214
Nasso, Anna & Jacob, 117
Newquist, August, 80
Newton, Arthur, , 50
Niemi, Arvid D., 154
Niemi, Frank, 188, 189
Niemi, Isaac, 189
Niemi, John, 191
Niemi, Lizzie, 191
Nilson, August, 118
Nord, Frank, 80
Novotny, Mr. & Mrs. Joseph, 136
Nyberg, Ony, 198
Nyrhinen, Jacob, 75
Oberg, Mr. & Mrs. John, 93, 94, 160, 161
Oberg, John F., 175
Oberg, John, 220
O'Brien, Michael, 66
Oestriech, Mr. & Mrs. Paul, 99, 100
Olson, Mr. & Mrs. Albert, 124
Olson, Cornelia, 155, 156
Olson, Mr. & Mrs. Emil, 129

Olson, Mr. & Mrs. Franz (Frank), 95
Olson, Mr., 225
Olson, S., 182, 183
Osberg, John, 220
Osberg, Mr. & Mrs. Peter, 81
Paajanen, A., 186
Paanenen, Emil, 175
Paananen, John, 175
Paananen, Matt, 173, 174
Paananen, William, 173
Paine, Horace, 51
Parson, Peter, 24
Parviainen, Andrew A., 180
Parviainen, Matt, 171
Patrick, Joseph, 84
Pepin, Ben, 57
Perttula, John, 150
Peterson, Andrew, 118, 119
Peterson, Carl M., 97
Peterson, Mr. & Mrs. William, 154, 155
Pheffer, Mr., 130
Pohl, John, 69, 209
Pohl, Louis, Sr., 70
Pohto, Mr. & Mrs. Jacob, 51, 52
Prakos, Mr., 84
Rajala, Mr. & Mrs. Ivar, 186
Rajala, John, 178
Rantala, Mr. & Mrs., 194, 195
Raynols, Mr. & Mrs. William, 99
Raymond, Gust, 262
Reimer, John, 100, 101
Rentola, Santen, 189
Richard, Mr. & Mrs. Joseph, 89
Richarva, Anton, 107
Rogers, Joseph, 66, 67
Rosicky, Mr. & Mrs. Anton, 98
Royer, Jerry, 53, 54, 222
Ruse, Mr. & Mrs. Albin, 129
Rypka, Emil, 83
Rypka, Frank, 82, 83

Saarela, Charles & Sophie, 152
Saarela, Matt, 176
Saarela, William, 153
Saari, Abraham & Sophia, 193
Salenius, Nickolas, 193
Salo, John, 193, 194
Sallman, Mr. & Mrs. John, 156
Sangola, Daniel, 94, 153
Saukko, Henry, 158
Savage, John, 58, 59
Schafer, Hiram K., 106, 107
Schei, John, 80
Schin, Cornelius, 111
Schonover, Mr. & Mrs. Weslee, 255
Schroeder, George, 79
Selander, John Arthur, 129, 130
Skonders, John, 116
Skramstad, Christ, 81
Slezak, Caspar, 82
Smitberg, E. M., 182
Smith, Gust, 181
Smith, Henry, 59
Sparring, Emil, 119
Stenberg, Mr. & Mrs. Charles, 126
Stone, Alfred, 100
Stonelake, John, 173
Stoner, Martin, 81
Swanson, Axel, 76, 77
Swanson, Carl, 112
Swanson, Charles, 109
Swanson, Charles, 129
Swanson, Oscar, 112
Swanson, Swan, 77
Swanson, Theodore, 109
Tauren, Emil, 177
Tianen, Matt, 195
Thomasberg, Rev. J. N., 274, 275
Tossavainen, O., 195
Tuuri, John, 172
Vasanoja, Matt, 113, 114

Vigness, Edward & Clara, 127
Vilonen, Otto, 186
Violett, James, 216, 217
Walker, Edward T., 65, 66
Walters, Mr. & Mrs. Harvey, 257
Waverin, Joseph, 86
Webber, Gust, 67
Westerlund, Konstan W., 196,
Westola, Charles Theo., 197
197
Whitten, Daniel, 50
Whitten, Woodbury, 50
Wiherela (Wherela), Alex, 171, 219
Wilcox, Frank, 229
Wilson, Claude, 59, 256
Wilson, Clarence, 256
Wilson, Sarah, 255
Winter, John, 184
Wolf, Edward, 255
Wolf, Ely, 101-105
Wright, George, 33, 34
Wright, John H., 34, 60, 61, 181, 224
Wright, Thomas, 34, 35
Wydra, Mr. & Mrs., 99
Wyeat, Mr., 116
Yirean, Edward, 114, 115
Ylinen, Mr. & Mrs. Alex, 187
Ylen, Hjalmar, 220, 221
Ylen, Victor, 220
Young, D. L., 208, 209

ADDITIONAL SUGGESTED READING

Carlton County Historical Society. *Fury of the Flames.* Cloquet, MN, 1998.

Carroll, Francis M. *Crossroads in Time: A History of Carlton County, Minnesota.* Carlton County Historical Society, Cloquet, MN, 1987.

Carroll, Francis M. and Raiter, Franklin. *Fires of Autumn: The Cloquet-Moose Lake Disaster of 1918.* Minnesota Historical Society, St. Paul, MN, 1990.

Carroll, Francis M. and Wisuri, Marlene. *Reflections of Our Past: A Pictorial History of Carlton County, Minnesota.* Donning Co. Publishers, Virginia Beach, VA, 1997.

Holmquist, June Drenning (ed.). *They Chose Minnesota: A Survey of the State's Ethnic Groups.* Minnesota Historical Society, St. Paul, 1981.

Mattinen, John A., trans. Richard Impola. *History of the Thomson Farming Area.* Carlton County Historical Society, Cloquet, MN, 2000.

O' Meara, Walter. *We Made It Through the Winter: A Memoir of Minnesota Boyhood.* Minnesota Historical Society, St. Paul, MN, 1974.

Wasatjerna, Hans R. (ed.). *History of Finns in Minnesota.* Minnesota Finnish-American Historical Society, Duluth, MN, 1957.

*Co-op Gathering at Workers' Hall in
Eagle Lake Township, ca. 1931.
(detail of photograph)*